D1094297

# PARCEL of ROGUES

## HOW FREE TRADE IS FAILING CANADA

# MAUDE BARLOW

KEY PORTER BOOKS

**To my parents, Flora and Bill McGrath,**
**who taught me to care.**

**Canadian Cataloguing in Publication Data**

Barlow, Maude
    Parcel of rogues

ISBN 1-55013-254-7

1. Free trade – Canada.    2. Free trade – United
States.    3. Canada – Commerce – United States.
4. United States – Commerce – Canada.    5. Canada –
Economic conditions – 1971-    .*    I. Title.

HF1766.B37 1990      382'.0971073      C90-093716-5

Key Porter Books Limited
70 The Esplanade
Toronto, Ontario
Canada M5E 1R2

Typesetting: Computer Composition of Canada, Inc.

Printed on acid-free paper
Printed and bound in Canada by T.H. Best Printing Company Limited
90 91 92 93 94 6 5 4 3 2 1

# CONTENTS

Preface / v

Acknowledgments / ix

1. Corporate North America Takes Care of Business / 1

2. The Tories Deliver: Canada to Go / 24

3. The Economic Cost of Free Trade / 52

4. The Human Cost of Free Trade / 82

5. War Games: Running with the Pentagon / 107

6. Energy Betrayal: The Last Resource / 129

7. Environment at Risk / 150

8. The Choice / 178

Afterword / 203

Appendix: Job Loss Register / 205

Bibliography / 235

Index / 241

## A Parcel of Rogues in a Nation

*Fareweel to a' our Scottish fame,*
*Fareweel our ancient glory!*
*Fareweel ev'n to the Scottish name,*
*Sae famed in martial story*
*Now Sark rins over Solway sands,*
*An' Tweed rins to the ocean,*
*To mark where England's province stands —*
*Such a parcel of rogues in a nation!*

*What force or guile could not subdue*
*Thro' many warlike ages*
*Is wrought now by a coward few*
*For hireling traitor's wages.*
*The English steel we could disdain,*
*Secure in valour's station;*
*But English gold has been our bane —*
*Such a parcel of rogues in a nation!*

*O, would, or I had seen the day*
*That Treason thus could sell us,*
*My auld grey head had lien in clay*
*Wi' Bruce and loyal Wallace!*
*But pith and power, till my last hour*
*I'll mak this declaration: —*
*'We're bought and sold for English gold' —*
*Such a parcel of rogues in a nation!*

— Robert Burns

# PREFACE

In December 1984, only months after winning his landslide victory for the Conservative party, Brian Mulroney went to New York to speak to the corporate élite of America. In a major address to the prestigious Economic Club, the cream of the seven hundred top companies in the United States, Canada's spanking-new prime minister outlined his government's platform, and the policies that would drive it for the next eight years. Not for Brian Mulroney the boardrooms of Toronto, Vancouver, or Montreal; not for him the halls of Parliament, or everyday Canadians.

It was in New York that he announced the demise of the National Energy Program. "Canada was not built by expropriating retroactively other people's property," he said of Canadian land mined for its wealth by foreign multinationals. New tax breaks for foreign-dominated energy companies were on the way. Canada was "open for business" he declared, and the nationalist policies of the past were history. He lavishly praised the United States under Ronald Reagan as a blueprint for Canada, promising new ties in military co-operation. Canada was going to tear down barriers to American take-overs of Canadian resources and businesses, he said with enthusiasm.

The prime minister basked in the sweet sound of "wave after wave" of applause. American business leaders were surprised and delighted in their new-found, compliant friend from the north. The prime minister returned to Canada, the conquering hero of Wall Street, having received recognition from the only audience he values.

What a disappointment! U.S. media coverage of Mulroney's New York visit was relegated to one tiny column under the stock prices in the *New York Times*. To raise their profile in the *Times* and hold the attention of American business, Canadian corporate leaders and Conservative-held provinces had to buy a nine-page supplement. "Canada is under new management," a marriage of government and business, it proudly announced. "The Chamber of Commerce believes that any agreements between Canada and the United States must be a product of a consensus between the two governments and their respective private sectors."

Canada would be "a cheap place for Americans to invest in," the supplement promised, and would "lay out the welcome mat for foreign investment." The new "market-oriented style" of the government would develop policies in tune with the private sector, and set the right atmosphere for business. Tax breaks and other corporate incentives were promised, with corporate profits of over 100 percent as a lure. Wage settlements were being "dramatically" decelerated in Canada, the ad boasted, and Canada would "look to move" the Canadian dollar "gently higher" against the American, "with further measurable upward appreciation to follow in 1986 and beyond."

The sale of Canadian raw resources and the reimportation of American processed goods made from those resources contribute to the creation of millions of American jobs, the ad brightly pointed out. "In the steel sector Ontario ships, on order, about 600,000 tons of semi-finished steel a year to Pennsylvania, with much of it being milled and sent back to Canada at a profit. For every dollar's worth of steel Ontario producers ship to Pennsylvania, they buy back $1.25 in iron, coal and other related products." Said another pitch: "The U.S. consistently enjoys a significant surplus on trade with Canada in services and manufactured end products."

One ad reminded its readers that the first entrepreneurs in Canada were Americans. Another encouraged American investment, with the assurance that "with as much as 60 percent of the manufacturing sector and 70 percent of the mining and petroleum sectors under the control of foreign companies, Canada has been more dependent on foreign investment than any other industrialized country." Peter Lougheed promised to "sell" Alberta to the world, and invited American private investment in Alberta's health-care and other sectors. The supplement also helpfully pointed out that the Reagan administration, displeased with former "narrow, self-styled" concerns about too much foreign control, had made it clear that Canada would have to prove itself trustworthy in this area and be the initiator in a free-trade deal. The Reagan administration, said the ad, kindly let Canada lead the "pas de deux."

True to his promises, the prime minister made a series of unilateral concessions to American demands. He dismantled the National Energy Program. He gutted the Foreign Investment Review Agency. New legislation on drug patents cheered the American-dominated drug industry and made all Canadian health programs more costly. And, in deference to Jack Valenti and the American Motion Picture Producers Association, Canada first watered down and then permanently mothballed its long-overdue legislation designed to improve Canadian access to film distribution. And all this was done before the negotiations even began.

Corporate America had long sought unfettered access to Canadian energy, raw resources, and markets and had worked to eliminate nationalist policies Canadian governments had implemented to protect Canadian independence. Over many years, the United States had won some victories. Successive Liberal governments, for example, had allowed foreign industrial control to reach levels unheard of in other industrialized countries. But, by the early part of the 1980s, and for the first time in our history, Canadian corporations, having outgrown their home bases, joined forces with powerful U.S. multinationals to transform Canada.

The goal of these corporations is the total restructuring of the national economy to suit the free-market philosophy of the United States. To accomplish this goal, corporate Canada needed several things: the massive privatization of a range of public enterprises, from transportation to energy, so as to diminish government involvement in them; the deregulation of the service sectors, to render them accessible to private interests and remove them from public control; and free trade with the United States to cement these new practices in place and to force Canadian wages, social standards, and corporate taxes down to American levels.

And corporate Canada needed a federal government that was willing to abandon its responsibility to the Canadian people and ready to sell their birthright to the highest bidder. What it found in the Mulroney Conservatives was a government willing to serve the interests of the corporate sector, Canadian and foreign, to such an extent that it has become that sector's principal vehicle to promote its business agenda. In his first speech to the House of Commons, the prime minister said, "We have been in power two months, but I can tell you this. . . . Give us twenty years . . . and you will not recognize this country."

The process of transformation has begun in earnest. Social programs are being gutted. Our foreign policy now simply echoes the Pentagon's. The government has destroyed internal systems to protect our natural resources. Canadian industry is being taken over at an unprecedented rate. Manufacturing and high-technology companies are fleeing Canada. We are becoming a nation of warehouses.

*Parcel of Rogues* is the story of greed, ambition, and betrayal. It is the story of the transformation of a country and its deliverance to a system foreign to its history and culture. For American business *would* come to Canada, all right — but on its terms. The story most Canadians do not know is that of the collusion in the betrayal of this country by the most powerful business and political leaders of our day. No wonder a major Washington-based business group has given Brian Mulroney its top award for "free enterprise" and his government's support of the Canada–U.S. Free Trade Agreement. The award is a sculpted eagle.

It is not too late for our country. But Canadians will have to have extraordinary courage to alter what seems to be our fate. There are alternatives that will allow Canada to regain control of its destiny and recapture the values that form the base of its identity and culture. For it is in these values alone that we will find the national will to survive.

# ACKNOWLEDGMENTS

I am very grateful to many people for their inspiration, advice, and assistance in the creation of this book. Its genesis was their conviction that Canadians are not being told the real story of the economic and social revolution taking place in Canada today. Mel Hurtig first inspired me to understand the dimensions of this fight. I am indebted to him. Tony Clark and the staff of the Pro Canada Network and Catherine Morrison and the staff of the Council of Canadians understood the time constraints of this endeavour and took on extra work loads to permit me to finish it. I thank them.

Mel Clarke contributed his vast experience in international trade. Duncan Cameron's constantly fresh insights helped form my analysis. Steve Shrybman shared his extensive knowledge of the environment. Ernie Regehr sat patiently through many long-distance discussions on foreign policy. David Langille provided background information on the BCNI. Peter Langille shared his excellent defense thesis. Jeff Bickerton guided me through the politics of Canada Post. Steve Watson gave me detailed information on the current state of transportation issues. John Dillon and Scott Sinclair of Common Frontiers contributed their first-hand knowledge of the *maquiladoras*. Wayne Easter and Raye-Anne Briscoe of the National Farmers Union were wonderful role models and have helped me understand the special plight of farmers. Bruce Campbell and the Canadian Labour Congress graciously provided background documentation on job loss. Sheila Purdy reviewed and improved my environment analysis. Jim Stanford did the same on energy, having guided my thinking on it for several years. John Trent's wonderful work on Canadian values provided much background for this section.

The talented team at Key Porter showed great patience for a first-time author and I could not have been more fortunate in a choice of publisher. To my editor, Charis Wahl, I owe a very special thanks. She was kind, encouraging, and firm, and her unflagging sense of humour took us both through some long, hard days. A particular thank you is due to my friend and mentor, Ken Ward-roper, who provided technical editing and day-to-day advice on the content of the book. I would claim that all errors are mine alone except that Ken wouldn't permit me any.

Finally, I wish to thank my husband, Andrew Davis, for putting up with me. And for sharing a dream.

# 1.
# CORPORATE NORTH AMERICA TAKES CARE OF BUSINESS

"Companies need to use free trade as a catalyst to mobilize employees to cut costs. Nothing clears the mind so much as the spectre of being hung out in the morning."

*Ray Verdon, President of Nabisco Brands*

"I've got nothing to keep me here now."

*Cecile McAllister, employee casualty of Inglis move to Ohio*

A RESPECTED NEW BOOK BY AMERICAN FINANCIAL forecaster Dr. Marvin Cetron and journalist Owen Davies, *American Renaissance: Our Life at the Turn of the 21st Century*, describes the stunning nature of the Canadian decision to enter into a free-trade agreement with the United States. By the year 2000, the authors predict, Quebec will have seceded from Canada, and the United States will have added five new states. Puerto Rico will become the fifty-first, and the remaining provinces of Canada will be combined into states fifty-two through fifty-six. "Once the free trade agreement with the U.S. takes full effect, the next logical step will be to accept politically what has already happened economically — the integration of Canada into the U.S." The move may seem politically difficult when it comes, they admit, but the real decision was taken when Canada entered into the trade deal in the first place. American industry got what it wanted — "unrestricted

access to both Canada's people and its raw materials" to provide the "safe haven" it needs to support other trading ventures.

Canada has no choice, the authors argue. It is now part of a powerful North American trading block that will reach down through Mexico into Central America and will form the basis for a new, corporate-driven attempt at American economic world domination.

A North American free-trade zone has been masterminded by a handful of multinational corporate power-brokers for whom it is designed and who stand to make a great deal of money in the new world order. In Canada, the zone's chief boosters are also its chief beneficiaries — the big Canadian corporations who outgrew Canada and whose self-interest is now directly threatened by the country's national interest. These brokers, many of them tied to or representing foreign corporate concerns, view any legislation to protect Canadian sovereignty or workers as an impediment to their growth.

The push for this sell-out started with the blue-chip lobby group for corporate Canada — the Business Council on National Issues. The BCNI represents the 150 leading corporations in Canada. These companies administer $825 billion in assets, and represent the major banks, insurance companies, oil and gas firms, and many foreign multinationals, such as Xerox, IBM, and ITT.

The council was formed in 1976 because a number of corporate leaders believed that a long-term, co-ordinated effort was needed to establish a solid business agenda in Canada. The problems, as they saw them, were that business was not speaking with one voice, and its priorities were being lost in the rough-and-tumble of Ottawa politics. The council is headed by a former Trudeau adviser and international-law specialist, Thomas d'Aquino, who serves both as president and as CEO. D'Aquino, unlike the corporate executives who serve a term with the BCNI while operating their companies, has made the organization his life. It is largely under his influence that it has gained its high public profile.

Public sympathy was not with the big-business agenda through much of the 1960s and 1970s, as was shown in the polls.

Pierre Trudeau was always more interested in issues centred on the constitution and language rights than with those related to economics. His government, although very slow to respond to the growing concern over foreign control of industry, did eventually create the Foreign Investment Review Agency to screen foreign take-overs of Canadian companies. It also brought in the National Energy Policy and drew up a timetable for Canadianization in the oil-and-gas industry. Although these measures were not necessarily bad for Canadian business, corporate Canada opposed them on the grounds that they represented too much interference by government in what should be business affairs.

These years witnessed the rise in the fortunes of the NDP and David Lewis's "corporate welfare bums" campaign that touched a sympathetic chord in many Canadians. The period of minority government was one of much progressive social legislation, and big business felt increasingly isolated from the mainstream of Canadian thinking. Powerful lobby groups representing women's rights, environmental concerns, and the peace movement appeared in the halls of Parliament, and were partially financed by the government. The clout these groups had in Ottawa provided one of the catalysts that launched a formal business lobby in Canada.

Modelled on the powerful right-wing American corporate lobby group the Business Roundtable, the BCNI set out to create a more hospitable public climate for big-business concerns. Looking south for the blueprint, Canadian corporate leaders sought to create financial opportunities by removing much of government's right to create public policy. In the remaining years of the Trudeau government, the lobby was beginning to exert real power. It found a number of sympathetic cabinet ministers and some positive feedback on such initiatives as deregulation in the transportation industry and wage-and-price restraints.

The tools for the job were clear: public enterprise and government regulation would have to go. The twin gospels of privatization and deregulation were crucial to this process. But the BCNI understood that Canadians are deeply committed to their mixed economy and that free trade would place enormous pressure on

Canada to harmonize its system with that of the Americans, a system that is much friendlier to corporate welfare. The groundwork involved selling these philosophies to provincial and federal government departments and building long-term support.

The BCNI sought allies among conservative and right-wing think-tanks such as the C.D. Howe and Fraser institutes. It established ties with university business schools across the country, placing its members on the right boards and governing bodies. These institutes and schools provide much of the research on which the government depends and are influential in the halls of power. The council knows that attitudes take time to change and it is prepared to work with new generations to convert them to a "pro-business" perspective.

Education has become an important focus. Under the guidance of the BCNI and its allies, some educators are turning from the arts and humanities towards creating the corporate drones of tomorrow. Support and funding for disciplines not serving business ends are under attack in many school boards. A uniform economic perspective that does not encourage independent thinking is being introduced, along with corporate funding, into many university faculties. The political philosophy favouring the unfettered working of the market-place is gospel. The vice-chairman of Northern Telecom insists that our schools and universities be the training grounds for the "armies" our country needs in the global wars of international competition. The goal is no less than the eventual transformation of the traditional Canadian economic and social system to one resembling that of the United States.

The BCNI has become the most influential business lobby in Canada, although it represents primarily the interests of big corporations, many of whom are foreign owned, and the inner circle of business leaders, most of whom have very close personal ties with the Mulroney government. It has become so powerful that it puts itself forward as government's equal partner in establishing the policies of the day. Yet its work has to do only with making corporate profit, not with creating business opportunities or jobs. A seven-year study found that virtually all new jobs in Canada are created by small- and medium-sized Canadian-owned businesses. In fact, during the years studied (1978–1985), big business in Canada — companies that belong to the BCNI and their ilk — cut their Canadian work-force.

Considering the exclusivity of the BCNI, it was inevitable that its goals would eventually collide with the rights and needs of small business and working people. Behind the scenes, members quietly worked to establish political ties in Ottawa and the provinces. Then, background papers reflecting the corporate view were written in a whole host of government policy areas. Many became the basis for government legislation.

In public, the group cleverly cloaked its goals in the guise of concern for the common good: their commitment, they announced, was to "help strengthen the country's social fabric." This concern translated into a call for an end to universal social programs and created enough pressure to kill the national child-care system promised by the Tories in their first term. The BCNI line that "the government must resist pressure to create new entitlements or more programs which in better times would be appealing, but which today simply cannot be afforded," was reiterated virtually word for word by the government when it abandoned child care.

While paying lip-service to a stronger economy, the BCNI prepared the ground for a new tax regime that shifts a greater tax burden to small business and families, freeing big business to integrate Canada more easily into a North American model. "The Canadian tax system is becoming increasingly less compatible with [those of] other countries, especially the United States. This puts Canadians at a competitive disadvantage. If we fail to correct this situation, the consequences for confidence, investment, growth and jobs in Canada will be negative," states one BCNI document. Again, these words were echoed in Parliament. Said Don Blenkarn, chairman of the House of Commons Standing Committee on Finance, Trade and Economic Affairs, "There is already too much differential between Canadian and U.S. tax rates. You can't put yourself out of line with your biggest trading partner."

The BCNI was also formed to curb the ability of government to interfere in areas big business considers to be outside government jurisdiction. All political parties in Canada have recognized that Canada is viable only with an economic system based on a mixed economy. Strongly opposed to traditional government attempts to buffer Canadian companies against an increasingly harsh international trading climate, the BCNI knew that a free-trade agreement would hand over the balance of power to the market itself, regardless of the political party in power, leaving successive Canadian governments with dramatically reduced room in which to serve the true interests of Canadians. Indeed, the corporate élite of this country view their success and that of all Canadians as intertwined, precisely because they will assume the role of "guardians" once claimed by government. However, as their aims become government policy, the income and living standards of almost everyone else decreases with each passing day.

The powerful BCNI's broad policy objectives are often well ahead of government's in articulating the future agenda for the country. So it was with the free-trade agreement. During the early 1980s, the idea of free trade was gaining momentum in Ottawa, at first primarily in Liberal circles. It was one of the principal recommendations of the Liberal Royal Commission on the Economy and was formally endorsed by the BCNI as early as 1982. In 1983, Thomas d'Aquino, president of the BCNI, publicly began to booster a deal, and to approach American business and political leaders. As well, with the Canadian Manufacturers' Association and the Chamber of Commerce, the BCNI entered into a five-year campaign to convince Canadians that a comprehensive deal with the United States would lead to more jobs, a higher standard of living, and wonderful new opportunities for business.

To hoodwink Canadians into believing that a new lobby group had formed to fight for free trade, the BCNI launched the Canadian Alliance for Trade and Job Opportunities; its innocuous name hid an ominous mandate. Alliance members were largely those of the BCNI, committed to funnelling huge quantities of money and expertise to the Conservative party in order to secure free trade. To front for the group, two former politicians were plucked from retirement as co-chairs. Donald Macdonald had chaired the powerful Royal Commission on the Economic Union and Development Prospects for Canada and was a firm supporter of free trade. That he was also a Liberal was politically crucial: the initiative could not be seen to be exclusively Conservative.

Peter Lougheed, former Alberta premier, was given a golden opportunity to ensure that no future federal government should ever again be able to interfere in Alberta business. His years in provincial politics had left him sure that nationalism was his enemy, and he spoke like a stern father to a silly child when he encountered resistance to his reverence for the natural justice of the unfettered market-place.

Lougheed and Macdonald personified the conviction of the corporate élite in Canada that few are chosen to understand the workings of the economy; the rest of us are called merely to trust them to know what's best.

To get their deal, the major corporations decided to put the full weight of their economic clout behind the free-trade agreement. Alcan, the Royal Bank, and Noranda Inc. each put up $400, 000 in early 1987; 112 other corporations raised close to $3 million for a major advertising blitz to promote the deal. Nineteen foreign-controlled companies gave large amounts of money to the fight, directly interfering in the political process of a sovereign country. This early list of donors was leaked to the press; the alliance was refusing to disclose information on donors or amounts, in spite of a promise it had made upon formation in March 1986 to open its books to the public for full accountability. The leaked list clearly demonstrated that the major donors were almost all members of the BCNI and included, and were profoundly influenced by, American-based multinationals.

United in their support of a comprehensive agreement that would usher in a new era of American-style free-market, business-friendly policies and practices, the corporate brokers spent more than $5 million, blanketing the media with slick, high-priced advertising. A page advertising space in the *Globe and Mail*, for example, costs $26, 000: the alliance placed dozens of full-page ads in the *Globe and Mail* and other newspapers in the two years leading up to the election. They spent millions more supporting the Tories. For the first time, the Liberal party received significantly fewer major corporate contributions because of its anti-free trade position. It entered the election deeply in debt.

Alex Carey, a writer who has traced the growth of a corporate culture in other countries, particularly in Australia, describes the process this way: "The twentieth century has been characterized by three developments of great political importance: the growth of democracy; the growth of corporate power; and the growth of propaganda as a means of protecting corporate power against democracy."

Nowhere was the truth of these words more visible than in Canada in the years and months leading up to the 1988 election. Corporate North America had hit the motherlode in the Tory party. The country became starkly divided, the vast majority of citizens' groups on one side, and most business interests on the other. While only a few companies contributed funds to the anti-free trade side, many thousands of individuals gave small donations. Conversely, only about $9, 000 of Alliance advertising came from individuals. *This Magazine*'s detailed estimates of corporate spending to promote free trade placed it at more than $19 million. However, the total may be a great deal higher as, despite a promise to disclose fully all donations, many corporations refused.

It is an ominous threat to our system of democracy that those with access to almost limitless resources had such a profound impact on the outcome of the 1988 election. Revenue Canada established a dangerous precedent when it permitted groups that were openly partisan to claim lobby donations as business expenses. Perhaps most disturbingly, much of this wealth came from foreign-controlled interests whose agenda is in no way motivated by a concern for Canada. Some companies with foreign head offices — for example, Shell, who gave $250,000; Texaco, who handed over $100,000; and Ford, who donated almost $30,000 — disclosed how much money they pumped into the Canadian fight.

Others, such as Allied-Signal, AT&T, and Bechtel, refused. And these figures do not include the enormous financial influence that the American corporate lobby had on its own government in its final position on the deal with Canada or how much was spent selling this position in the United States.

What is certain is that corporate Canada, deeply influenced by continental pressures, waded into this election as never before. The usually quiet, behind-the-scenes mode of operation of the corporate lobby was replaced by a very public confrontation. "We're damn proud of what we've given and we want to be up front about it," said Alf Powis of Noranda. Thus, whenever the groups aligned against the deal raised enough money to put their message out publicly, the alliance was able to inundate Canadians with highly personalized responses, targeting their interests by region, occupation, or age. Although the messages were often dense with jargon and stilted language, the sheer numbers of them overwhelmed the opposition.

While the anti–free trade movement operated out of kitchens, warehouses, and small basement offices, the alliance and the BCNI managed the corporate strategy from corporate boardrooms. Anti–free trade protesters organized spontaneously all over the country, braving the chill winds of an early Canadian winter to tell the politicians and each other about their fears for their country. Near the end of the campaign, the Tories organized counter-protests for the media to attempt to show grass-roots support for the deal. When the television cameras arrived, busloads of young people would pull up, pro–free trade sweatshirts and buttons would be donned, the young people would shout their support for the prime minister; then, as soon as the parade of politicians and media had left, the young people would give back their sweatshirts and buttons and climb back on their buses. It was the quiet, smooth hum of money at work, the sweet siren call of power not yet wielded, of favours not yet dispensed.

And so, they delivered the election. With one final push following the televised leaders' debates, the alliance, the Chamber of Commerce, and the BCNI launched a last, vicious, fear-mongering campaign that warned of economic collapse, reprisals from the Americans, and a retreat into isolationism if Canada rejected the deal. "It would be dangerous, very dangerous to reject free trade," said Paul Desmarais, head of Power Corp.

The corporate leaders had spent money in unprecedented amounts. But the stakes were very high. They correctly understood that free trade would forever free them of responsibility to the Canadian people. From now on, just like grown-up multinationals, they would be free to move production to anywhere in the world where labour was cheap and compliant, and where environmental regulation awaits an economically sounder time.

Their victory coincided with a revived continental movement emanating from the corporate boardrooms of the United States. In fact, their victory and this movement were parts of the same large plan, and the two sides worked in tandem. Common Canadian greed delivered what history had not. Over the years, U.S. desire for military dominance over Canada had been slowly replaced by the reality of economic integration. It hadn't always been so.

The United States invaded Canada twice in its history — both times before 1867. In 1775, and again in 1812, Canadian forces repelled the invaders. The dream of Manifest Destiny, however, guided the United States in its relations with the whole continent, and rapid expansion took place in the Southwest, against Mexico and land that belonged to Spain (now Florida), and in the Northwest, against British settlements, moving the American boundary substantially north. As military invasion declined as an option for Americans who still dreamed of one nation, sea to Arctic sea, economic union increasingly seemed to be an alternative route to the same goal.

The Americans were abetted in their pursuit of this goal by a Canadian fifth column — these nineteenth-century counterparts of Mulroney's Conservatives were the rogues of their time — called Annexationists. Made up of 1,000 of the wealthiest families in Montreal, the Annexation Movement succeeded in its push for a free-trade agreement, although it failed in its ultimate goal for full union between the two countries. A reciprocity agreement that had been in place since 1854 was cancelled in 1866, as a lever for the Americans to use to try to force Canada into a more vulnerable position, and, ultimately, into annexation. The nationalist forces in this country, however, held their ground, and Canada was declared a nation in 1867.

But the push in the United States for what many Americans considered Canada's destiny didn't die. From the purchase of Alaska to aggressive interference in Manitoba's troubled struggle during the Riel Rebellion, American political designs on Canada were clear. As John A. Macdonald said, "It is quite evident to me that the U.S. government is resolved to do all it can, short of war, to get possession of the Western Territory, and we must take immediate and vigorous steps to counteract them." Calls for commercial union between the two countries increased, particularly during the financially troubled last decade of the century. In a mood of deep pessimism about Canada's future, many felt that only one option lay before the country — becoming part of the United States. In fact, between 1881 and 1891, more than one million Canadians moved there.

The U.S. Senate passed a commercial-union bill, and the Liberal party in Canada adopted reciprocity as its central platform. As it would in 1988, American money poured in to further the cause in Canada. The influence of "Yankee gold" on Canadian politics became a central rallying cry for the opposition. In 1891, and again in 1911, the forces of Canadian nationalism defeated the powerful drive for union with the United States. In both elections, the pivotal issue was described in terms that made it seem nothing short of the future destiny of Canada.

In the years following, the economic bonds between the two countries deepened. At the time of the Laurier defeat, less than one-quarter of Canada's trade was with the United States. This situation was to change dramatically. Quite deliberately, Canada's industrial development was encouraged as a complement to American industry, but not to be permitted to grow as competition. U.S. trade policy was designed to subsume Canada within the American orbit.

According to the U.S. ambassador to Canada in 1935, it was vitally important to develop trade ties in such a way that Canada would be clearly supporting the United States internationally. Canadians must feel that "in a thousand and one ways they are bound to us in political things," he said. In a 1948 editorial, *Life* magazine forecasted: "The next step we should take is a complete U.S.-Canadian customs union. . . . Political integration may be desirable, and welcome, someday but it is not now an issue. Economic union makes sense now. It is right and desirable for both countries."

Canada became, like no other industrialized nation on earth, a branch-plant economy, and our resources were developed under foreign control. The rate of establishment of branch plants, through direct investment and by take-over of existing Canadian companies, grew dramatically. From an annual average of 10 to 20 companies in the 1940s, acquisitions swelled to 150 a year by the 1970s. The massive inflow of American capital into Canada since the Second World War has left half of the country's mining, oil, and manufacturing industries American owned. The vast majority of foreign investment in Canada goes unregulated and unscreened.

Canada has by far the greatest foreign domination of industry and resources of the twenty or so developed nations of the world: 99 percent of our tobacco industry is foreign owned, as is 92 percent of our automotive sector, 76 percent of our chemical industry, 78 percent of our electrical-apparatus industry, 84 percent of transportation, and 53 percent of our combined manufacturing and petroleum industries.

This is not foreign investment. This is foreign control. And most of it — almost three-quarters — is American. The price for Canadians is very high. More than half of the profits of the five hundred biggest corporations in Canada go to non-Canadians. High foreign ownership and high unemployment go hand in hand. Non-Canadian companies don't buy Canadian goods or invest in research and development in Canada. That's one reason why branch plants are so profitable for their parent companies.

The dream that fired military continentalism in North America has been replaced by a practical reality. Despite predictions like those made by Marvin Cetron and Owen Davies, most American leaders believe that it is no longer necessary or desirable for Americans to annex Canada. Corporate Canada has, in all practical senses, voluntarily merged its interests with those of corporate America; there is no need for force. The American push for free trade was driven by a desire to remove remaining impediments to total economic integration of the two systems, and a powerful business alliance grew up to push the agenda in the United States.

That alliance, the American Coalition for Trade Expansion with Canada, was made up of six hundred powerful corporations and industry associations, with ties to sixty million employees. Led by the giant American Express, the coalition was formed in 1987 in response to what Harry Freeman, executive vice-president of the company, saw as lack of sufficient commitment to the concept on Capitol Hill. With key companies and sectors representing food, finance, chemicals, oil and gas, pharmaceuticals, forest products, auto parts, defence production, and telecommunications, the coalition was an unprecedented alliance of corporate interests coming together to lobby for a common goal.

Former U.S. trade representative Bob Strauss called it the "Lord's work." Harry Freeman was a little more specific: "The right of market access should be considered paramount . . . and U.S. firms should have the right to offer their services from either within Canada or from across the border . . . the ultimate goal would be a convergence of our two nations' domestic financial relations." The coalition's stated goals included an open market for energy. "The U.S. is guaranteed non-discriminatory, duty-free access to Canadian supplies, even during shortages." It promised a "close economic/political/strategic relationship of the two countries" and declared that, "when fully implemented, FTA [the free-trade agreement] is expected to add as much as 1 percent to the U.S. GNP. The U.S. gets guaranteed access to a market the size of California."

Many members of the American Coalition for Trade Expansion with Canada became directly involved, financially and strategically, with the Canadian pro–free trade lobby. Industry leaders such as Shell, IBM, Weyerhaeuser, Allied-Signal, AT&T, BP, Cargill, General Motors, 3M, General Electric, and Dow Chemical not only spent undisclosed millions of dollars promoting the deal in their own country, but also joined the Alliance for Trade and Job Opportunities in Canada, and gave money through their subsidiaries to the Conservative party. They lobbied in the state and federal governments while the alliance did the same in Canada.

Since so much of the trade between our two countries is intra-corporate trade, that is, Canada shipping its natural resources south and the parent companies selling the finished product back to us, these multinationals had everything to gain from a co-ordinated strategy to remove the border. "We purchase much of our inventory from suppliers in Canada and distribute them throughout the United States. The opportunity to re-export to Canada is a potentially attractive market for our company," said the owner of one company. Said another, "Ply*Gem is dependent upon the Canadian market for sustaining a constant supply of specialty wood products for worldwide markets. We import large quantities of wood products from Canada. . . . We would like to re-export finished wood products back to the Canadian market. . . . a trade agreement with Canada will open a re-export market for Ply*Gem."

An example of the co-operation between corporate Canada and corporate America can be seen in the approach to free trade taken by the Grocery Products Manufacturers of Canada. This is one of the most powerful groups in the country, a $50-billion industry, which employs 230,000 Canadians. Food processing is the second-biggest industry in Ontario, with annual sales of $15 billion. Like many other industry associations in Canada, the GPMC is heavily dominated by foreign-based multinationals. Eighty percent foreign owned, it is controlled by such giants as Kellogg, General Foods,

Nabisco Brands, Campbell Soup, Kraft, Nestlé, Procter & Gamble — a long and familiar list to Canadian consumers.

These companies have ruled the Canadian food scene for many years; but they have been required by legislation and tariffs to provide jobs and net benefit to Canada in return for access to the market here. Consequently, in the years and months leading up to the free-trade agreement, their position on such an accord was watched with considerable interest in business and government circles.

To find out what their members thought, several months before the 1988 election, Grocery Products Manufacturers of Canada prepared and distributed a detailed questionnaire on the possible ramifications of a free-trade agreement, with instructions that the answers would be treated anonymously. Well over 80 percent of those who responded expressed grave concerns about the impact of such a deal on their businesses. Many said that, under the current system, they could live with the marketing boards and Canadian wage packages but that, under a free-trade regime, they would not be able to compete. Not only did the membership not give GPMC permission to support the agreement, but many urged the association to speak out against it.

Yet, the multinationals that dominate the association wanted to support free trade publicly, and urged GPMC to do so. Only fierce resistance by a few small Canadian firms forced the organization to a compromise: it took no official position on free trade, in spite of the fact that a majority of the members had strong concerns about its impact. The large American corporations had to find another forum for their strategies, so they joined the free-trade lobby and donated money to the cause. Nabisco Brands, for example, gave more than $100,000 to the Conservative party in 1988 alone. A number of them — companies such as Kraft, Gerber, Coca-Cola, Nabisco, and Pepsi, and the leading industry associations — supported the American pro–free trade lobby in a prominent way.

It became very clear during this time who was calling the shots for this group, and it is not their Canadian members or customers. In this situation, as in every other where there is a conflict between the interests of the country in which they are located and the country of their head offices, these companies serve American interests.

During the year following the ratification of the deal, the big multinational powers within GPMC applied pressure on both the Canadian and the American governments to speed up the removal of tariffs in their sector, as did the big players in the Confectionery Manufacturers Association of Canada. Nestlé, Rowntree, Hershey, Mars — the sugar giants, some American, some multinationals headquartered elsewhere — wanted the process accelerated. They had waited a long time to integrate their North American operations and were eager to get on with the next phase. They understood, as most Canadians still did not, that the free-trade agreement was a green light to "rationalize" their production facilities and move out of Canada.

Ann Hughes, then with the U.S. State Department, now the chief American trade negotiator with Canada, explained this process very clearly in an article she wrote during the negotiations. Calling the free-trade agreement one of "stunning proportions," Hughes explained that its primary function was to permit American companies full access to the market-place in Canada without having any rules placed on them. Essentially, the market would be left alone to operate, she explained. "Investment and trade are inseparable. Trade barriers can be used to promote investment in order to gain market access. Conversely, investment restrictions can be used to choke off trade where a local presence is essential to sales and/or service." Therefore, she said, the elimination of both trade and investment restrictions had been necessary for the Americans in any deal.

Noting that U.S. investment had not always been as welcome in Canada as it now was, Hughes said that former legislation requiring that foreign investment must have some benefit for Canada ("you had to invest or to forgo the potential business") had rendered the business climate "unstable, unpredictable and decidedly unfriendly." The new climate was of such significance, she said with enthusiasm, because now American companies were no longer to be considered foreign firms, and, consequently, the government could not force them to use Canadian supplies, create jobs in Canada, or invest in research and development here. Most new investments wouldn't even be screened, and Canada could no longer require minimum levels of Canadian-equity holdings. The companies were assured of "free transfers of profits, proceeds of sales, and their remittances."

But, Hughes warned, the United States must have "an insurance policy that a future government won't undo all the good Prime Minister Mulroney has done." Hence the hurry for the food giants and others to take advantage of this new friendly-to-multinationals atmosphere. Now, American business is not only free to invest where it chooses, with very few questions asked and no requirements seeking benefits to Canada imposed, but also free to continue to sell in Canadian markets without creating any jobs or wealth here. Campbell Soup executives had forecast years before the free-trade agreement was signed that, as soon as it was law, Campbell would close its Canadian operations and service all of the Canadian market from a Sunday evening's overrun in its Chicago plant. The process has started. Campbell has closed three plants so far and is "consolidating" many others.

Given the unacceptably high level of foreign domination in Canada and the dramatic potential for expanded exploitation by U.S.-based multinationals in the future, the single most important aspect of this agreement for Canadians must be the collusion that took place between the American coalition, the Canadian alliance, and our own government. At the time that American Express formed the U.S. pro–free trade lobby, Public Affairs Resource Group (PARG) was a Canadian holding company that owned Public Affairs International (PAI) — a well-connected Ottawa-based consulting group with strong Liberal and Conservative ties; Decima, the exclusive Conservative polling company headed by Allan Gregg; and a strategy group called Public Affairs Communications Management, run by Nancy McLean, a senior Tory insider who has helped Bill Davis, Grant Devine, Richard Hatfield, and John Buchanan to gain and maintain power.

This group formed the key strategy team for the Canadian Alliance for Trade and Job Opportunities, McLean on tactics and Gregg on polling. The deep and long-standing links between these individuals and the Conservative government guaranteed that the corporate lobby was being advised by Mulroney's finest, and the way was cleared for a joint strategy involving the most senior levels of government and business in this country. Not only did the government help co-ordinate the corporate strategy to sell free trade, not only did it receive many millions of dollars from its allies, not only did it spend tax-payers' money to then hawk this deal back to them, it participated in joint planning with the American coalition to seal the fate of Canada.

PARG had another subsidiary, Government Research Corporation, located in Washington. It was hired by Harry Freeman and American Express to do the strategy work for the American Coalition for Trade Expansion with Canada. Undoubtedly, the coalition knew the importance of having a key adviser with close corporate links to the Canadian government. Nor did it hurt to connect its planning to the Canadian pro–free trade lobby groups, since so many of its members were owned anyway by these multinationals. And American Express was well acquainted with the services of this company. It was a PAI client in Canada.

The free-trade agreement was a corporate bill of rights. For those who were to benefit personally, it didn't much matter which side of the border they were on. To ensure that concerns about Canadian sovereignty didn't interfere with business in Canada or the United States, PAI was careful not to accept any contracts with anti–free trade companies in Canada until the election was over. And so, in the end, it was a core group of Canada's corporate and political élite, a small circle who had always had access to and had taken the best from Canada, who helped the United States to realize its long-standing dream of Manifest Destiny on the North American continent.

This was Manifest Destiny with a difference. Historically, American expansionism has been built on a fervent belief in the inherent superiority of the American system and way of life and has grown from the conviction of divine mission. But corporate goals have become the fundamental basis for American society — what is good for GM is considered to be good for all of America — and this reality has been one of the most important distinctions between our two countries.

The goal of the new Manifest Destiny is financial and corporate, the freedom for global corporations to compete internationally without the interference of national borders, standards, or rules. Like many other big corporations, American Express, which headed the American lobby and was to be given its reward by the Canadian government, saw the free-trade agreement with Canada as a stepping-stone to a world market. This view was particularly important for the service sector, which had been excluded in the GATT negotiations but was an important part of the free-trade agreement. Said Allan Taylor, CEO of the Royal Bank, "A Canada/ U.S. agreement which includes services could be the catalyst for multilateral cooperation. Freer trade breeds more free trade — putting pressure on other countries to come into line as the multilateral negotiations proceed."

The chairman of the American Stock Exchange explained it this way: "The free trade agreement negotiated by President Reagan and Prime Minister Mulroney establishes a new standard of trade policy essential to an international economy. It continues a trend begun by financial institutions like the American Stock Exchange to integrate world financial markets and ease restrictions on the flow of goods and services . . . this agreement continues an important trend to link the economies of the world." Because of the profound and fundamental change that telecommunications has brought to world trade, the companies in this sector have the most to gain from international deregulation.

The world is being reshaped by these companies in their own image and on their own terms. The United Nations tracks transnational corporations and says that a select group of six hundred international companies, each with annual sales of more than $1 billion, produces 25 percent of everything made in the world's market economies. They will merge, however, to fewer than half that number in the next decade and will consequently grow in status and sheer untouchable power. One major bank has predicted that, by the year 2000, there will be as few as ten international banks, forming a small élite that will totally control the industry.

Northern Telecom, a Canadian company that increasingly perceives Canada as insignificant in its future plans, parrots the new gospel. David Vice, its president, speaks lovingly of a "world without borders" in a publication for Canadian Airlines. The editor of the report, James Gillies, writes that no natural advantage of a country can any longer render it secure. Rather, he states, each country has to try to "supply goods into world markets at lower cost and prices than anyone else."

A world without borders is a euphemism for a tightly controlled corporate system, where there is no power strong enough or international enough to protect the needs and rights of people. Those in control can play workers in one country off against workers in another, and governments will not be sufficiently strong to regulate on behalf of their populations. Because the companies are private, they are not required to disclose their financial status. A nation has no way of knowing if their annual reports have any basis in fact. Because they are global, they can transfer money from country to country, loading debt where they wish and avoiding costs. They do not have to consider the effect of their actions on a country, nor are they in any way accountable to its population. In their world, the rules will come from the top down, not from the bottom up.

In this system, such terms as "good government/business relations" take on a new meaning. Decoded, such phrases really mean that government must not interfere with the goals of big business. Economist Carl Beigie says that if wages and taxation policies don't serve the needs of business, "production (and employment) will be forced to seek a more favourable environment elsewhere." Economist Mark Holmes calls any subsidy that fosters local growth, creates jobs, or maintains incomes a "disloyal form of competition." Disloyal to whom? To American Express? "This definition of 'free trade' means that transnational conglomerates may use ... technology however they wish: without fear of any government interceding, ever. The terms outline a carte blanche charter of rights and freedoms for corporations which supersedes national law," says Lanie Patrick, a cultural-policy consultant from Winnipeg.

In a global economy, the power of these corporations supersedes the power of the state and, therefore, democracy itself. Patrick says their rivalry will displace national struggle and pit transnational against transnational. People everywhere, and the world environment, will be the losers: "The transnational conglomerates are co-opting the world's nations, and negotiating with them on a one-by-one basis, through sponsors." In Canada, these sponsors were the Business Council on National Issues and the Alliance for Trade and Job Opportunities. Through them, Canada is becoming a willing participant in the creation of a world system in which the most influential institutions are transnational corporations, above national law and beyond the control of any international agency.

For corporate America, then, the free-trade agreement with Canada was a first step to regaining trade dominance in the world. The creation of a legally enforceable model was an important step towards an international policy of free trade, tailored to serve American interests, a "wedge with teeth." For instance, including trade in services was essential because the United States still enjoys a comparative advantage in this area, and it can now by-pass the GATT system of multilateral trade if any country tries to impose conditions. The United States will not have to subordinate its goals to a world-trade body. As then U.S. Treasury secretary James Baker said, "Other nations are forced to recognize that the United States will devise ways to expand trade — with or without them. If they choose not to open their markets, they will not reap the benefits."

It could not come as a surprise, then, as political economist Duncan Cameron puts it, that the free-trade agreement with Canada passed through the U.S. Congress like a hot knife through butter. Or that the only study of the deal that has called it a success was American. The Institute for U.S.–Canada Business Studies, of Pace University in New York, in a report commissioned by the Canadian division of Prudential-Bache Securities, declared that the deal had had an "extraordinary" effect in stimulating the Canadian economy in the same week that Canada recorded its first merchandise-trade deficit in thirteen years. Why does the institute think the results of the trade deal are so positive? "The FTA has made it easier for foreign companies to reorganize their Canadian subsidiaries in line with changes in the world economy and integrate them into global production systems."

For Harry Freeman of American Express, it was well worth the effort. The Canada–U.S. Free Trade Agreement gave him what the GATT did not. A world without borders is next. For the political-consulting élite of PAI/Decima, there was a happy ending too. The company merged with an American public-relations firm, Hill & Knowlton, owned by British giant WPP Group Plc (London), in a deal valued at up to $43 million, including $12 million in cash up front. David McNaughton of PAI and Allan Gregg of Decima, between them, owned 70 percent of the company and took the lion's share of the profits.

Membership does, indeed, have its privileges.

# 2.
# THE TORIES DELIVER: CANADA TO GO

"They looked pretty happy to me. Everybody seems to be doing pretty well."
*Brian Mulroney, on a tour of an Atlantic fish plant.*

DEREK BURNEY, THE CANADIAN AMBASSADOR TO Washington, loves to tell the story about a Maritime fisherman carrying a pail of lobsters up from the wharf. On the way, he meets a friend who warns him that the lobsters might escape because there is no lid on the pail. "Oh no," says the fisherman, "These are Canadian lobsters, boy. As soon as one makes it to the top, the others drag him down." Canada's ambassador believes that free trade will change Canada's attitude.

Canadians have a deep attachment to a way of life that they have built up over many years. Our ancestors knew that our harsh environment and small population required sharing for survival. Our very existence depended on helping each other. We established some of the finest social programs in the world, based on a sense of responsibility to others. Thus we rejected the American ideology founded on the supremacy of the individual. Instead, we attempt to balance the rights of the individual with those of the group. This system was also born out of desire to foster tolerance and respect for two founding nations, each of whom could promote its own way of life.

The Mulroney government knew this and did not have the courage to present its changes honestly. The assault to come was never talked about before either the 1984 or the 1988 elections.

Instead, it embarked on a free-trade agreement with the United States, fully aware that, with time, the pressure would grow on both sides of the border to harmonize our two economic systems.

Before the 1984 election, Joe Clark warned that unrestrained free trade with the United States would put thousands of Canadian jobs at risk. Brian Mulroney said that Canada had rejected free trade with the United States in 1911, and would do so again. Michael Wilson said that bilateral free trade with the United States is simplistic and naive: "It would only serve to further diminish our ability to compete internationally."

By the time of the 1988 election, the party that had originally come to power on a platform of patronage reform, that had promised renewed access to the political process, that had historically fought for Canadian sovereignty, had exchanged its integrity and independence for massive infusions of money, without which it could not have won its second mandate. Never before had the lobby groups representing big business been so powerful and almost exclusively listened to in Ottawa.

Brian Mulroney was quite prepared to trade away the historical authority vested in the federal system and entrusted in the office of the prime minister. To the provinces, he was prepared to give jurisdiction over shared-cost programs and increased export authority; to the Americans, Canada's vast resources, high-tech companies, and farms; to his corporate friends, assurance that his government would never again require that they link their success to the national interest.

A 1985 cabinet strategy document that was leaked to the press outlined the government's slick, low-keyed campaign to convince Canadians that free trade was benign, and to promote as little dialogue and information exchange as possible, lest a grass-roots coalition grow up to fight the initiative. The document called on the government to focus exclusively on the benefits of a deal, to discredit opposition members who raise concerns about it, and to "divide and neutralize" groups that oppose the agreement. Calling for "communications control" of the situation, the cabinet brief

said that the best the government could hope for was "benign neglect" of the issue by Canadians.

Another leaked internal memo, prepared by the PC corporate fund-raising strategy committee in 1986, shows the progress of the relationship between the government and its corporate friends in the intervening year. The document recommended that corporate donors who contribute more than $5,000 a year were to be given élite treatment, invited to private dinner parties with the prime minister and senior cabinet ministers, and sent special "insider" newsletters explaining government policy. Emphasizing the need to reserve special recognition for the top echelon of this group, the report warned: "Even within this elite, it might be necessary to discriminate on the basis of donation importance for the scarcest of rewards."

"Invoices" seeking "contributions" were to be sent to specific corporations, reminding them of federal government contracts and grants the company had received. Although the party denied that either practice was ever carried out, the committee's recommendations were approved at a 1986 meeting of the fund's board of directors, and were an indication of the deal that was to take place between the corporate power-brokers and the Tory party in the election of 1988.

Once its corporate friends delivered the election, it was time for the government to pay up. Immediately after the election, the big-business lobby called for severe cuts to social spending. The government found itself in a difficult situation. Brian Mulroney had assured Canadians that all charges by the opposition that free trade would place Canada's social programs in jeopardy were false. "As long as I am Prime Minister of Canada, social benefits, especially those for the elderly, will be improved — not diminished — by our government," he said a month before the election. He even brought his mother up onto a public platform and solemnly vowed to her on television that he would not touch the entitlements of seniors.

And he described the now-cancelled child-care program as "a program that the nation can afford in our current fiscal circumstances and within the budgetary framework we have set." So the government could hardly start right in, breaking its promises to the voters. Yet neither could it ignore or postpone the urgent corporate agenda that would end universality, dismantle marketing boards, and leave the regions to fend for themselves.

The government had another serious problem. Unable to come to any resolution on what constituted an unfair subsidy during the free-trade negotiations, it had left these key disputes for future discussions. (This is a little like buying a house, closing the deal, and agreeing to decide on terms later.) By agreeing to give away its ability to negotiate terms, the government surrendered the agenda to U.S. business interests. What those interests think of our social programs is a matter of record. All through the negotiations, and in fact for years, American business and government leaders had made it very clear that they consider many, many Canadian practices to be trade distortions; these practices would have to cease before free trade could remove the threat of reprisals against Canadian producers.

They objected to our unemployment-insurance system; our entire agricultural structure; protection for our cultural industries, including Canadian-content laws; a whole host of regional-development programs; our exchange rate; and countless other practices established by successive governments in accordance with Canadian values and aimed at providing equality of opportunity for all Canadians. The very act of leaving the definition of subsidies unresolved was an admission by the Canadian government that eventual harmonization of the Canadian and American systems was inevitable. Quite simply, the Americans wanted free, unimpeded access to our market and were not prepared to deal with a different system across the border.

In the introduction to the implementing legislation that accompanied the free-trade deal in the U.S., the intention was startlingly clear: "The Administration has no higher priority than the elimination of Canadian subsidies that adversely affect U.S. industries." Needless to say, there was no mention of offending American subsidies or of any commitment to making the process work to the advantage of both countries. After all, the agreement is only one more step in a long process that has been building for years and will last for many more. Fifteen new bodies directed to oversee more than twenty sets of negotiations were established, including a mandate to eliminate "arbitrary governmental impediments to economically sound U.S. investment decisions in Canada."

In other words, American business interests now control the U.S. position on what constitutes unfair trading practices in Canada. And crucially, the goals of corporate America coincide with the goals of corporate Canada. In both countries, the government has transferred its primary obligation from the people to the corporations. In both countries, corporate interest is the government. The difference is that our corporate world is controlled by the U.S. corporate world.

American priorities were clearly set out in their legislation, and included an end to all remaining screening of American investment in Canada, and the expansion of free trade to remove remaining protection for Canadian cultural industries and energy. As well, the document established that provincial laws and practices would also be open to challenge, defining subsidies as anything at all that might have an adverse impact on American producers.

At the top of Washington's list were future negotiations to curtail Canadian industrial subsidies and to rewrite the Auto Pact. And, the administration promised to report to congress on developments in trade in services, intellectual property, and government procurement. A senior Washington official warned Canadians very bluntly: "It would be a serious political mistake for the Canadian government to come to the negotiations demanding further limitations on the application of U.S. [trade-remedy] laws, without offering major concessions in return in the form of substantially reduced subsidy programs." The American government was unequivocally stating that there was no chance it would stop countervailing actions against Canada until Canada agreed to substantially change its economic and social systems to resemble those of the United States. The U.S. government, unlike our own, was always up-front about its objectives.

The Mulroney government was caught in a web of its own making. Flanked on one side by the Canadian corporate élite, fresh from its victory at the polls, ready to call in its debt from the Tories, and, on the other, by an aggressive American business community, eager to flex its new-found muscle in Canada, it had very little room to move. Brian Mulroney knew that, although he had won another majority government, more Canadians voted for parties opposed to free trade than for the only one supporting it. He also knew that the support he did receive was based on trust in his promise that social programs would not be touched.

And so, the Mulroney Conservatives embarked on one of the most singularly dishonest campaigns ever waged by government in this country. They launched a crusade to convince Canadians that Canada was suddenly facing a major crisis in the form of its deficit. Every Tory MP and cabinet minister was conscripted into service of the "new" crisis — a serious issue that had been developing for years but that the government had deceitfully neglected to address during the election.

Important politicians and government officials fanned out across the country, sounding the alarm, carrying dire warnings that, if Canada did not lower its spending, future generations of Canadians would be crippled economically. To sell its 1989 budget, the first after the election and the child of this new crisis, the government spent almost $3 million on a slick media campaign designed to "educate" Canadians to the urgency of the deficit. "I think it's very important that Canadians understand the nature of the problem we're facing," said Michael Wilson. (To sell the Goods and Services Tax two years later, the government allocated $13 million of tax-payers' money for an advertising blitz extolling its virtues; to collect it, the government is creating a whole new tax centre.)

What Canadians were being educated for is, quite simply, the beginning of a radical departure from our historic social and economic way of life. The government is preparing us to accept a profound change in direction, away from the distribution of wealth to the regions, which is our historic and constitutionally mandated responsibility and a reflection of our deeply held belief in the inherent fairness of the universality of social programs. The blame has been conveniently laid at the altar of the deficit; as quickly as the words "free trade" entered the Canadian vocabulary, they vanished.

The people who brought us free trade now never talk about it. Free trade has nothing to do with the assault on our social programs, they insist. We will have to wait at least ten years to see the results of the deal, announce the very people who had promised scant months earlier that the positive benefits of free trade would be felt immediately. John Crosbie called free trade critics "hyenas."

It would have been more honest if the Business Council on National Issues and the government had admitted that, if assessment is irrelevant, it is because this is a game where the rules keep changing to suit predetermined winners and losers. In fact, the creation of victims whose presence aids in the ability to impose a harsh new system is considered a benefit by those corporate interests that backed free trade.

The losers were identified well before the 1988 election. According to a document leaked to the Canadian Inter-Church Coalition for Economic Justice, during the free-trade negotiations, Simon Reisman, the chief Canadian negotiator for the agreement, had made an offer to the Americans to limit regional programs in order to gain exemption from U.S. countervail actions. He informed those attending a meeting with the provinces that the government was prepared to restrict targeted programs and that "it would be up to the provinces to find new ways to deal with specific problem situations." Ironically, the Americans turned him down because they did not want to limit their bargaining power in the future. The break-down in bargaining almost scuttled the deal, which had to be rescued at the political level: the tough talk was merely postponed.

Soon after the 1988 election, the *Financial Post* made the clear link between the upcoming cuts to the regions and the free-trade agreement: "It is long past time to dismantle the malodorous pork-barrel maintained under the name of 'regional development.' The government can start now, and seize the offensive. Or it can wait, and let the bilateral discussions on export subsidies, however beside the point, make reform impossible."

In other words, the government could start the inevitable process itself or wait to be forced into it by the Americans. But the message was crystal-clear: there would be no choice. The free-trade agreement would see to that. The deal prevents Canadian governments from regulating key sectors of the economy or introducing measures to promote Canadian enterprises. For ever and ever, or for as long as the agreement is in force, successive Canadian governments will find their hands tied to the agenda of the American-dominated free-market system. Foreseeing that some would not forget free trade so easily, the *Financial Post* editorial contained a warning: "The government must not shy from the rest of its economic agenda for fear of accusations it is all somehow linked with free trade."

Well, shy away it did not. The budgets of 1989 and 1990 started the process of Canada's wholesale capitulation on subsidy questions: the government had taken the initiative. To avoid the public spectacle of backing down to the Americans in area after area, the Tories set in motion the means of effectively harmonizing our system with that of the United States. And, true to the party line of denying the impact of free trade, the government passed on the *Financial Post*'s admonition to bravely admit the connection of the deal to a larger agenda. The finance minister declared, "There is no connection with this [1988] budget and the free trade agreement."

Yet government budgets are in harmony with the gospel according to free trade: regional transfer payments have been slashed; universality of social programs has been undermined; women's centres are starved of funds; native presses have been shut down; and farm communities have been left to fend for themselves. The simple reality is that Canada could not have retained the system of regional and social support it had built and remain free of American harassment. The very principles upon which the free-trade agreement was founded predetermined that these practices would have to go.

The head of the Western Diversification Fund said that, even before the deal was signed, lawyers from the departments of justice and external affairs vetted large expenditures to determine if they would have adverse consequences vis-à-vis the United States. Ensuring that our habits don't interfere with corporate practice, U.S.-style, has become routine.

The Mulroney Tories have adopted all the rhetoric of hardball economics. The wealthy create wealth, they wrongly assert. Therefore, to empower the wealthy is to advance the country. There will be hard times for a while, they admit, as the country sinks deeper into debt and trade deficits; but only by making life easier for the multinationals and selling off our assets to lure foreign "investment" will we find the money to share future wealth. Canadians have become lazy and undisciplined, they insist. Hence the need for the "cold shower" of competition with countries and states that have a history of exploiting the work-force to make profit and where legislation to protect employees is non-existent or minimal. Anyone who disagrees is a "communistic socialist," according to Don Blenkarn, the Finance Committee chairman.

Free trade has not been the only tool available to the government to force the country to conform to the new system. The privatization of public enterprises and the deregulation of services to the Canadian people are the others. For this new system to work, it is essential to reduce the public role in the running of our country, and the government has been accomplishing this quietly for several years. The Tory ideology is simple: if it makes a profit, sell it; if it doesn't, starve it; if it talks back, cut it.

The privatization of public enterprises in Canada is a central goal of the free-trade agreement; in order for there to be a smooth transfer of our economy to that of the United States, strict limitations must be put on the ability of the Canadian government to exercise its economic power in the interest of the country. The Canadian tradition has been to use our resources, financial and otherwise, to promote the values of Canadians and to establish as wide a base as possible for participation in economic life. For free trade to work, however, this role of the federal government must end.

Harmonization means adopting the values of American business attitudes: needless to say, these are traditionally deeply hostile to public-run enterprise. The Tory government has committed Canada to decreasing the role of public service; programs that were administered as non-profit government-sponsored services are now available for private take-over.

Canada and the United States have very different economic systems. Our distinct economy not only has served to foster a different way of life in Canada but has prevented us from being absorbed into the United States. The mix of private and public enterprise established services at low prices in areas business alone would not have been able to enter profitably or maintain affordably.

Because these enterprises were Canadian owned, they conducted their research and development in Canada. They became innovators in many areas, from large dam construction and the first experimental diesel locomotive to rural telephone systems and the Candu reactor. To have permitted the market-place to dictate all economic decisions would have doomed the young country. It was simply too expensive to run railways to the north or to provide basic services to Atlantic Canada unless those services were underwritten by government. The very existence of Canada depended on this early understanding of sharing, community-based entrepreneurial action and the distribution of wealth and opportunities.

Many Canadian Crown corporations were conceived not only to serve a Canadian perspective, but to retain control of decision-making in Canada. The CBC was established to prevent network radio in Canada from falling into the hands and world-view of U.S. companies. "The state or the United States," Graham Spry, the father of the CBC, used to say.

But now everything is for sale: parks, forests, municipal phone utilities, shelters for battered women, public services. Since assuming power, the Tories have sold off eighteen Crown corporations, and the sale of a number of others is imminent. Such Canadian institutions as Air Canada, the CN hotel chain, CNCP Telecommunications, and Petro-Canada are being turned over to private control. The government has received more than $3.3 billion for these sales (not including Petro-Can), and 64, 000 employees have been transferred to the private sector.

The delicate balance between public and private ownership, a balance without which Canada could not have been built and could not have survived, is being tipped by the government in favour of the same forces of corporate greed and concentration that fuelled the free-trade fervour. Corporate Canada wants to get its hands on profitable and essential sectors — public enterprises that belong to the Canadian people, who have paid for them many times over through their taxes. In this, as in other issues, these large companies have much more in common and much stronger ties with U.S.-based multinationals than with the Canadian people, so they are willing to weaken the national fabric that Crown corporations have helped to weave.

In a statement that would have been inconceivable a decade ago, the finance minister has announced plans to step up privatization of Crown corporations and the minister of state for privatization, John McDermid, has said that any and all are up for sale. He told a Conservative riding association that the government no longer feels that it is obligated to "be the landlord" of public services.

Let us look at just some of the many examples of what happens when the government is no longer the "landlord." In recent years, a fierce battle has been growing in Canada over control of the food supply and the future of life-patenting. Until recently, genetic material was universally considered to be a public resource and not the domain of private interests. Seeds and other reproductive material, even if altered through selective breeding, were seen to be products of nature to be cultivated for the benefit of all. In fact, Agriculture Canada has a seed bank of hundreds of thousands of plant species for the development of improved farming and food sources for all Canadians. Companies can sell the seeds, but they do not own the patent to them or have exclusive rights to market them; that would be like owning the power of creation itself.

Canada has just joined a small group of countries who recognize the right of corporations to patent life-forms and to exclusively market the "products" they develop. Recent advances in bio-technology have led to the discovery of many new varieties of plants and animals, and the results have created a huge international business. This approach turns all of nature into a commodity waiting to be discovered, patented, and sold for profit.

The future of bio-technology and world agriculture is now in the hands of a small group of chemical and food giants — corporations familiar to Canadians, such as Pfizer, Sandoz, Upjohn, Ciba-Geigy, and Cargill, who have spent $10 billion in the last decade to take control of the world supply of seeds. Many of them also sell fungicides, herbicides, insecticides, and chemical fertilizers.

GROW, the rural lobby that fought the legislation, says that to move ahead with plant-breeders' rights is to "relinquish society's control over this powerful new technology, and to place it in the hands of people whose primary concern is making money and not society's increasingly urgent concerns with environmental protection, eradicating world hunger, and preserving small-scale farming upon which so many people depend for their very livelihood."

The new Canadian legislation harmonizes our system to the American system, in which plant-breeders' rights have been accepted for many years. Not surprisingly, the United States has, for some time, been demanding that Canada recognize "intellectual property rights." The principal beneficiaries of monopoly rights in Canada will be the multinationals, most of which are U.S. based. Over 90 percent of all Canadian patents are owned by multinational corporations. Under this new legislation, Canadians will have access to these life-enhancing materials only through a small group of foreign corporations who will no longer be required to do research and development in Canada in order to retain control of the sale for their "discoveries" in Canada.

In fact, the Canadian government has stated that a principal goal of the legislation is to shift participation in plant breeding to the private sector, and it has made substantial cuts to Agriculture Canada's research program. As in countless other areas of Canadian life, the government has transferred control of genetic research, and, as a consequence, Canada's food system and its long-term environmental impact, from public to private hands.

The decision to privatize Petro-Canada is another example of the Mulroney government's willingness to cater to its big-business sponsors and sacrifice the Canadian public interest to private control. It also illustrates a government strategy that involves several stages and the softening-up of public opinion prior to privatizing a Crown corporation. The company was established by the government in the mid-1970s as a Canadian presence in the energy sector and to invest in long-range frontier exploration. Canada was at the mercy of the development plans of the private oil and gas companies, for whom the only long-term strategy was maximizing the bottom line. Petro-Canada was created to represent the long-term energy needs of the Canadian people. It gave the government insight into the petroleum industry, and became a symbol of the Canadian people's desire to Canadianize the industry.

In 1984, however, shortly after coming to power, the Mulroney government cut off all federal funding to the company, and laid off hundreds of employees. The board of directors was told to shelve its original mandate. Instead, the board was to start operating the corporation like a private company. By demoralizing the company and making its future uncertain, by leaving it in need of cash to complete politically motivated projects, the government made Petro-Canada's Crown status indefensible; thus, the corporation was ripe for privatizing. In fact, Petro-Canada was high on the hit-list of the original, pre-1984 election, little-known Conservative task force on privatization that laid the groundwork for the Tories' massive privatization program. Senator William Kelly and former MP John Thompson, a powerful Calgary oilman, were the co-chairs of this task force, and made it clear to Tory insiders at the time that a commercial Petro-Canada, even foreign-owned, was to come.

The government is assuring Canadians that there will be a 25 percent foreign-ownership restriction on shares of Petro-Canada, the same assurance they are offering in the privatization of Air Canada. Such an undertaking is deceitful and misleading. Under Article 1602 of the free-trade agreement, such restrictions do not apply in subsequent sales. The government can control the initial share sales. But those buyers can resell without restriction. As well, the privatization minister has stated that it wouldn't bother him one bit if all of Petro-Canada ended up in foreign hands. "If Petro-Canada went foreign, it wouldn't reduce Canadian ownership in the oil industry that much."

As for corporations not yet privatized, consider Canada Post. The legislation governing this Crown corporation requires not that it make a profit but rather that it provide quality, affordable, and accessible postal service to Canadians, no matter where they live. However, the government has determined that it should turn a profit — which it did in 1988–89, to the tune of $96 million, and again in 1989–90, of $149 million. It did this by eliminating thousands of jobs, closing rural postal stations, increasing postal rates, hiring privately at very low wages, and selling off assets of the corporation. Privatization is under way.

Canadians might expect these profits to be used to improve services or lower postal rates, in other words, to fulfil its original mandate. Wrong. In his 1989 budget, Michael Wilson recommended that the corporation be operated under a private-sector definition of financial self-sufficiency. A government-appointed review committee said, "Canada Post has evolved into a commercially oriented and profit-conscious company."

As a consequence, this supposedly non-profit public corporation must adopt a target return on equity in the 15 percent range, the rate expected of a comparably sized private company. Suddenly, $149 million profit is a serious shortfall. The committee openly recommends raising rates for revenues. "The totality of rate increases planned for implementation on January 1, 1990, would produce $17 million of additional revenue in 1989–90 and an additional $72 million in 1990–91." These numbers go a long way to closing that "shortfall." In future, capital costs will also be factored in when defining profit. "If rates do not include the cost of capital, then Canada Post benefits from an indirect subsidy from the federal government which has provided it with capital free of charge." Because the government funds the corporation through tax revenues, "the general tax-paying population indirectly subsidizes users of the postal system."

This is Tory talk. What it means is that the government is getting ready to sell the post office. First, you change its mandate behind closed doors (but you leave its official public mandate untouched). Then you structure it to look and act like a private corporation. Then you sell. Who would fight to keep public a company that continues to raise rates, not in order to improve service, but to make a profit?

Not only is the whole concept of mail delivery as a basic service destroyed, but clearly the silent hand of the free-trade agreement is present. A Crown corporation, with its mandate to use tax-payers' own money to provide them with essential services in an equal and accessible manner is an unfair subsidy — a bump on the level playing-field so beloved of American corporate games players. Public enterprise is simply not how Americans do business; therefore, it will not be for Canadians either.


In a country such as Canada, one with a relatively small population and smaller pool of private capital, the death of public enterprise will lower the standard of living for many. Those with money will be able to buy superior services once available to all: lower-income earners will depend more and more on welfare. Workers transferred to the private sector will be paid lower wages and receive fewer benefits, while prices for the goods they produce will increase, as privatization inevitably leads to increased monopoly and less competition.

As our public enterprises are privatized, Canada will lose not only its past but the right to re-create these institutions or other services we deem essential. Article 2010 of the free-trade agreement states that, in order to establish public enterprises (or, in the new jargon, to "deprivatize"), Canada would have to gain U.S. government approval and compensate U.S. companies for potential losses as a result of the formation of these Crown agencies or corporations. And without cancelling the deal, no future government will be able to undo this government's massive program of privatization.

Free trade not only cements the concept of privatization into an international agreement, it increases the inevitability of Canadian enterprises falling into foreign hands. For example, Edmonton is considering privatizing and selling its telephone system, which has a value of close to $500 million, and the city council sees no reason to prohibit Americans from tendering. The Alberta government is selling its telephone company, and although the premier, Don Getty, is promising a share limit on foreign ownership, it is a promise he cannot enforce. In Saskatchewan, where the government has been massively privatizing provincial public enterprises, one important public enterprise has already been sold out of Canadian hands. The Prince Albert Pulp Company was privatized and then sold to the American giant Weyerhaeuser, one of the big free-trade backers.

Once public enterprises leave public hands, there is no government presence or agency overseeing where they end up. Canada has given up one of its most powerful tools to retain control of key sectors of its economy without so much as a national discussion of the impact on our future of such a radical departure from our past.

Harmonization with the free-market ideology of the United States includes another American import — deregulation. Just as free trade shifts economic control from government to corporations, and privatization shifts national policy to private interests, deregulation of Canadian services transfers profitability and accountability from the public domain to that of large corporations, leaving key decisions regarding quality of services and the health and safety of Canadians to multinationals.

The prime example of the effects of deregulation can be seen in Canada's transportation industry. The government bowed to pressure from Canadian transportation and manufacturing corporations who wanted to drive costs and wages down, using the U.S. model — transportation has been deregulated there for more than a decade — and began the process of leaving all decisions about routes, prices, and standards to the industry. By the time the process had been formalized in legislation early in 1988, another strategic part of Canada's unique history and economic structure had been undermined.

Canada had originally regulated its transportation system during the 1950s in recognition that transportation is a public utility, and should provide all parts of the country with service. Such regulation was seen by government and the industry alike as a powerful means of curbing dangerous practices, preventing price gouging, and discouraging destructive competition. Regulating our transportation industry protected consumers and less economically developed regions of the country. It also helped build a strong Canadian industry, one that was as good as any in the world. But regulated transportation, however efficient a service, was not tolerable to the Tory government's corporate ethos.

The government promised air travellers great benefits from deregulation — lower fares and better service, because of greater competition for the travellers' dollar. Yet, Wardair couldn't compete, leaving two private carriers to control 95 percent of Canadian skies. Prices rose in 1989, and Andrew Roman, a regulatory lawyer, predicts that they will rise again by 30 percent by the end of 1990. The cost of a ticket used to be based on the equitable cost over distance. Now, each route has to be profitable. A number of smaller Air Canada routes have been cancelled, deepening regional isolation and harming local economies.

More important, however, is the other harmonization taking place. As is typical, "harmonization" means a move to the lower standard. According to the maintenance workers responsible for air safety, Canadian safety and maintenance manuals are being down-graded to U.S. levels, and inspectors are being laid off or not replaced as they retire. The results won't be apparent for a number of years, as our highly trained workers will continue to keep the planes flying. "You won't notice it," said one worker, "but we see the way they cut corners. People here are just watching things deteriorate."

In the United States, deregulation has resulted in the bankruptcy or sale of more than two hundred airlines, reduced service to smaller regions, and sharply increased travel costs. The pilots' union says that accidents are on the rise and blames deteriorating safety procedures: cut-throat competition after deregulation doesn't allow for the cost of keeping standards high. Canada and the United States are moving to an unregulated, integrated North American air system, dominated by a small number of very powerful carriers: it is they who will dictate the safety standards for the aircraft, the services for customers, and the working conditions for employees. Neither governments nor the flying public will have much influence on these corporations or their operations.

When the government privatized Air Canada and deregulated the industry, it precluded itself and future governments from having a say in the development of the industry. Already, Canada's airlines have given up their Canadian computer reservation system in favour of an American-made system controlled by United Airlines of Chicago. It is believed that the largest block of Air Canada shares are in American hands. The vice-president of American Airlines has called on Ottawa to liberalize its investment rules (transportation was left out of the free-trade agreement and will be a subject for future talks) and conclude a "bilateral agreement" with the United States, allowing for wide-open competition over North American skies. American Airlines is "holding talks" with the small Montreal carrier Intair, which is integrated with American's computerized reservation system.

In fact, since both of Canada's major airlines are relatively small in comparison with the big U.S. carriers, it is not inconceivable that, in an integrated North American system, one or both may be taken over.

The situation in the trucking industry is even more unsettling and demonstrates the clear link between deregulation and free trade. Says Michael Lynk of the truckers' union, "The trucking arena in the U.S. has been littered with the corpses of bankrupt and merged companies, on a scale unprecedented since the Great Depression." The big centres received enhanced services and transportation rate increases, and caused industries to move from smaller and less prosperous centres. Between 150,000 and 200,000 truckers lost their jobs, and safety standards have suffered a drastic decline. Interstate trucking accidents and trucking-related fatalities rose dramatically following deregulation.

Similar symptoms are now appearing in Canada. Bankruptcies in the trucking industry jumped almost 50 percent during the first year of deregulation here. Moreover, with the free-trade agreement in place, the very future of a Canadian transportation industry is jeopardized. "Deregulation and free trade have not created a level playing field in the trucking industry. The U.S. carriers have a clear advantage and we're being creamed," says the Ontario Trucking Association. Lower wages, lower taxes, and bigger markets give American companies a distinct advantage, and many Canadian manufacturers are using American rather than Canadian trucking firms. This has forced Canadian trucking companies to set up shop in the United States. The association says that most of the major carriers have moved all or some of their operations to the United States. "Somebody has to make some moves to correct this situation or there won't be any Canadian carriers left," says the vice-president of a major trucking company.

Canada's transportation market is now seen by American trucking companies as "easy pickings." Deregulation means that anyone who wants a licence to transport goods can get one, and American companies, who once had to prove public necessity to receive a Canadian licence, now enjoy total freedom of movement in Canada. Between free trade and deregulation, the Canadian market is being Americanized. Canadian companies dominated the market only a few years ago. Since deregulation, U.S. trucking on Canadian roads has dramatically risen. The president of Thompson Trucking notes that, concurrently, Canada's trailer-making and van-manufacturing industries have been destroyed. J.B. Hunt and Schneider National — the number-two truckload carrier in the United States — have moved into Canada in a big way. More than 85 percent of the transborder truckload market will be solidly in the hands of U.S.-based carriers by the end of 1990. And, of course, the transborder parcel market is virtually sewn up by United Parcel Service, a U.S. company.

The union representing the truckers warns that 400,000 jobs are at real risk. Said one industry executive, "I don't think Canadian-made means much any more and it's going to mean less. . . . The real world is that we're the 51st state and the longer you fight it, the longer you're going to suffer."

The Mulroney government's determination to impose a harsh, corporate-controlled agenda on Canada, and in the process destroy Canada's national transportation structure, includes the dismantling of its passenger rail system and potentially its freight rail system. Throughout history, our railways have been the personification of our national soul. John A. Macdonald's national dream was founded on the practical fact that Canada could survive as a nation only if a railway linked the country from sea to sea.

Although passenger-use and VIA earnings steadily improved during the last few years, our rail system is doomed. The former chair of the House of Commons Transport Committee, Tory Pat Nowlan, admitted that the deep cuts announced in 1989 were the first step to killing off passenger rail service in Canada: "I just can't see how you can cut 50 per cent of services and have the thing survive." The National Transportation Agency is being besieged by applications to close freight lines throughout Canada; it has recommended that the service be deregulated so it can stop serving unprofitable routes. Canadian National and Canadian Pacific applied in 1989 to close more than twice the number of lines that all fifteen rail companies in Canada had closed the year before. Hardest hit is Atlantic Canada, but any route that is not profitable will not survive.

No other nation in history has ever deliberately destroyed its own railway system except to forestall invasion during wartime. The government claims the railways are a luxury we can no longer afford. But their cost is small compared to those of the alternatives: greatly expanded highways, upgrading airports to handle increased traffic, the lay-offs of thousands of employees, and the isolation and impoverishment of whole communities. Who is counting the environmental impact of shutting down a clean mode of transportation when all the world is seeking to create one? Says an American visitor to Canada, "Americans may now question the seriousness of Canada's commitment to curbing acid rain since the VIA cuts are expected to result in one million extra car trips a year. . . . Will the real Canadian position on global warming please stand up?"

Ever ready to accommodate when Canada loses ground, an American company is coming to the rescue. Because western Canada now has virtually no rail service, Washington-based Amtrak has launched an aggressive advertising campaign for their service that buses Canadians south to catch U.S. trains bound east or west. Ironically, of course, the very existence of Amtrak as an alternative will provide an opportunity for the government to continue cutting Canadian routes. Says Transport 2000, "This is part of the north-south realignment of trade and commerce under free trade." Western leaders are fearful that the cuts could eventually hamper the transportation of western Canadian grain. The loss of the Canadian railway system is inestimable. Not only will many communities be cut off from the nation's business, but, says Michael Lynk, the loss "softens the national glue that holds us together."

That this is part of a corporate agenda, and one that will allow the subsidization of American companies while denying it to Canadian services, is evident by a decision of the Canadian government to provide a favourable $100-million loan to Amtrak to purchase new coaches and dining cars from Bombardier. Some of the stock will be built in Vermont. Our government is not only providing an American company with passengers, but financing a good part of the operation. Why are we not financing our own future?

There is one more Canadian sector being starved, a sector that is vital to our future. As the world aligns into global trading blocks, erasing borders, it is imperative that we continue to support a rich cultural community in Canada. But art isn't a commodity. The creative expression of a country with a small population doesn't generate corporate wealth. So the Mulroney government is slowly abandoning its responsibility to our writers, artists, and musicians.

The struggle to develop a Canadian cultural industry has been an uphill battle. Canada is dominated by a powerful American entertainment industry. Foreign companies control 90 percent of the Canadian feature-film market, and 97 percent of the profits from distribution of film in Canada go out of the country to fund someone else's industry. Canadian films occupy only 5 percent of total screen time, and 75 percent of all programs on English-language television are American.

Of the total drama programming on television, 98 percent is American, as are 75 percent of the entertainment programs seen on our screens. By age twelve, a Canadian child will see 12,000 hours of television, 10,000 of them American. Aided by government policy of the last decade, American networks have been imported whole-sale with no accompanying safeguards to provide for at least an equal choice of Canadian programming. Canadian children, whether they live in St. John's, Newfoundland; Toronto, Ontario; or Tuktoyaktuk, in the Northwest Territories, share with American children the sexual and social role-models of Teenage Mutant Ninja Turtles and Freddie Kruger.

As well, although Canadian publishers produce three of every four Canadian books, 80 percent of all books sold in this country are foreign, mostly American. So even though we have a home-grown Canadian publishing industry, Canadian consumers are inundated with American books when they shop. Canadian publishers cannot compete against American low costs and sheer volume.

In spite of these figures, the government is dismantling the structures put in place by successive governments to stem the tide of American media influence and promote a Canadian cultural vision. The CBC has served as the principal vehicle for this expression. Yet, since coming to power in 1984, the Tories have cut its parliamentary allocation by 16 percent in purchasing power — the largest cumulative cut suffered by any national cultural organization. They announced cuts worth $140 million over the next four years, a move that former CBC president Pierre Juneau calls "a catastrophe." The corporation has had to lay off five hundred employees, and more may have to go.

More ominously, however, Canada will soon have a new broadcasting act, and it may kill public broadcasting in this country. First, the CBC will be stripped of its mandate to promote national unity. Second, the act will allow foreign broadcasters to do business in Canada without making any contribution to the country, and will permit the entry into Canada of American broadcasting services that will compete head to head with our industry. In fact, Canadian broadcasters will be disadvantaged because they will still have to produce Canadian programming not required of their American competitors. The government rejects a call to place restrictions on American broadcasters as being counter to its policies of deregulation. MP Sheila Finestone points out that for Canada to introduce such restrictions would be a violation of the spirit of the free-trade agreement.

Further, the act will substantially increase the direct power of cabinet over the decisions of the CRTC. (This trend to politicize regulatory agencies is also evident in the energy sector. The government has stripped the powers of the National Energy Board.) Decisions relating to culture and broadcasting will increasingly be made for political reasons, behind closed doors, with the same small group of corporate leaders, Canadian and American, that influence this government in every other sector. Increasingly, the

CRTC will become irrelevant as decisions will be made privately, outside of the licensing process, and Canadian broadcasters will come to resent having to submit to regulation not required of their U.S. competitors.

In the long run, the east-west imperative, the fundamental reason for the CBC, will disappear. And so will the Canadian dream. But it is not the only cultural institution in trouble. The Canada Council had campaigned strongly for a badly needed increase in operating grants, and was refused. As a result, grants to artists are steadily declining, and many are not able to continue their work.

And in spite of a pre-1988 election vow that it would not tamper with the hundred-year-old practice of providing a postal subsidy for Canadian magazines, the government has slashed $220 million from this fund, a move the industry calls "a betrayal." It had come under fire from the American publishing lobby as an unfair form of trade subsidy, and in this case, as in so many others, the government caved in before it was forced to. Several magazines have already folded, and more will follow. The Goods and Services Tax will be an added body-blow to many small publications. The direct beneficiaries are American magazines.

Film production has been cut by 25 to 40 percent in one year. The government's long-promised film-distribution legislation, which would give Canada some control in this field, has been buried. Daniel Weinzweig, a spokesperson for the Canadian industry, says that "U.S. distributors do not invest one dime in Canadian productions while taking almost $1 billion a year in revenue out of the country." Jack Valenti, the American film-industry bully, has repeatedly warned Canada not to attempt any legislation that would give Canadian film distributors access to our own studios. Valenti has ordered Ottawa to stay out of his film business. He is a strong proponent of American-dominated international free trade and does not hesitate to use threats: "The prospect of pain must be inserted into the equation, else the solution will never be suitable."

These are just the opening shots in an ongoing war. The American government and industry have made it abundantly clear that they neither understand nor will tolerate Canada's obsession with this thing called "Canadian identity." Cultural industries are named in the U.S. free-trade legislation as high on the list for inclusion in the agreement in future talks. A powerful Democrat, Michigan congressman John Dingell, has taken on the government's Canadian book-publishing policy — the so-called Baie-Comeau policy — as a personal crusade. He labels the attempt to maintain a Canadian presence in the industry as "repressive and one sided" and is urging the American trade representative to take action against Canada.

The bottom-line reality is that corporate America regards culture as entertainment. The Canadian government must dismantle the structures that have created a different perspective in Canada.

Using deregulation, privatization, and free trade to smooth the way, the Mulroney government has transformed the alignment of the country from east-west to north-south. It has made it easy for Canadian companies to leave Canada for greener pastures and has laid out the red carpet for American corporations. And, in some cases, the government has blatantly discriminated in favour of American companies to the detriment of our own.

For American Express, the Canadian election of 1988 was a sweet victory. And its reward for its help was immediate. While Canadians were busy voting on November 21, 1988, the federal cabinet approved a request to allow American Express to become a bank in Canada. The junior finance minister admitted that his government had to bend its own guidelines to do so as Amex is not a bank in its home country, and therefore is not eligible to be considered one here. The Canadian banking community and many others rightly pointed out that granting Amex Bank a licence in Canada gives it special privileges not now held by Canadian banks, while Canadian banks in the U.S. are still restricted in their activities there.

The Canadian Bankers' Association expressed its "grave concerns" to the finance minister and said that, if the government granted this application, it "will be creating a precedent whose

ultimate consequences for the Canadian financial system are profound and disturbing." Many expressed outrage that the government would have made a private deal with the company before
introducing long-expected legislative changes to allow Canadian
banks to compete. Amex will be able to carry on business activities,
such as insurance and merchandise retailing, that Canadian banks
are unable to do. And Canadian banks will not have the same
powers to operate in the United States that Amex will possess in
Canada.

Given that the banks had fully endorsed Mulroney's free-trade
agreement, many began to wonder about the motives of a cabinet
who would doggedly pursue this course of action. "This was done
because [American Express chairman] Robinson supported free
trade. This was the deal that I guess the Prime Minister made with
him, and it would appear that he didn't think of the implications of
this policy-on-the-run-for-my-friend-approach," said Robert
Korthals, the chairman of the Toronto-Dominion Bank. (He later
apologized for but did not withdraw the remark, after intense
denials from the government.) But it was undeniable that blatant
favouritism was involved in the government's decision, which was
politically motivated.

For, in spite of government denials of favouritism, documents
show that American Express had received support in principle for a
Canadian banking licence in a private meeting with then junior
finance minister Tom Hockin, in September 1986, two years before
it reached cabinet. Only months later, the company formed the
pro–free trade coalition in the United States. It seems that Conservative lobbyist Bill Neville, then of PAI, had successfully intervened
on behalf of his client, American Express. The rest is history.

Korthals said that Canada was facing an invasion of its banking system by huge American corporate conglomerates. And the
senior vice-president of the Bank of Nova Scotia had warned a year
earlier that any American financial holding company could now
control Canadian banks and other financial institutions, by-pass-
ing Canadian legislation on ownership limitations. "That holding

company would be as free as any collection of Canadian share-holders to own the Bank of Nova Scotia."

Yet the government held its ground, in April 1990 granting Amex its licence to operate, with no financial-reform legislation for Canadian banks in sight. As an additional favour, Mulroney's Conservatives granted its corporate backer a $50-million deal to supply the federal government with travellers' cheques.

A global conglomerate operating in over 140 countries, American Express has 31 million cards around the world, which covered $89-billion worth of transactions in 1988 alone. Its profits are growing at a rate of 17 percent compounded annually, and the company has set a target of more than 60 million cards and billings of $300 billion by the end of the decade. It sees itself on the cutting edge of sophisticated consumerism and has made it clear that it intends to service only upscale clients in Canada. "Amex Bank won't be making loans to farmers and fishermen, that's for sure," said one bank official.

The new agenda for Canada, which was set in the boardrooms of the nation, was delivered by the Tories, for whom the Canadian people and their sovereign rights were less important than the politics of power. Promises made during the election campaign masked a hidden agenda. The transformation started immediately.

# 3.
# THE ECONOMIC COST
# OF FREE TRADE

"There comes a time to take a profit."

*Paul Desmarais*

"THE POLITICS ARE OVER," THE PRESIDENT OF THE
American Association of Exporters and Importers said with a sigh
when the free-trade agreement was signed. "Now business will do
their thing." His relief was echoed by business leaders on both sides
of the border.

For good reason. The passage of this historic agreement was a
watershed. For American-based multinationals, there remained
very few impediments to the take-over of Canadian companies and
resources, and no constraints if they wanted to shut down their
Canadian operations. For Canadian corporations, this deal signalled the beginning of a new era. Using the threat of international
competition, they could now mount a steady assault on Canadian
working standards, wage laws, social programs, and taxes. They
now had a powerful weapon at their disposal. If government didn't
comply, they could leave Canada.

They quickly made their intentions clear, and heralded the
onset of a total restructuring of the Canadian economy. "With free
trade, the geographic area for Heinz Canada is now North America.
We either make products coming out of the Leamington facility
cost competitive or move production to Heinz plants in the
U.S.A.," William Springer, Heinz president, said as a warning to
his employees.

A major Ontario truck-parts firm warned female employees
not to push the province's new pay-equity law, although "we're not

against women," said John Doddridge, then president of American-controlled Hayes Dana. The threat was clear. If they demanded equal pay for work of equal value, he warned, the company would likely move production to its U.S. plant.

A photo-engraving company in Toronto warned its employees in a memo that free trade posed a serious threat to the company's competitiveness: to protect their jobs, staff would have to lower their demands for better wages and fewer hours. The Automotive Parts Manufacturers' Association of Canada said that the lower taxes, wage rates, and unemployment insurance in the United States were attractive to the industry; Ontario was becoming too "expensive and complacent" for investment. The association hired a U.S. firm to "prove" that Ontario must lower its social standards or risk losing this industry.

Alcan, a big free-trade booster, has demanded a two-year wage freeze from its Laval, Quebec, workers, warning that Alcan's U.S. operations could easily satisfy the Ontario and Quebec markets for aluminum products. The message to Canada is clear now that free trade is a reality: corporations don't have to keep production in Canada to do business here.

The message is clearly stated in a report from Wood Gundy: "If Canadian workers are to compete effectively for jobs in an increasingly integrated North American market, wage gains in Canada . . . must be constrained to even more austere settlements in U.S. industries." An analyst for the Royal Bank warns that Canadian wage settlements are too high to permit the country to take advantage of free trade. The head of the Business Council of B.C. called for a mobile pool of jobless workers who would shift across the country to serve the needs of business, but receive no benefits or regional assistance.

Although Brian Mulroney had promised the "finest" readjustment programs in the world to help workers displaced by free trade, his blue-ribbon panel set up to recommend how these programs would operate let the government off the hook. The chairman of the task force, Jean de Grandpré (then head of telecommunications giant BCE Inc.), refused to deal specifically with people thrown out

of work as a result of free trade, although just months later he admitted that "thousands of Canadians" would lose their jobs because of the deal. Instead, he said that the best way to help displaced workers would be to give more tax breaks to corporations for worker retraining. Employees, he explained, are like machines that depreciate and need to be upgraded. Adds Mike McCracken, president of Informetrica, the consulting firm that prepared a report on free trade for John Crosbie, "Plant closings may be an indication that the deal is working."

Suddenly, the corporate agenda became clear: free trade was for the big companies able to move production out of the country if Canadian wage demands and taxes did not decrease. The CEO of Du Pont Canada had laid out this rationale in a 1986 speech to sell free trade to American business leaders: "In my view, there would be attractive benefits to an open border for Du Pont and for most multinationals. Market forces would determine where goods would be produced more economically. The market would decide whether this would be in the U.S. or Canada."

The pressure to compete against multinationals paying poor wages and low taxes in other countries was a welcome weapon for corporate Canada. Business could cry that it was unable to coexist with Canada's social programs or wage rates while paying lip-service to the principles of equality and responsibility. If government suggested corporations pay a larger share of taxes, there was nothing to stop the corporations from pulling up stakes and moving away. Before the 1989 budget, Michael Wilson, the finance minister, admitted his government's vulnerability: "If we followed that route . . . the incentive to invest in Canada would be lowered relative to other countries and corporations would move down into the United States or other countries, set up businesses down there, create jobs in other countries, take job opportunities away from Canada."

And moving they are. An early *Business Week* assessment of free trade monitored the flight of Canadian capital and jobs to the United States. "Canadian executives are rushing across the border to set up manufacturing bases in what they see as a more hospitable climate. . . . The unexpected shift to U.S. production by potentially large numbers of companies comes as Canada's exports to America are flattening. . . . One thing is for sure, free trade already is spawning much deeper economic ties along north-south corridors. . . . Canadian companies are looking south."

A number of American states have opened offices in Canada. They have two aims: to find new markets for their products and to lure Canadian companies south of the border. More than one-quarter of Canadian manufacturers have been invited by individual states to move to the U.S. Even small Canadian companies are welcomed by high-level state officials. Willy Tencer, a Canadian who has just opened a small woodworking factory in Meadville, Pennsylvania, instead of Toronto, where he was originally planning to build, was impressed not only with the wide array of loans, training grants, cheap land, and low-cost labour put at his disposal at his U.S. location, but with the fact that he was greeted at his plant's opening by the state governor. Says Tencer: "I was quite surprised. . . . They act like businessmen there, not like politicians."

Attracted by a very aggressive local business campaign trumpeting cheap labour, inexpensive land, and low taxes, hundreds of Canadian firms are shifting production to Buffalo, New York State, and New England: hundreds of others are looking into the possibility. Free trade and the removal of tariffs means that these companies can produce or assemble goods nearer to big U.S. markets and still sell their products back in Canada. "With free trade passed, we think a lot of industry will be relocating all or part of their operations in Buffalo," said one Toronto real estate agent who is putting up office buildings there. A big plastics-equipment maker was planning to add a product line in Canada but has decided to put the new plant and all future jobs in Buffalo. The brother of federal cabinet minister Otto Jelinek has decided to open a new chalkboard-manufacturing plant in Buffalo instead of Toronto.

Many large furniture makers are heading south. Kaufman of Collingwood, Ontario, has built in Winston-Salem, North Carolina. Braemore set up shop in Medina, N.Y. Bilt-Rite Upholstering of Toronto opened a 150,000-square-foot facility in Mississippi in 1989 and then its Canadian company went into voluntary bankruptcy in March 1990. "With high costs and free trade removing a 12 per cent duty on imports, I don't see a very rosy future for large furniture companies in Canada," says one manufacturer. The Canadian Council of Furniture Manufacturers contends that an original estimate of job loss in the furniture sector to the United States of 3,500 by 1994 is too low.

Varity, a farm-machinery manufacturer (formerly Massey-Ferguson), is moving its entire operation to Buffalo, N.Y., in spite of its having accepted a $200-million federal and provincial government bail-out in exchange for a promise to employ 1,500 people in Canada and keep its head office here. The site was chosen so that Canadian employees could still live in Canada and receive all its benefits, but work in the United States. The company has retained a Buffalo lawyer and public-relations firm and has applied for state tax incentives that would exempt Varity from $700,000 (U.S.) in real estate taxes and allow the company to avoid $50,000 (U.S.) in sales tax on renovation work.

Buffalo immigration authorities receive hundreds of calls a week from Canadians seeking work in the expanding industrial Canadian sector: 92 percent of all new businesses established in Buffalo in 1989 were started by Canadians.

The local people in upstate New York and Vermont talk about the "Canadian invasion," hundreds of Quebec entrepreneurs moving their businesses to the United States or setting up branch plants there with the intention of closing the operation in Canada when all the tariffs are down. They point out that Americans are quite nationalistic and want to buy from an American firm. The president of a Quebec furniture company is foresaking Ontario for what he calls Quebec's "natural" trading partners, Boston and New

York. Free trade will lead to a weakening of Ottawa's powers, he said, and ultimately to the sovereignty of Quebec.

A study by economist Prem Gandhi of the State University of New York in Plattsburgh confirms that many Canadian companies are locating near the border so that the executives can live in Canada but operate in the United States.

The story is repeated with chilling regularity all over the United States and Canada. And it includes the many American-based multinationals that are closing their Canadian subsidiaries and moving their production south. From St. John's, Newfoundland, to Mission, British Columbia, Canadian companies are quietly closing their doors or converting their facilities to warehouses, leaving whole communities devastated.

Peter Newman calls the process the "accelerated deindustrialization of Canada." "We've gone straight from smokestacks to warehouses. . . . With the free-trade agreement in place, Canada is establishing an unheard-of precedent. We are about to become the only country in recorded history to reverse the traditional evolution from underdevelopment to a manufacturing economy. The 20th century never did belong to us; now it seems we will not belong to the 21st."

The economic loss to Canada is high. As manufacturing flees south, Canadian workers will be pressured to lower their quality of life. Jobs in the service and natural-resource sectors will increasingly be the only alternative for displaced employees. Research and development and high technology will be exported with these companies, and all Canadians will be the losers.

Weston Foods president David Beatty laments that Canada's business climate is forcing Canadian companies to set up shop in the United States. Noting that "something psychological" has happened in the country as a result of free trade, Beatty acknowledges the dramatic increase in competition from foreign companies who see Canada as simply an extension of their markets. "If you are to survive and prosper you've got to be looking south."

The Canadian Importers' Association predicts that a customs union with the United States is inevitable because of Canadian business pressure for access to low-cost goods from outside the country. "So we're going to start to see Canada start to resemble the U.S. and start to move towards harmonization of even some of their external tariffs," said the vice-president. The minister of national revenue has announced that Canada has accelerated proceedings to establish a joint customs commission with the United States. The U.S. customs commissioner points out that a joint system will save both countries money and enhance joint law enforcement. These moves, and the fact that free trade has rendered Canadian business less competitive, set up perfect conditions for an even closer economic union with the United States. The pressure will become irresistible to merge the systems virtually seamlessly.

The food-processing industry is experiencing massive change. Even though it is one of the most vital industries in the country, it is also one of the most vulnerable. Caught between farm marketing boards and the prospect of massive cheap American imports, it is scrambling to stay afloat. The country's largest food processor, Canada Packers, is to fall into British hands, as London-based Hillsdown Holdings merges it with its Canadian operation, Maple Leaf, to form a super-company capable of competing in the United States. The company admits there will be Canadian job loss, and operations will be cut sharply. Analysts predict that western beef slaughterhouses will be the first hit.

Campbell Soup has announced that all of its Canadian plants will answer to the U.S. parent: the company is forming one unit for North America. The Canadian president put a brave face on the move, expressing hope that it would afford "great opportunity" for Canada. But he admitted that the rules for success have been changed and that "we are no longer competitive." The American head office made it clear that all decisions regarding Canada's future were its exclusive prerogative, although a spokesperson for the U.S. company added charitably, "Maybe nothing needs fixing in Canada."

Most food companies will follow suit. Says the executive vice-president of the Ontario Food Processors Association, "It doesn't make sense to have two companies operating on both sides of a non-existent border." The president of Campbell Soup speaks enthusiastically about a "common market arising from the Canada–U.S. free trade agreement." The CEO of Heinz says that when their company merges, he will leave a marketing branch open in Canada, but he doubts whether it will be financially feasible to continue to manufacture in Canada. If his company can't lower costs to match those of the United States, "the [Canadian] equipment will be disassembled and moved to the United States." Even a voluntary wage freeze by workers in the Leamington plant in June 1990, won't likely lower costs sufficiently, says the company.

Grocery Products Manufacturers of Canada (the association that could not take a pre-election position on free trade because its executive, the big multinationals, was backing the deal) warns that many food processors will be forced to close their operations in Canada and move south in the very near future. "We cannot stress too strongly that we are working with a time frame of weeks and days, not months or years."

And so the plants close: Campbell Soup, Gerber Baby Food, St. Lawrence Starch, Rowntree McIntosh, Hostess, Lowney (Hershey), Kraft, Cobi Foods, to name just a few. Borden Inc. of New York forced its Montreal workers to take a cut in pay. David Clark, Campbell Soup's CEO, explained the scenario to some of his employees: "I sat down with the folks at Listowel [the company's TV-dinner plant] and told them they would probably be out of a job unless they brought costs down."

The multinationals say that Canadian branch plants are too expensive to maintain. Canadian-owned companies are vulnerable; their rivals supply Canada from the United States, where the price of farm products is 40 to 60 percent lower than in Canada. One independent food producer predicts that at least 50,000 Canadian jobs will be lost in this industry alone within the next two years. Many Canadian operations are planning "twin" plants in the United States; they will close their Canadian companies when the new facilities are up and running. The Canadian food-processing industry is now controlled by a handful of multinational and U.S.-based corporations who no longer have to consider Canada as a separate country.

Buddy L. Pratt lives in Delta, a community of four hundred, tucked in the rural farmland of eastern Ontario, Loyalist country. For thirty-one years, he worked at the only major employer in the town, United Maple Products, packing bulk syrup and commercial blocks of maple sugar. His son joined him at the plant sixteen years ago. Owned and operated by a local family since it was founded in the 1930s, United Maple was bought by Labatt's in 1977; it was employing eighteen people full time and providing much spin-off employment when Canada signed the free-trade agreement. In July 1989, just six months into the deal, the U.S. multinational Borden bought the company. Within days, Borden had closed down the plant and moved production to Vermont.

The town has been devastated. People are moving away. Pratt's son has become severely depressed. Pratt expresses anger, frustration, and sadness. "I'm fifty-four years old. Where will I go? How will I start over? Does anyone care?"

Buddy L. Pratt is a statistic, a victim of the new system in Canada. His story will be repeated in sector after sector. For example, the multinationals who dominate the chemical industry in Canada, corporations such as 3M, Bayer, CIL, Cyanamid, Dow Corning, Du Pont, and Kodak, have requested that the government of Canada speed up the removal of tariffs on their products. As most of the Canadian chemical industry consists of branch plants duplicating products manufactured in U.S. factories, acquiescence by the government will allow the industry to restructure and consolidate production in the United States. The effect on Canadian workers will be dramatic. Considering the "enormous economies of scale in chemical production," notes the United

Steelworkers of America, and the size of the industry, "the problems with employment adjustment . . . are potentially massive."

It is not only the multinational corporations that are restructuring to profit from this new environment. Several large Canadian companies are "going global," and the cost will be borne by the Canadian people who get left behind. One such company is Northern Telecom. The story of Northern Telecom is the story of Canada itself. It describes a source of pride for the country, and is a parable of what happens when a Canadian company outgrows its roots and the government looks the other way.

The country's premier high-technology company, Northern Telecom has annual revenues of about $5.1 billion and sells telecommunications equipment in more than one hundred countries. It has spawned a whole telecommunications industry, creating, through its genius, spin-off work for hundreds of high-technology firms and job opportunities for generations of Canadian scientists and engineers. This company had a lot of help from Ottawa. Yearly research tax credits worth many millions of dollars, the wise use of special tax concessions, and help from the Export Development Corporation in the form of loans to foreign governments to secure contracts have helped build Northern into the fifth-largest telecommunications manufacturer in the world. As well, for years, the company was supported through a deal whereby its parent, Bell Canada, contracted to buy its subsidiary's telephone equipment exclusively.

But trade liberalization, deregulation, and free trade in Canada have made the climate less pleasant for Northern, and it is gradually seeking a warmer home. It recently shut down its plant in Aylmer, Quebec, putting 600 employees out of work, and cut 107 jobs at its Belleville plant. The major union of the company, the Canadian Auto Workers, estimates that Northern has transferred 15,000 jobs out of the country in recent years to low-wage, non-unionized states. The company now has more employees in the United States than in Canada, and the U.S. operation produces 60 percent of its annual revenues. The company now reports results in U.S. funds.

Northern Telecom was building a massive new research and development facility in Richardson, Texas, funded in part by a $200-million tax write-off from the Canadian government, when the company shut down part of its Canadian operation. Although it has announced an expansion of its Ottawa site, the project involves a consolidation of smaller locations scattered throughout the region, and no new jobs will result from it. New research jobs are being created elsewhere.

The company's new CEO, Paul Stern, who has come to Canada for a three-year term, is a tough-talking American businessman with strong ties to the White House and the Republican party. He wears gold-rimmed porcelain-inlaid cufflinks bearing the official seal of the President of the United States. He has moved the U.S. executive office to Washington where his political connections can be well utilized. His mandate is to shape Northern into a global corporation capable of competing against the telecommunications giants that control the industry world-wide. He has reorganized the chain of command so that the manufacturing subsidiaries all report to him, replacing the Canadian management in the hierarchy. He is clearly in charge.

Stern has no time for national concerns. "International boundaries are inconsequential or a mere inconvenience," he says. He has cut back the percentage of revenues to be spent on Canadian research. Indeed, Northern Telecom's massive expansion into the United States has "uncoupled the corporation from the country," according to *Report on Business* magazine. "Canada no longer comes first."

There is no question that the heat is on in the telecommunications industry. Ten years ago, there were thirty major companies in the world; today there are fifteen. By the year 2000, there will be four or five. Northern cannot survive alone in the new game. It is vulnerable for take-over or it may have to merge with another company, probably one that is seeking entry into the American market. The products Northern develops are increasingly sophisticated, and customized service is crucial. As 60 percent of all Northern sales are now in the United States, it will continue to move research, production, and head-office jobs to be near its major customers.

David Vice, Northern's president, says that trade wars are going to replace Star Wars and that his company is readying itself for that reality. He apparently believes that, as the power of government everywhere declines, business will replace it, and trade will be the weapon. He is readying his company to compete in this international war from its recently secured American market base. Northern is spending heavily on international expansion in China, France, and Australia. In its view, the company's best "home base" is the United States, with its low wages, low tax base, and lower transportation costs.

Moreover, many states have a "buy American" policy, and the company must become as American as apple pie to land major contracts. Northern has launched a huge global ad campaign, and the ad series for North America is targeted directly at American congressmen. Its purpose is to show Northern as a good U.S.corporate citizen. One headline reads "Northern Telecom helps keep the U.S. Air Force flying into the wild blue yonder." Canada is not included in the campaign or mentioned in the ads.

Selling itself as an established, American-based company helped Northern Telecom Inc., the American arm of the company, to secure a landmark deal with the Japanese government to build Nippon Telegraph and Telephone. Capitalizing on Japanese concerns over their country's huge trade imbalance with the United States, the company assured Japan that the switches — a vital ingredient of the contract — would not be made in Canada but in the United States. Ironically, the choice for this contract was between AT&T and Northern, and the fact that Northern was Canadian was a major influence on the Japanese government's decision.

The Canadian government has warned that the deficit makes it difficult for it to assist Canadian companies seeking export contracts. It does not warn us about the pressure it is under from the

American government for such past assistance. In the 1990 budget, the federal government announced that it was going to cut aid to exporters by $75 million over the next two years, seriously limiting its help for Canadian companies trying to secure overseas contracts.

A potential bid for work in China may seal the fate of Northern's future in Canada. With the help of funding from the Canadian government, the company secured the first part of a major contract to supply China with telephone-cable and switching equipment. However, future contracts in China may not receive government funding, and the company may have to sell this bid from its American base. The U.S. government has just announced it is going to start funding this kind of project (called "tied-aid," it is the kind of funding just cut by the Canadian government). If Northern gets the China contract and American government aid, it will be with the condition that the switches are manufactured in the United States.

In the United States, Northern goes to great lengths to prove it is a fully American company so it can secure American defence contracts. Paul Stern, who served on Reagan's National Security Telecommunications Advisory Committee and on the Pentagon's Defense Policy Advisory Committee on Trade, is bringing in other Americans to serve as directors and to toughen up the Canadian company. Former Reagan defence secretary William Carlucci is now on the board of directors. The very nature of Northern is changing, tuned to American political and defence needs. Stern says that there are "huge" business opportunities in the new Pentagon emphasis on telecommunications.

Northern Telecom was a big supporter of the free-trade agreement. It donated $107,000 to the Alliance for Trade and Job Opportunities. The ex-premier of Alberta, Peter Lougheed, prominent Tory government adviser on free trade, is on Northern's board of directors. After years of support and funding by Canadian taxpayers, Northern welcomes the new regime for two reasons: wage restraints and mobility.

The threat of world competition will pull down worker demand in Canada and instil "discipline." Already, the company is giving its employees an object lesson on what global competition means. A program called the President's Council on Competition takes workers to Northern sites in other countries, where workers who are paid much less are grateful for their jobs and work hard to keep them. The message is not lost on the visitors.

The lessons of wage restraint for employees apparently weren't meant for senior management. Retiring chairman Edmund Fitzgerald received a cash compensation of $1.06 million (U.S.), a raise of 85 percent from the previous year; David Vice got a 37 percent pay raise; consultant Paul Stern, who is paid $3,000 a day to whip companies into line and keep employee costs at rock bottom, received $1.18 million (U.S.) and options on 130,000 Northern shares.

Northern has also gained mobility. Having taken the best Canada has to offer, it is moving on with the blessing of the Canadian government. For the next generation of young scientists and engineers, the decision will be whether to follow Northern or to stay home with reduced prospects. There is no other option when a company's sole allegiance is to profit, and when government chooses not to interfere in the working of the "free" market.

The restructuring of corporate North America is part of a larger plan: the formation of a free-trade zone from Canada's Far North into Central America. Of major importance to the regeneration of U.S. economic pre-eminence are Canada's vast resources and the abundant, cheap labour of Mexico and Central America. Such an alliance will form the most powerful trade block the world has ever known and will enable the United States to compete with Europe and Japan. The United States and Mexico are now openly moving towards a free-trade agreement, fulfilling Ronald Reagan's dream. "The U.S.–Canada free trade agreement is a New Economic Constitution for North America. It will, I believe, inaugurate a similar continent-wide economic expansion," he said in his 1988 State of the Union address.

This agreement with Mexico will have profound implications for Canada. Of special concern is the tariff-free industrial strip in Mexico, running along the American border, known as "the Maquiladora." A haven for Fortune 500 companies seeking to avoid the higher labour costs of Canada and the northern United States, this industrial zone has a free-trade arrangement with the United States. The *maquiladoras* are component-assembly plants (the word means "twin") of North American, Japanese, and West German corporations. Final assembly of the products usually takes place in the home country of the company. There are at least 1, 800 *maquiladoras* in Mexico, and the number is growing by 20 percent every year.

The plants employ about 500,000 workers, mostly young women earning on average $6 a day. So low are the wages and so docile is the labour force in poverty- and debt-stricken Mexico that many companies prefer it to the traditional centres of cheap labour — South Korea, Hong Kong, Taiwan, and Singapore. Sexual harassment in the Maquiladora is rampant, working conditions often hazardous, and environmental safeguards almost non-existent.

Encouraged by the United States, Mexico has radically transformed its economic policy in recent years from a nationalist system to one dependent on foreign investment. It has implemented a massive program of privatization, selling the vast majority of state-owned enterprises in just a few years. The buying power of workers' salaries was cut in half during the 1980s, while business profits more than doubled in the same period.

Companies often side-step North American environmental and safety laws by assembling the most hazardous components of a product in these factories: guns, ammunition, chemicals, insecticides, fungicides and herbicides. Then the components are shipped back to the United States or Canada for final assembly or packaging. This area of Mexico is an environmental cesspool. As many as 86 percent of the Tijuana *maquiladoras* produce toxic waste; more than 100 different industrial wastes are dumped into the New River in Mexico.

Rosa (her last name is not used to protect her) is a Maquiladora worker. She explains why women put up with these conditions: "Women very often don't do anything to risk their work because they have to care for their children. The fear of losing your job is very real. So instead you do the best you can to survive — eat very little, work double shifts, and get other members of the family to work." By "other members of the family," Rosa means her children. Birth certificates are often falsified, and few questions are asked. Rosa and her co-workers also put up with dangerous working conditions. They suffer rashes, burns, and nausea working in the chemical plants; if they miss a day, the are docked for two. If a worker's child gets sick, he or she can be fired.

Several years ago, as reported in a series of articles by Jack Todd in the Montreal *Gazette* in July 1989, the head of a school in the town of Matamoros noticed that there were twenty children about the same age with a condition resembling Down's syndrome. She discovered that the mothers of all the children worked in a plant owned by a company called Mallory Capacitors that manufactured batteries, and had been exposed to acid fumes over a long period. The union refused to help the children, as did the government. Not surprisingly, the union movement is tightly controlled by the Mexican government. Any real worker protest ends in firing.

A new wave of excesses rivalling those of the Industrial Revolution is rolling over Mexico, and many blue-chip North American companies are the perpetrators. Unlike the European Community, where strict social and environmental standards have been set, the emerging North American trade block has none; short-term economic necessity will drag everyone down to the lowest common denominator. Whichever country has the lowest wage, safety, and social program will attract the big corporations, placing pressure on the others to lower their standards in order to compete. This issue is of singular concern to Canada and Canadian workers. Under free trade, many goods assembled in Mexico will now come into Canada duty free, as long as 50 percent of their value was added in the United States. Canadian companies will have to try to compete against these products in both the Canadian and the U.S. markets.

No one in Canada could live on *maquiladora* wages; nor should the people of Mexico have to accept such conditions.

Two trends are apparent. Some companies are closing all or part of their Canadian operations and are moving to Mexico. Fleck Manufacturing of Centralia, Ontario, whose president is a prominent member of the Business Council on National Issues, is but one example. In the dead of night, hours after its mostly female workers went on strike for decent working conditions and wages, the company backed trucks up to its factory doors, loaded them up, and moved the whole operation to Ciudad Juárez. When the employees came to the factory in the morning, they found only a boarded-up building — no settlement, no recourse.

Bendix Safety Restraints Ltd., an auto-parts maker, has shifted production out of Collingwood, Ontario, to the Maquiladora, putting four hundred Canadians out of work. It also employed many women, women whose husbands had lost their jobs in the local shipyard. In one family, the husband lost his pension and all his benefits when he had to find another job, one that pays considerably less. His wife, who had worked at Bendix for fifteen years, lost all her benefits when the company left; she has been able to find only part-time jobs since. Their family income has been halved. They are bitter about the long years they spent building a dream now shattered, and they are very worried for their children's future.

The second trend is the growing chorus of voices warning us to down-grade our standards so Canada can compete. The threat of Mexico will be a silent participant at every future negotiation between employee and employer and between the corporations and the government. "Going global," the catch phrase of the 1990s, means that Canadians will have a new standard against which to measure their jobs. The image of Rosa, paid a wage she can't live on to work in unsafe conditions, hovers as the competition for every Canadian in a manufacturing job.

In fact, "the maquiladoras are key to making North America competitive in the global marketplace," says the pro–free trade *Financial Post*. Mexico's national unemployment rate of over 20 percent is a labour pool of unlimited depth. "To labour-intensive companies in the U.S. and Canada, Mexico's slogan could be: 'Cheap labour and lots of it.' "

U.S. business is already forming a coalition to promote free trade with Mexico that is much like the group that promoted free trade with Canada. The signs of a silent integration of Mexico into the American economy are unmistakable. But American business has learned from its experience with Canada. In order to avoid the backlash that free trade has caused in our country, it is prepared to go slowly and maintain a low profile. Corporate leaders have as their goal extending free trade and the *maquiladora* concept into Central America, and they know it will take time.

Terence Corcoran, writing for the *Globe and Mail*, calls it a "powerful idea that is slowly gaining breeze-like momentum in some political, business and academic circles." The vice-president of corporate relations for the Business Council of British Columbia enthusiastically supports trilateral free trade, as "Mexico would provide a large and relatively inexpensive labour pool. . . . Ultimately, this will rationalize industry on a continental scale." These polite words mean that American multinationals and Canadian corporations recently given the free-trade go-ahead can move production to Mexico and pay absolutely no price for displacing thousands of employees in their countries of origin.

The federal government is actively exploring a scheme called "outward processing" — giving trade concessions to encourage Canadian clothing manufacturers to farm out sewing to foreign factories. The clothes would be designed and cut in Canada, then shipped to Mexico and other low-wage countries to be stitched. The loss of jobs in Canada could run into thousands, mostly for unskilled, immigrant women.

Companies have already been set up to help with this transition. A U.S. firm with the forthright name of Bottom Line Technologies Inc. has opened an office in Toronto. It helps Canadian companies to relocate with "start-up programs that smooth the transfer of your personnel, operating procedures and equipment to Mexico." As their corporate clients are likely to be as uninterested in the well-being of the new country in which they will locate as in that of the country from which they are fleeing, this firm also advises on a "shelter plan that allows you to operate without legal/ financial involvement with Mexico."

Extensive job losses to Mexico in the manufacturing sector will force Canada to turn increasingly to the production of raw resources, deepening our dependence on their exploitation. Moreover, we will have no leverage with which to fight the United States when it starts to buy from Mexico products traditionally bought from Canada. We gave away all our bargaining power in the free-trade agreement.

Now that their Canadian branch plants are no longer part of the business structure of a foreign, sovereign country, American multinationals can treat Canada as just another domestic market, one about the size of California. The Canadian operations can be closed, specialized, or converted to warehouses; they no longer have to be consulted. Rendered the political equivalent of a regional interest, Canadian branch plants have neither autonomy nor clout: what is good for them, or for Canada, is irrelevant.

Unfortunately for Canada, there is no shortage of experts willing to hasten the process. Isaiah A. Litvak, a Canadian academic and business consultant to multinationals, has much advice for American-based corporations with branch plants in Canada in the post–free trade era. Free of the historical necessity to treat these subsidiaries as "Canadian-centred" operations, he says, the parent companies "will have to exert greater control over their Canadian subsidiaries. ... it is not practical to leave decision-making" to them. He advises the American members of Canadian boards of directors to sensitize Canadian members to the "probable role to be assigned to the Canadian subsidiary."

Recognizing that labour groups and many others in Canada had serious concerns with the free-trade agreement, Litvak suggests that the Canadian board members can play a pivotal role in allaying these fears while facilitating the transfer of power to head office. "Many Canadian subsidiaries have been managed as relatively autonomous units and their integration with the much larger U.S.

operations will require time and diplomacy by parent management." He counsels his U.S. corporate clients in this piece of
corporate etiquette: "While making these consolidations, maintain
a Canadian president as 'country manager.' " Common interests
on both sides of the border has brought about a long-standing goal
of American business. Greed greased the political wheels.

The Canadian government is doing everything it can to hasten
and smooth the fundamental and profound corporate restructuring taking place in North America. It is also encouraging the sell-
out of Canadian industry. Since scuttling the old Foreign Investment Review Agency and replacing it with Investment Canada in
June 1985, the government has made Canadian history. The
agency has not turned down a single application for take-over, and,
between 1985 and 1989, more than 2,000 Canadian-controlled
companies, worth almost $50 billion, were sold to non-residents.

"The renewed interest in Canada is being driven by enthusiasm for the free-trade pact with the United States and the relatively
low asking prices for many of Canada's premier companies," reported the *Globe and Mail*. The head of Canada Trust warns that
U.S. firms are gunning to buy Canadian trust companies as a wedge
into the Canadian market.

The giant Consolidated-Bathurst of Quebec has been sold for a
cool $2.6 billion to Chicago-based Stone Container. The president
of the parent company, Roger Stone, who has a reputation as a
tough employer, has announced he wants to lower Canadian labour costs to bring them in line with those south of the border. The
union is already gearing up for a fight. But some people have done
very well, indeed, from this take-over. Oscar Strangeland, the head
of former Consolidated-Bathurst and now head of the new subsidiary, Stone-Consolidated, earned $2.3 million (U.S.) in 1989, and
was the highest-paid executive in Canada. Maurice Sauvé (husband
of the then governor general) received a massive finder's fee — a
good portion of $26 million — to clinch the deal according to
reports in the *Toronto Star* and Douglas Fisher's column in the
Toronto *Sun* in 1989.

Power Corp., the firm that sold the company, now says that Canada is a poor investment and the company is looking to spend its profits "elsewhere."

Federal Pioneer, the largest electrical-parts manufacturer in Canada, was bought by a Paris-based multinational for $300 million. The largest gas distributor in the country, Consumers' Gas Company of Toronto, is being taken over by British Gas.

Company after company in the high-tech sector is being sold, ironically to firms based in countries that would never permit foreign control in this key sector. Such well-known companies as Lumonics and Mitel were sold. A leading software computer firm, HCR, a Canadian success story, was sold to Santa Cruz Inc. of California. Connaught Biosciences, Canada's most influential medical-research company, is now under the control of the French government. That this company, such a significant part of Canada's history, because of its major investment in pharmaceutical research, and its subsidiary, Bio-Research, the only company in Canada doing primary research in toxicology, were allowed to be sold to non-Canadians stands as an indictment of this government for all time. Connaught was a healthy company. The year before it was sold, its shareholders' profits increased by 37 percent.

The executive of Connaught were given a golden parachute for their part in facilitating the deal. Brian King, the president, was given three years' salary (his 1988 salary was $478,000), an undisclosed executive bonus, three years of health and insurance benefits, a stock option pay-out of $915,000, and a yearly pension of $95,000. The others received similar prizes. Norma Michael, executive vice-president, was given a pension credit for thirty-seven years of company service although she was only thirty-nine years old at the time.

Yet, the federal government stands on the side and watches. Leigh Instruments was a healthy Canadian high-tech company before it was taken over by Plessey PLC of Great Britain, which then sold it to General Electric and Siemens of West Germany, who shut it down, putting 750 people out of work. In the House of Commons, Benoit Bouchard, the industry minister, said there was nothing he could do because the deal was between two foreign companies, and none of the government's business.

In some sectors, the selling off of Canadian companies has felt like an assault. The advertising business in Canada is quickly being eaten up. Six of the top ten advertising agencies in Canada are now American owned, and 70 percent of all Canadian contracts are to non-Canadian companies. The government quietly dropped the requirement that advertising agencies bidding for government contracts (government is Canada's largest advertiser) be 100 percent Canadian owned, asking only that they be majority Canadian owned. Heralded by foreign-based advertising agencies as the first of a two-step process to deregulate the industry, the guidelines were also greeted with warnings that they will invite abuse. "Games will be played and subsidiary relationships will be created so that nobody will know who is doing what to whom," said the head of an American firm.

Now that they are no longer required by law to encourage participation of Canadians, foreign multinational companies such as General Electric, Westinghouse, and Nabisco are "going private" and buying out minority shareholders of their publicly traded Canadian subsidiaries. They thereby remove yet another safeguard of Canadian interests.

The vice-president of a major American mergers and acquisitions firm summed the situation up this way: "Many business people in the U.S. now feel that Canada has turned into just another state. They think Canada will simply become part of the U.S." An economic study by the Washington-based National Planning Association on Canada–U.S. Relations argues that Canadian financial planners and politicians will have to mimic their American counterparts as a result of the free-trade agreement. Our banks will be forced to follow the American bank rate and policies, it said, because our two countries are now economically one and the larger's policies will prevail. James Rill, a senior American antitrust official, predicts that the two countries will have to compare and review competition policy, as different rules will lead to problems.

The price of this growing domination of our economy is a diminution of our very sovereignty and our ability to make basic decisions about our lives. The *Financial Post* says that foreign ownership of Canadian financial assets has put a "strait-jacket" around the Governor of the Bank of Canada in establishing Canadian monetary policy. The Bank has never been confronted with such daunting foreign financial power in Canada before, says a Prudential-Bache Securities analyst. Foreigners own about 30 percent of all Canadian government bonds, 36 percent of all provincial bonds, and 50 percent of all corporate bonds. A U.S. investment banker warns that Canada has a "Third World currency."

But such domination of our economy also carries a terrible financial toll. Our huge merchandise-trade surplus of recent years has shrunk dramatically. So has our current-account balance, which includes the cost of paying for our foreign debt. The cost of servicing our rapidly increasing foreign debt is racing out of control and our merchandise-trade surplus is plummeting. Our current-account position with the United States has deteriorated from a surplus of over $2 billion in the first half of 1987 to a deficit of over $3 billion in the same period of 1989. And Canada's current-account deficit doubled in 1989 as the country had its worst-ever year in balance of payments with the rest of the world. Doug Peters, chief economist with the Toronto-Dominion Bank, says that our current-account deficit could run up to $25 billion in 1990.

If this situation brought new investment dollars into Canada or established new economically profitable enterprises here, there might be an argument to offset these appalling figures. But the vast majority of foreign investments are in the take-over of existing companies. Of almost $70 billion of foreign investment in Canada between June 30, 1985, and June 30, 1989, 96 percent was spent in the take-over of existing Canadian businesses and only 4 percent was for new business investment. And most of this is accomplished with the retained earnings of these corporations in Canada, financed by Canadian banks with Canadian savings, so that money for new activity is raised right here. Between 1974 and 1986, almost 80 percent of the increase in foreign direct investment was financed in Canada.

The government has initiated other financial measures favourable to the large multinationals that are having a devastating impact on small-business people and exporters. It is beginning the process of dismantling the border, planning some shared customs facilities with American border offices, streamlining regular cross-border travel, especially for businesspersons, and working to a system of pre-inspection of goods. Eventually, most people will pass back and forth with only a card to flash, and Canada Customs will regularly allow all goods through without inspection unless tipped off by American authorities that drugs or other banned goods are contained in the shipment.

Traffic congestion at border sites attests to the dramatic growth in travel to the United States. At several border crossings, traffic volume has increased 400 percent in 1989 and may again in 1990. Canadians are driving south to buy gas, clothing, appliances, and even food. It is not only at border cities that this is happening. Residents of Thunder Bay are travelling 320 kilometres and a time zone away to find bargains in Duluth, Minnesota, much to the distress of the merchants of their home town. Same-day visits by Canadians to the American side increased 20 percent in 1989, as have purchases. But far fewer Americans are coming to Canada.

While many Canadians are finding bargains in the United States, the decision to open up the border has enormous ramifications. Canadian store-owners are reeling from the loss of business. The *Windsor Star* calls it a crisis: "The traditional seepage of Canadian consumer dollars into the U.S. has become a tidal wave which threatens the economic life of border communities." The Canadian Council of Grocery Distributors reported recent losses of $300,000 weekly in grocery dollars in one border town alone. And about 1,100 retail jobs have disappeared in the Niagara region in the last year as a result of lost business.

It is true that, on average, prices for goods are higher in Canada than in the United States. But much of the reason for that is the high amount of foreign ownership of Canadian business. Says Mageed Ragab, an economics professor at the University of Windsor, foreign parents of Canadian firms insist that their offspring charge higher prices and show a big return on investment for the parent. The more Canada is bought out, the more this will be the case. Prices will stay high in Canada, and Canadians will continue to suffer job loss as a result of consumer dollars going south. It is a vicious cycle that can only get worse as our ties with the United States increase.

An open border smooths the way for a North American economy. One integrated business system works to the advantage of the very corporate élite who masterminded the free-trade agreement. Merging to gain strength for the global wars ahead, Canadian business is already concentrated in the hands of a few. This concentration of power gives these corporations enormous clout in influencing the economic and political agenda of Canada to their benefit. Economic integration with the United States serves their overall goals.

These goals include lowered competition, higher consumer prices, and lower wages for employees. And, not surprisingly, they include harmonization with another American practice — paying much higher salaries to corporate executives. Several reports predict that Canadian practices will soon come in line with those of the United Sates and will bring corporate benefits into line with them. "Integration of our two economies . . . will increase the pressure to equalize compensation at the executive level," says one report, which notes that Canadian executives now earn about half what their American counterparts do.

Another deliberate harmful government economic policy is the high Canadian dollar. Although it is deeply hurting Canadian exporters, the Bank of Canada continues to punish the economy by keeping the dollar high. A higher Canadian dollar that would remove any advantage Canadian exporters had over American companies was part of the pre–free trade bargaining that went on between Canada and the United States and was added as a carrot in the business supplement that was placed in the *New York Times* the week of Mulroney's famous visit to New York.

Indeed, Senator Max Baucus clearly stated the U.S. position on the dollar at a speech to the Brookings Institute in Washington in 1987: "In my judgement, the exchange-rate issues should be addressed before any agreement is struck. The Canadian dollar currently is about 25 percent below parity, giving Canadian exporters a tremendous price advantage in the U.S.market. . . . such an imbalance against U.S. producers creates a bad climate for Congressional approval of any free-trade agreement." And the U.S. Manufacturers' Association wrote to the U.S. Secretary of the Treasury in 1988, calling for the government to use the free-trade talks to force Canada into line on the dollar. Now, as a further indication of who this policy serves, the Canadian government is saying that wage settlements in Canada must come down before the issue can even be discussed.

But perhaps the most disturbing economic policy this government has introduced in favour of its corporate friends is the bill the Canadian people have been handed for free trade — the Goods and Services Tax. Inherently unfair, it will collect enormous revenues for the government.

This government has been steadily shifting the burden of taxes from richer to poorer since it came to power. Tax changes from 1984 to 1990 have had a devastating impact on low- and middle-income families, who are bearing the brunt of deficit reduction. By the end of 1990, working-poor households will pay $1,000 more taxes than they paid in 1984. Taxes on a traditional family earning poverty-line income have gone up more than seven times faster than the taxes paid by a high-income family. And taxes on families with children have steadily increased more than taxes on families without children.

The middle class is suffering too. Taxes have reduced middle-class incomes more than any other factor since the Tories came to power. Squeezed between high interest rates, high housing and child-care costs, and the declining value of their paycheques, the middle class is increasingly less able to use tax breaks designed for a wealthier group. The 1989 budget's announced surcharge on personal income is a flat tax, and as such, will have disproportionate effects all the way up the income ladder.

But these figures are trivial compared to the favouritism this government shows to its corporate friends. These friends receive enormous tax breaks and subsidies, in direct comparison with the amount given the families referred to above. In 1988, there were about 60,000 profitable corporations that paid no tax in this country. Many are BCNI members. Algoma Steel (profits $80 million) and Brascan (profits $263 million) are members who paid no taxes. Goodyear Canada (profits $75 million) is one of the group members that received a tax credit that year ($2.86 million), as did Power Corp. (profits $214 million; credit $2.12 million). Subsidies, loan guarantees, and grants helped BCNI members Noranda ($16.3 million) and Domtar ($10.1 million).

In fact, the Canadian corporate sector has been getting quite a break for a long time. In 1950, direct tax revenue from both the personal and corporate sectors was approximately equal. By 1988, personal taxes had dramatically risen to 47 percent of government expenditures, whereas corporate taxes declined to just 9 percent. In other words, the corporate sector has managed to cut its relative tax liability by 75 percent since 1950. If the corporate sector had just kept pace and paid its share, instead of finding itself with a deficit, Canada would be in a fairly healthy surplus situation now.

As well, a Library of Parliament study shows that, in recent years, business's share of federal subsidies has steadily grown, whereas support for social spending has declined. The biggest breaks, however, are happening right now. Ottawa is allocating about $30 billion annually in tax shelters, special grants, and incentives to business.

The new tax is entirely consistent with the agenda of this government and its corporate sponsors. Once all the tariffs come down, as a result of the trade agreement, the government will lose billions of dollars annually. The GST is, in part, a replacement for this lost revenue. It places the tax burden on families and small business and begins the harmonization of Canada's tax structure with the American system. Because of the "level playing-field" required by the free-trade agreement, the government has ruled out levying a meaningful corporate income tax, or removing all the loopholes and concessions now given to corporations. "The GST is designed to adapt Canada's tax system with the economic environment created by the free-trade agreement," says the Pro-Canada Network.

As well as replacing the tariff revenues, and as the government has repeatedly stated, the open intention of the tax is to make large Canadian corporations more competitive, particularly in the American market. Under the GST, government will be able to remove taxes from exports, helping them to compete against countries with lower corporate taxes. Canadian consumers will make up the difference.

But, the GST will hit small Canadian businesses hard. Not only will it significantly raise the price of most goods and services in the country, it will increase the disparity in consumer prices between Canada and the United States. And the Conference Board of Canada estimates that the GST will reduce the real disposable income of Canadians by over $7 billion annually.

The reality of this tax is that it was designed for the kind of corporations, Canadian and American, that belong to the Business Council on National Issues, not the small- and medium-sized companies who create the jobs in Canada. The BCNI has been lobbying for such a tax for years. The GST is a major step towards a more regressive tax system, mirroring the orientation of the U.S.-style system. The president of Dow Canada says that Canada will lose under free trade without this kind of tax harmonization. David Buzzelli says that, without this adjustment, "investment and jobs will gradually shift to the U.S."

The tragedy for Canada is that many of the very small- and medium-sized businesses that fought this tax are being forced to move out of the country as they are no longer able to compete. Such is the nature of the deal between the Mulroney government and its corporate bosses that, in spite of the overwhelming opposition to the GST in Canada, the government will not — cannot — back down.

This is the economic legacy of the Mulroney government's free-trade agreement — job loss, flight of Canadian investment and research dollars, increased competition on small business, a regressive tax, and a trade deficit. Tragically, as always, the social legacy mirrors the economic one.

# 4.
# THE HUMAN COST OF FREE TRADE

"This is not pleasant stuff. You've got to say, Atlantic Canada, you're on your own. Northern Canada, you're on your own."

*Micky Cohen, President of Molson's*

NO SUBJECT WAS MORE CONTENTIOUS DURING THE 1988 Canadian election debate than whether a free-trade deal with the United States would affect Canada's social safety net. Political leaders called each other liars on television. Justice Emmett Hall went in front of the cameras to say that he could see no reference to social programs in the agreement. Former health minister Monique Bégin held a press conference to express her fears that free trade would compromise medicare.

The intensity of this disagreement highlighted the centrality to Canadians of our social programs. In contrast to the United States, Canada has developed a complex network of social programs that provide some security for seniors, families with young children, the unemployed, and those in need of health care. They are founded on the belief that services should be equitable throughout the country. Although these programs have often been uneven in their delivery, equality has been a fundamental goal.

Any assessment of the impact of free trade on our social programs must take into account the promises that were made regarding them. Those opposed to free trade feared that the deal would affect social programs. Those who supported free trade promised it would not do so. In fact, both government and business promised that the free-trade deal was going to create the wealth necessary to maintain and enhance Canada's social safety net.

Time and again before the election the Business Council on National Issues and the Canadian Alliance for Trade and Job Opportunities maintained their commitment to Canada's social system and standard of living. In their primary election advertising vehicle, the alliance took great exception to the charge that Canada's social-security system was jeopardized by a wide-open agreement with a superpower whose values are so very different. "But won't the agreement gradually force us to align our policies along the lines of the larger and stronger partner? Won't Canadian business lobby to reduce spending on social and other programs?" they were asked. "Not at all . . . On the contrary, it will help to generate the wealth that will allow us to continue to develop a rich, rewarding and diversified society," they responded.

"But don't our social benefits add up to higher labour costs than in the U.S.?" No, they replied, "It is a myth to say that the costs of our total compensation packages are uncompetitive with the U.S. because of our social benefits. . . . We've proven that our workforce can be more cost effective than that of our friends in the U.S. . . . With access to the United States markets we become an even more attractive location for manufacturers from throughout the world." The FTA will bring "More jobs. Better jobs. More wealth to improve government services such as daycare."

What a difference an election makes. Within weeks of winning and before the deal was even signed into law, these same people discovered the deficit they had assiduously ignored before the election. The deficit was the means by which they turned their mollifying pre-election message into an alarmist and highly co-ordinated campaign to cut Canada's social-security system. The Canadian Manufacturers' Association called for a royal commission on social spending. "How can we make the manufacturing sector more competitive," they lamented, unless we overhaul our social programs "in their entirety?" Laurent Thibault, the association's presi-

dent, said that, without social-spending cuts, Canada's transition to free trade would be undermined. The Chamber of Commerce called for the elimination of universality and cuts to unemployment insurance. Roger Hamel, then head of the chamber, demanded cuts to old-age security and guaranteed income supplements of $2 billion and cuts to unemployment insurance of $3 billion. He also recommended expanding the sales tax to cover everything, including food.

In a pre-1990 budget speech, the president of the C.D. Howe Institute, a think-tank that advises government, said that the concept of universality must be abandoned. The BCNI called for wage restraint, and in a ruse to appear fair, also called for government restraint in hand-outs to business. But that call is self-serving. A recent report for Kodak Canada also called on business to become less dependent on government in Canada. Why? Because such assistance has inhibited Canadian firms from investing in "more favourable locations" in other parts of the world.

The government responded with speed by attacking the fundamental concept of universality. It brought forward two pieces of legislation: one to change the universal nature of unemployment insurance, and one to end universal payments to seniors and families with children by "clawing back" these entitlements from higher-income groups. Both bills are still working their way through the House of Commons and the Senate, which is attempting to force major revisions in them.

While many Canadians would agree that our public funds have to be better targeted to help those most in need, as a country we have long believed that family allowance and old-age security are essential rights to be enjoyed by all. If this principle is destroyed, these programs will be diminished, aimed only at those the government and its corporate advisers consider "in need." Limiting these programs to those at the very lowest end of the economic scale transforms them from a right to a charity. The middle class, under increasing assault, will lose this security, at a time when it cannot afford it; as well, the programs themselves, which now enjoy such wide support and respectability, will lose the backing of the influential middle-class. Furthermore, there will be no basic principle that will inhibit successive governments from dipping into this seemingly bottomless well for revenues, "clawing back" the most basic of Canadian social-insurance programs.

The legislation to limit family and old-age benefits to individuals with incomes of under $50,000 was condemned by the National Council of Welfare and many other social advocacy groups as "the most significant change in social policy in a generation." By not fully indexing entitlements to inflation for the first time, the council warned, in less than ten years more than a million Canadian families could lose all or part of their family allowance, and workers now in the $40,000 range could get as little as 25 percent of what the pensioners can now expect when they reach retirement. This is not only an assault on hard-working, middle-income Canadians, but a betrayal of seniors who paid into these funds for years to provide security for their retirement. As Jean Woodsworth, president of the seniors' network One Voice, said, "It's unfair to change the rules of the game when we seniors can't change the way we've planned our retirement income."

Cuts to subsidized housing, federal social assistance, and legal aid will also hurt older Canadians disproportionately. Particularly mean-spirited was the decision to increase the payments for room and board that Canada's veterans must pay to remain in veterans' lodgings. Those who served Canada in two world wars will also lose their once-a-year spring cleaning and maintenance service. Says economist Stephen Triantis, "The federal government, in a shocking display of callousness, plans to unstitch, rip apart and finally dismantle the whole system of the Old Age Security, the Canada Pension Plan, Medicare and other entitlements, which generations of Canadians struggled for and a succession of governments have honoured."

The wealthy political and corporate élite of this country will never notice the loss of these programs, and several generously declared their willingness to give them up for the benefit of the "poor." Not only have we now eliminated one of the major support structures for the middle class — a shift that will, as it has in the

United States, widen the gap between rich and poor — we have removed the dignity that universality brings to a social-security network.

The major changes contained in the government's legislation to fundamentally abandon our system of unemployment insurance is a sign of the Americanization of our social programs. Our UI system particularly rankles the United States and, if left intact, would be a source of much friction at future free-trade discussions to define subsidies. At issue was the American belief that our federal government's support of the UI program constitutes a subsidy and therefore presents an unfair advantage to Canadian companies and employees. So, once again, the Tory government moved to head off the U.S. challenge by lowering our standards to U.S. levels. The Tories have reneged on their commitment of almost $3 billion a year to unemployment insurance. Now the total costs are to be borne by employers and employees.

This move is significant for several reasons. Unemployment insurance has always been seen as a means for the federal government to achieve equality across the country and buffer sectors or regions experiencing hardship. By removing the federal presence from the program, this government is balkanizing the country. Without federal funds in this system, there will be little incentive for regions to assist one another or share a commitment to job-creation in Canada as a whole.

This is the American way. There is no federal funding for unemployment insurance in the United States and each state sets its own standards. The lack of government interest encourages low support for the concept. In Canada, over 80 percent of unemployed workers collect UI; only 25 percent of unemployed Americans receive it. Moreover, in Canada, the average weekly payment is significantly higher, as is the average length of time the average worker can receive benefits. In recent years, America has experienced a steady erosion in support for the program.

Our government is running headlong in the same direction. In the interests of harmonization, it is lowering our UI standards, cutting eligibility and benefit periods, and putting up obstacles to provinces and regions that have traditionally depended more on these entitlements because of the nature of the available work. As well, the government has frozen employer/employee contributions at rates lower than they were in 1984, which will likely drive the UI fund into a deficit. Future support for such a program will be weakened as the benefits themselves will be fewer. As numerous observers are predicting a serious downturn for our economy, this could leave many thousands of Canadians in desperate straits if they are laid off or unable to find work.

But the government is not limiting its attack to individuals and families. Whole communities and regions are being deserted too. No more convincing evidence of the government's heartless, business-oriented agenda exists than its betrayal of the concept of regional equality. It had predicted that central Canada would benefit most from free trade — a bitter irony considering the extent of job losses in Ontario alone (see Appendix) — but vowed that free trade would not hurt the regions. In fact, regional equality was one of the benefits of his deal that Mulroney regularly promised.

    The government is hitting the regions with a number of cuts. It has cut federal transfer payments for health care and post-secondary education in every budget since 1986. According to the Canadian Association of University Teachers, the federal reductions will amount to almost $24 billion by 1994 — a shortfall that will leave the provinces with a difficult choice between higher taxes and declining services. As well, deep cuts to programs such as the Atlantic Canada Opportunities Agency and the Western Diversification Fund will increase the growing disparities between rich and poor regions in Canada. Dozens of regional programs, from forestry to fish-processing, to tourism, are being axed, and, with the sharp decline in fish stocks, many in Atlantic Canada, like Wesley Stubbert, a Cape Breton County Council member, are expressing the region's desperation: "The Government of Canada has no concept of the destruction and calamity it is laying on Atlantic Canada. ... We have had in Cape Breton heavy-water plant closures, closure of CN Express, severe reductions in the coal and fishing industries, closures of post offices, lay-offs at Marine Atlantic, grants eliminated." National Sea Products and other Atlantic-based international fishery conglomerates laid off thousands of plant workers during the last two years, people who will be hardest hit by the tough new unemployment-insurance rules. The seasonal nature of the fish industry and the depletion of the stocks has rendered these communities more dependent on UI for security.

Whole communities are devastated by these closures. Although Ottawa has come forward with an aid package, it comes nowhere near supplementing the funds the government has cut from the industry in the last few years. For example, in May 1990, Ottawa announced that the Strait of Canso region will receive $26.7-million to offset job losses. But, in 1989, Ottawa allowed a five-year, $28-million regional-development agreement for Canso to expire and it is not being renewed.

But neither the government nor the fish-processing companies supports the fish-workers' demand that all fish caught off the Atlantic coast be processed in the area. Such a move would run afoul of the free-trade agreement; so would government aid. Premier Clyde Wells has said that the Newfoundland government considered buying one of the companies but didn't because, under the free-trade agreement, the Americans wouldn't have tolerated it.

Apparently unmoved by the plight of unemployed fish-plant workers, then National Sea president Gordon Cummings said, "Canadians have to get off their butts and get out there and find out about the American market and win. Any aid to laid-off workers will only pay them to stay home so we'll feel better." Perhaps Mr. Cummings has forgotten the subsidies his company received from successive Canadian governments. The program to revive the industry, launched under the former Liberal government in 1983, committed hundreds of millions in tax-payers' dollars in direct support to the big, mostly international, privately operated (therefore not publicly accountable) fishing corporations like National Sea. They were guaranteed stable access to large fishing stocks, and their abusive harvesting methods are a major factor in the depletion of Maritime fish stocks. They now close down Canadian plants while shifting profits and investment outside the country.

But to Gordon Cummings's way of thinking, when corporations get such help it's called an "incentive." When laid-off fish-plant employees get the same thing, it's called "dole." In Newfoundland, the new labour-force development strategy is based on the "bottom line." People on the scarcely populated northern peninsula call it the "resettlement program." Simply put, people are being trained to work elsewhere. Says a local official for the federal government, "What they're asking us to do, and let's not beat around the bush about it, is train and move them off the island."

Bev Butler is a fish-processing worker in St. Mary's Bay, Newfoundland. She has watched the fish stocks diminish for many years as the government gave fishing rights to foreign fishing operations and allowed the export of unprocessed fish to the United States. When she first worked here in 1969, the plants stayed open all year. Then, the plants closed half the year, and now, in St. Mary's, the inshore fishery operates for only six weeks. As a result, Bev is now dependent on unemployment insurance, as are most of her neighbours. She knows what the changes to the system will mean.

"You stand up on top of that hill over St. Mary's and you look way out over it and try to figure out where she's goin' to all be in five years time. Fifty percent of Newfoundland youngsters that come out of school, they don't have no work, as far as I know. I know down there they don't. They all heads to Toronto. To Toronto and work probably for minimum wage and then come home. We're being classified as a lazy bunch, but we're not lazy. We don't have jobs to go to."

Stats Canada figures clearly show that Atlantic Canada is by far the poorest region in the country. And a recent study compiled by a Halifax-based economic council shows that the myth that this region gets an unfair proportion of government subsidies is just that — a myth. In fact, business grants to Atlantic Canada are significantly below the level of subsidies to businesses in the richer regions.

But this is the cost of the government's free-trade agenda. Increasingly, the unregulated, foreign-dominated market-place will determine the conditions of life in regions like Atlantic Canada.

So, too, the North. Mail rates to the North have been sharply increased, and federal subsidies for northern isolation and hardship have been done away with. Northern seasonal workers will be particularly hard-hit by the UI changes. And northern tax breaks are being limited to fewer communities. The prices of southern goods are steep enough and for some will be crippling with the start of the Goods and Services Tax. The roughly 30 percent increase in postal rates could bring more than hardship. Medicine, fresh fruits and vegetables, and fresh water may be at a premium. A family of five, for instance, that now has a grocery bill of $1,300 a month will pay $1,600 for the same products after the new rates come into effect — a cost well beyond the means of most.

No single group stands to lose as much under the new regime as farm families. Promised by the Tories time and again before the election that their fears of negative consequences of the free-trade agreement were unfounded, this community has been hung out to dry. Lauretta Rice is a dairy farmer in Ontario's Renfrew County. She runs a 120-hectare operation with her sixteen-year-old son, Michael John. Together, they have struggled, working long hours, to keep the farm. Lauretta is the only female member of the Renfrew County Milk Committee, and an active member of the National Farmers' Union.

Free trade, and this government's insistence on abandoning farmers to the play of free-market forces, may destroy farmers like her, she says. She warns that the family farm may be dying. What will take its place will be a handful of transnational giants, committed to pesticides and other harmful farming practices, and supported by cheap labour.

Canada established a system of marketing boards in most agricultural sectors to protect farmers against the price swings caused by international price fluctuations and weather conditions. They were also created to provide a secure source of food for Canadians. Marketing boards are typically Canadian in that they are a unique blend of private and public enterprise. The Canadian Wheat Board, for instance, was established in 1935, and whereas its powers are granted by government, it is supported and controlled by the producers themselves. Its goal is to maximize the return to the primary producers, unlike a big agribusiness company, whose goal is corporate profit.

But, these boards, and the philosophy behind them, are in danger. American multinationals have long made it clear that they want the right to operate freely in Canada, buying and selling at whatever the market will bear. The free-trade agreement gives them a powerful tool. As their products start coming into the country unregulated by the Canadian marketing system, the role of the boards will be compromised. Eventually, pressure to kill them will grow.

Cargill, Inc., headquartered in Minneapolis, is the world's largest grain trader. Cargill and its subsidiaries operate in 800 locations around the world in 55 countries and have 46,000 employees world-wide. It is the largest private company in the United States. Its corporate trading company, Tradax, was set up in Panama in 1954, but serves only as a tax shelter. As the company is privately held, Cargill trading activities are obscured from governments in the countries in which it operates. It is the personification of the faceless transnational with no loyalty to anything but its own profit. It is companies like Cargill that free trade really serve and the price must be the sacrifice of practices or people who get in the way.

Cargill is now by far the most significant private trader in Canada, and it wants the freedom to do business without government interference. Economist Brewster Kneen reports that Cargill and its corporate and ideological companions are now the major architects of Canadian agriculture and transportation policy and that Cargill executives have great influence in government circles.

Cargill was represented on the negotiating committees of *both* the United States and Canada for the free-trade agreement. The company had a keen personal interest in seeing that the deal passed.

U.S. agriculture analyst Mark Ritchie explains it this way: "The Free Trade Agreement is a bill of rights for big capital. Agribusiness wants bidding wars on both sides of the border to shave prices." He says that the farm marketing boards will have to go and it won't just damage farmers. "Consumers will have to accept the lowest common denominator in environmental, health and safety standards. Already, Canada has lowered its pesticide standards and has agreed to get rid of irradiation labelling." Cargill is an integrated company, which means that it controls the whole process of its products, from farm gate to finished product. Says Kneen, "Consequently, it is simply unrealistic for a Canadian farmer, or a corporation or co-operative, be it a mill, elevator, feed company, fertilizer company, meat packer or grain buyer, to assume that they can compete directly against Cargill in the marketplace."

Not surprisingly, although Cargill publicly trumpets the superiority of what it calls the "back to the market" theory of business, the company recently accepted a $4-million grant from the government of Alberta to build a massive meat-packing plant in High River, and a loan guarantee of $305 million from the government of Saskatchewan to open a fertilizer plant in Belle Plain.

Canada's harsh climate is one of the reasons we created security for farmers in the first place. Edna Russett has a mixed farm in Manitoba, about 320 kilometres north of the Canada–U.S. border. "This year, for instance, winter started in October so that from then to May we must feed all of these animals from grain and hay that we put up over the very short summer. You can see that most of the year our 'level playing-field' is covered with snow."

The Barrett family in Muenster, Saskatchewan, struggled in the courts for six long years to save their family farm. They found out that they had lost in the local paper — an ad offered their farm for sale. Marlene Barrett says that only their stubborn will to fight kept them from hanging themselves from a tree. Saskatchewan farmers are so desperate that they say they will need $1 billion in government assistance just to survive this year. The number of farm foreclosures in Saskatchewan has tripled during the past five years. Farm incomes dropped dramatically in the last two years, and will drop a further 40 percent in 1990; in Saskatchewan, the drop will be 87 percent.

The National Farmers' Union estimates that as much as 600,000 hectares of farmland may be under title to the federal Farm Credit Corporation (the agency that oversees farm loans, credit, and foreclosures), and to chartered banks on the prairies alone. The size of Prince Edward Island, this farmland represents thousands of families who lost their fight to retain their farms.

The message coming from this government is clear: if farmers cannot adjust to the harsh climate of international trade they will lose their farms to the big companies that can. There has been a steep drop in government aid in recent years: 57 percent in 1990 alone. As the National Farmers' Union explains: "In implementing the corporate business agenda of the food industry, the federal government has Canadian farmers firmly secured to its rack for policy change and is slowly but relentlessly advancing the ratchet — notch by notch."

The ability of a country to feed itself is a fundamental definition of sovereignty. Yet bowing to pressure from a powerful American lobby that has launched an aggressive assault on Canada's supply-marketing system, the government is turning its back on the wisdom of history and abandoning the food producers of this country. Brigid Pyke, president of the Ontario Federation of Agriculture, sums up the situation: "Farmers across the country are extremely anxious that what we have struggled to put together for decades is being systematically dismantled." In its place, there will be corporate control over food production, farm depopulation, and domination of the food business in Canada by American food corporations.

The social cost includes job loss in the sectors relating to agriculture. Canada was founded on the national principle of building strong communities and regions to serve the needs of their residents, not depleting these communities in order to supply land and factories for economic interests. Lay-offs and closures are rocking the meat-packing industry as American giants take over. Twelve big plants process 70 percent of the cattle in the United States, and Canada is following this pattern. The head of the Canadian Turkey Marketing Board says that American industry has its eyes on Canada, and is poised for a take-over of our turkey production, a take-over that could be accomplished in a weekend, maintains one official. About a dozen large poultry conglomerates have driven out the family producers in the United States and they are targeting the 2,500 small processors in Canada who are now protected by marketing boards. The banks in Canada know this, and have tightened up credit to turkey farmers. They know that in the face of these big operations, the small producers are a bad risk. They are more valuable bankrupt than functioning. In this, the banks are serving government's end. Without the support of Canadian banks or the Canadian government, there will be precious little power for the farmers to prevent their demise.

The Canadian government's policies that have led to this deteriorating situation for the agriculture sector have also pitted food processors in Canada against farmers. The largest manufacturer of dairy products in Canada, Ault Foods, warns that it may have to close down: it is not against marketing boards, it insists, but in face of U.S.imports, it cannot compete under free trade with them in place.

Yet fears that such negative changes would occur were systematically denied by the pro–free–trade lobby before the election. "Will our agriculture industry bite the dust?" asked the Canadian Alliance for Trade and Job Opportunities in their literature. "No. . . . We're not giving up our right to set and maintain our own high agricultural and health standards." In a letter to food producers in Saskatchewan just before the 1988 election, the premier, Grant Devine, declared that he was "setting the record straight" on the effects of free trade on the agricultural industry, especially in light of "unfounded and misleading allegations" being made by many in the farm sector. The premier vehemently promised that existing protections would remain and even be enhanced: "For hog and beef producers, the Agreement [Article 401] removes tariffs on Canadian sales in the U.S. This ensures that Canada's higher quality animals will be able to penetrate the U.S. market on a level playing field."

Within a year, the United States had slapped a hefty counter-vailing duty on Canadian pork. Saskatchewan hog farmers will lose as much as $5 million a year, and Ontario farmers up to $250,000 a week; as many as 30,000 Canadian jobs will be lost. When the government of Alberta (which was an avid free-trade booster) took over the troubled Gainers meat-packing plant, the governor of South Dakota said it amounted to an unfair subsidy, and warned that the United States would likely slap large duties on Canadian meat as a result.

Insisting that there is nothing in the deal referring to dairy products, Saskatchewan premier Grant Devine said, "Both Canada and the U.S. retain their tight import controls on dairy products," and pointed out that, since the agreement was signed, Canada had extended import controls on ice cream and yogurt. This proves, Devine said, that the free-trade agreement affirms that Canada and the United States both retain their right under the General Agreement on Tariffs and Trade.

Since then, of course, the United States took Canada to the GATT on this very issue. Canada was told that it could no longer place import controls on these products, a ruling that places thousands of dairy farmers at risk. However, the United States obtained a waiver under the GATT years ago, permitting it to continue to place import quotas on a range of food products, including dairy, leaving Canada with no option to retaliate. The free-trade agreement could not protect Canada as Devine said it would, nor was it intended to. Through deep cut-backs in the federal commitment to the industry and the twenty-month freeze it placed on Canadian milk prices until the end of 1990, our government is deliberately destroying the national dairy policy to harmonize it with the American system.

Perhaps, however, the most outrageous statement of Devine's document (he was also a big free-trade proponent and worked closely with the Mulroney government) had to do with the Wheat Board. "In unequivocal terms, I want you to know that the Canadian Wheat Board is completely protected under the Free Trade Agreement with the United States. . . . the Board will continue to be the sole exporter, both to the United States and to offshore markets, of western Canadian wheat, barley and oats." Within months of the election, the federal government, backed by American grain buyers, some Canadian companies, and some provincial governments (including Devine's), much reduced the power of the Wheat Board and removed the oats trade from its jurisdiction.

The decision to privatize oats comes, not coincidentally, at a time when consumer demand for the product is growing. Agribusiness wanted government out of the way. The Wheat Board's concern for the Canadian farmer was a hindrance. Now Cargill and its ilk, backed by their Conservative friends in Ottawa and the provinces, are getting the return on their pre-election investment: complete freedom to do business without considering the growers, the community, or the country. Months after the deregulation of the oats industry, the federal government ended import restrictions on U.S. oats. Said a senior official with Agriculture Canada, "It's strictly as a result of the free-trade agreement."

According to Washington trade lawyer Elliot Feldman, the way trade disputes are solved under the free-trade agreement almost always favours the United States. The dispute panels must adhere to the laws of the country where the dispute arises, so they will almost always follow U.S. laws because the United States initiates most of the disputes, and their law is procedurally more complex. He points out that there is a history in the United States of fighting imports in the courts and complainants usually have the support of an aggressive Congress.

The large multinationals also want common U.S. inspection standards introduced in Canada. Committed by the free-trade agreement to harmonize inspection practices at the border, the Canadian government is, indeed, lowering our standards in food supplies. Canada Customs used to inspect every shipment of meat and poultry from the United States because conditions on American farms and plants are so much lower than in Canada. For example, because U.S. poultry growers are not required to disinfect after every "generation" of poultry, as are their Canadian counterparts, many U.S. chickens are raised in generations of filth counteracted by strong doses of antibiotics. Fred Coates, head of the agriculture component of the Public Service Alliance of Canada, warns that there is danger of tainted meat coming into Canada. He says that, in the past, customs officers have turned back shipments of meat shipped side by side with photocopying chemicals and hairspray. Yet, rather than protecting Canadian farmers and consumers, the government has bent to U.S. pressure and is now inspecting only one in twenty shipments of these goods.

The Mulroney government was pro-active in the assault on farm programs just as it had been on regional development. In its decision to place countervailing duties on Canadian pork, the U.S. International Trade Commission blamed eighteen Canadian subsidy and farm-stabilization programs, key elements of our marketing system, a system that is very clearly unacceptable to the United States. This is just one volley in the aggressive and orderly assault by the United States on our regional programs, our agriculture policies, and even our right to protect established industries. Knowing it cannot fight back because of the free-trade agreement, our government is preparing Canadians for the new reality.

"The food marketing system that has protected and nurtured a generation of Canadian farmers and processors is on the verge of a far-reaching overhaul," says the *Financial Post*. Don Mazankowski, the agriculture minister, recently warned Canadian farmers that they will have to make "sacrifices" to remain competitive. Certainly, he and Michael Wilson have been doing just that. From the elimination of Canadian rail subsidies for agricultural products to a $90-million cut in crop insurance, the government, since the 1988 election, reduced or destroyed programs that will cost the farm sector $500 million over the next two years. The same conditions that led to the crisis in the U.S. farm community are building here. As farmer Barry Robinson of Renfrew County says, "We're in the last half hour."

This story of whole communities being cut loose by the smug, buffered, and greedy alliance of the Canadian corporate and political élite is told again and again across the country. For eighty years, Canada supported a lively West Coast fish-processing industry by requiring that salmon and herring caught in its waters be processed at fish-packing plants in Canada. In many communities on the West Coast, one would be hard-pressed to find a single family that doesn't have at least one member working in the fishery. For many years, the Americans have been seeking direct access to these fish stocks for their own processing factories, where wages and working conditions are substantially inferior to those at Canadian plants. Using both the GATT and the free-trade agreement successfully against Canada, the Americans pressured the Canadian government to drop its support of the industry. In the first free-trade settlement, it was ruled that, in effect, Canada must give one-quarter of its fish stocks to the United States. In acquiescing without a fight to this loss of sovereignty, Canada abandoned the hard-won principle of the Law of the Sea, which gives coastal states the right to manage their own resources.

The president of the United Fishermen and Allied Workers Union and the Prince Rupert Amalgamated Shoreworkers and Clerks Union warns that 90 percent of the West Coast fish-processing jobs could be lost. "The loss of assured supplies of Canadian fish will undermine or destroy an industry which competes successfully in global markets, generates thousands of Canadian jobs and has enormous potential for growth," he said. An economic-development officer in Washington predicted that it is inevitable that "some" operations will have to move out of Canada. The British Columbia fisheries minister sounded an ominous warning. "The loss of these regulations could mean the collapse of the entire B.C. industry." The sad irony is, of course, that his government sided with the Mulroney Tories in their push for this deal.

Kathy Schultz has worked in a fish-processing plant for fifteen years. This is the end. She and her family are leaving Vancouver. "My family can't survive on welfare and we can't survive on the U.S.-style poverty wages that the companies want to impose on us. With the free-trade deal in place the companies tried to lower the starting rate for shore workers by five dollars an hour. On those wages we couldn't feed our family."

Perhaps the most disturbing and far-reaching change being made by the Mulroney government to Canada's social foundation is the death of national health care. Medicare is the social program of which Canadians are most proud. Canadians receive high-quality, universally accessible health care, and although costs are rising, we utilize our health-care dollar better than does the United States.

Opponents' fears centred on two issues. The first was entering into a binding agreement with a superpower whose whole approach to health care is based on profit. At least one-third of all U.S. physicians are now on salary to private health-care enterprises, and the trend is growing. Around 37 million Americans have no health insurance, and if they need hospital treatment, they must find $500 or more a day. The American Medical Association has waged an expensive and aggressive campaign to discredit our system to Americans as it is gaining supporters in the United States. The vice-president of the AMA says, "Your solution wouldn't be appropriate here where the individual is king. No one wants to pay higher taxes to help somebody else." Many Canadians were concerned that, with time and the harmonization already so apparent in our economic life, our medical systems would start to merge.

The second apprehension lay in the fact that within the free-trade agreement, private U.S. health-care companies are permitted to own Canadian health facilities, thus establishing the principle of privatization within our system. When Justice Emmett Hall declared that he could not find a reference to health care in the free-trade agreement, it was because the subject was deliberately obscured. The free-trade document referred to a list of services eligible for private take-over covered by the agreement, but the list was contained in a code number. To discover the services included, one has to go to a government list called the Standard Industrial Classification. There the list of services included in the agreement, many dealing with health care, covers 100 pages. Clearly, no one showed that list to Justice Hall.

Sadly, many signs point to the steady erosion of medicare in Canada. The trend started under the Trudeau government when it relinquished its responsibility to contribute fifty cents of every provincial health-care dollar. But the Mulroney government sealed the system's fate by capping Ottawa's health-care contribution at two, and then three, percentage points below the growth of the economy. Ottawa's share of medicare dollars has been shrinking every year, and, according to journalist Francis Russell, sometime between 1998 and 2014, the federal government will no longer pay any funds directly to the program in any province. At that point, it will surrender all authority over health care to the provinces.

Canadian health care is already dividing into ten different systems. Quebec is questioning the viability of free health care. Daniel Johnson, the chairman of the provincial Treasury Board, says that cut-backs in regional transfer programs are forcing the province to look at alternatives to the present system. Alberta's Commission on Future Health Care has recently tabled a set of radical proposals that would introduce a two-tier health system in that province. A private insurance program may be established, and the province would monitor people's use of doctors and hospitals with a view to constraining an individual's use of these services. Alberta has also permitted U.S.-based firms to set up shop in the province and to deliver services formerly reserved for hospitals.

The federal government has guaranteed the now accepted principles of universality, portability, accessibility, and public administration. How will it continue to do so when it no longer has authority over the health-care spending of the provinces? The office of the minister for international trade sent a memo to all Conservative members of Parliament shortly before the 1988 election, outlining the government's position on free trade and health care.

The document strongly denied that our health care would be dismantled under free trade, but it did provide a very candid look at this government's stand. The government clearly permits the provinces to privatize the management of health-care facilities, and to allow the entry of U.S. firms into their health-care systems. "It is entirely up to each provincial government to prohibit or permit private management."

The memo also supports the concept of privatization, while insisting "there is no reason to believe that private management endangers equal access to health services in Canada." But, of course, it does exactly that. A public health-care system is created to serve the needs of the public. Money collected by government is used to improve the quality of these services, and is also used for research and upgrading equipment. When health care is privately owned, services must return a profit. Business decisions, not need, become the determining factor and, inevitably, privatization leads to two kinds of systems — one for the rich who can pay for top-quality services, and another for everyone else.

Small wonder that the head of the Canadian Medical Association's ethics committee recently stated that, under free trade, our system is going to be eroded. Dr. Eike Kluge says that Canada will not be able to maintain a public system when we have to compete with a commercialized U.S.-type system. The government vigorously denies that our medicare system is endangered; yet, the prime minister himself admitted in an interview with an Ottawa newspaper that no universal program was safe: "We're overhauling them one by one."

As usual, there is a foreign-based corporate interest eager to profit from the situation being created by the Canadian government. This time it is the multinational drug companies. The Pharmaceutical Manufacturers Association of Canada (PMAC) is an industry group of 130 companies; 85 percent of them are foreign firms. Generally, their Canadian operations only package, label, and market products produced off-shore.

They are eager to clip the wings of Canadian-based generic-drug firms who are capable of manufacturing the drugs here and selling them at lower prices under their chemical names. The drug companies make great profit on their products, and resent the lower-cost, high-quality competition from the generic firms. Government curbs on the generic companies is in the interest only of the foreign — mostly U.S. — firms; nevertheless, the government legislated long-term patent protection for the drug companies.

The Tories were paying much lip-service to the need for business to increase its research-and-development spending, as Canada invests less than any other industrialized country in R and D. The big drug companies wanted more patent protection from the generic firms, which had garnered some of the profits the multinationals claim as their own. So they made a deal. The government sold ten-year patent rights to the drug companies in exchange for promises of short-term and inadequate research-and-development funding.

PMAC promised that its members would increase their research-and-development investments in Canada to 8 percent of their Canadian sales by 1991, and 10 percent by 1996. But the average R and D investments by major corporations world-wide is 16 percent, and even if these companies meet their targets, Canadian subsidiaries will be allowed to spend well below the research dollars spent by their parent companies in other countries. For instance, Johnson & Johnson reported R and D investment in Canada in 1988 of 8.6 percent, but its parent spent 13.3 percent. Ciba-Geigy spent only 5.7 percent in Canada, but 16.4 percent elsewhere. Squibb spent a pathetic 2.6 percent of its sales in Canada on research and development, but saw fit to invest 12.4 percent world-wide.

The ministries of health in Ontario and Alberta report that drug prices have soared 16 percent annually during the last two years. The Patent Act gave foreign drug companies a licence to protect high drug prices, make fortunes in Canada, and give back just a fraction of what they take out of the country, say Canadian-based generic firms. "It does nothing to build a domestic industry," they say. Not surprisingly, the drug companies played a leading role in the American Coalition for Trade Expansion with Canada. The president of Pfizer, one of the biggest drug companies in the world and a key player in the life-patenting fight, was not only in the coalition, but a high-profile member of President Reagan's free-trade negotiating team. At the same time he was serving as an adviser to his president, he was taking care of business. The deal between the American-dominated drug companies and the government of Canada was clear: no Patent Act, no free trade.

In its policy of free trade, and the resulting process now leading to the destruction of the Canadian social network, the Tory government has sacrificed Canada's heritage, history, and sovereignty, and is leaving a bitter legacy of unemployment, poverty, and inequality. Although we live in the midst of wealth, our society is becoming distinctly harsher. Those able to thrive under this new system are doing very well indeed; but a gaping chasm is emerging between rich and poor, young and old, men and women, and among the regions. The Economic Council of Canada has reported on the disappearing middle class, citing only two areas of growth in the work-force: high-paying, highly skilled jobs, and low-wage, unskilled jobs. The council calls them "good" jobs and "bad" jobs, and warns that the resulting polarization severely strains the fabric of Canadian life.

Since 1984, wages and salary increases have trailed inflation for every category of Canadian worker except management and senior executives. During the same period, more than 60 percent of the new jobs created were in the two lowest-paid categories. And yet, Michael Wilson insists that nurses, teachers, and welfare workers must sacrifice wage gains to help Canada fight inflation. The rise of the service economy accounts for almost all net employment growth and is a key factor in the growing poverty of women and young people. As public services are privatized, and as the goods-producing sector of our economy declines, more and more Canadians are going to be among the service-sector working poor. The benefits of economic expansion that took place through the 1980s, and is now ending, were startlingly unequal. Senior executives and managers enjoyed major increases in their real earnings, while the average family with one parent working outside the home had the same after-inflation income in 1988 as it had a decade before. Canada faces almost certain economic hardship ahead, and life for our citizens is sure to get tougher.

The quality of jobs is a vital issue facing Canada in this decade; but so is their number. In spite of the promises that free trade would lead to the immediate creation of thousands of jobs, employment growth slowed markedly in 1989: the number of jobs created was 100,000 below the average since 1984. From May 1989 to May 1990, Canada lost 165,000 manufacturing jobs, 43,000 in May 1990 alone. All predictions are for an acceleration of this trend over the next several years. The new reality is that 400,000 Canadian children depend on food banks to eat. And proportionately more of the poor are women. In 1984, when Brian Mulroney came to office, two-thirds of all poor seniors were women. In 1988, three-quarters were. This all sounds disturbingly like another country that has become more ideological, less compassionate, and more desperate: the United States.

A Senate report states that half of the jobs created in the United States in the last eight years were at wages below the poverty level for a family of four. Between 1978 and 1987, the poorest 20 percent of U.S. families became 8 percent poorer; the richest 20 percent became 13 percent richer. Since U.S. tax reform, each of the richest 1 percent of Americans are paying $82,000 less than they were paying before it; yet all but the most affluent Americans are paying significantly higher taxes. Twenty million Americans lack sufficient food; yet the country is estimated to have a million millionaires — nourished by the "blood from the wounds of the Reagan era," says one housing activist.

The sharp differentiations in the labour force in the United States are even more pronounced than in Canada's; the top 20 percent are extremely productive and skilled; the bottom 25 per cent are functionally illiterate and a drag on the economy. The number of families living below the poverty line jumped more than 25 percent in the last decade. There are as many as 750,000 homeless on the streets of America. In such circumstances, we shouldn't be surprised that murder is the leading cause of baby deaths in the United States. A leading U.S. economist, University of Southern California's William Davidson, approves of our GST but says that we should follow the U.S. practice even more closely. We must strip our unions of power and further reduce our social programs. He explains his country's extremes of wealth and poverty this way: "You can either have a viable, competitive economy or a social policy."

As our two countries harmonize our economies and our social structures, Canada will increasingly mirror the humanscape to the south. A Canadian steel executive shares his concerns about what that will mean for us. In Canada, his company pays hourly rates of $12 to $20 (U.S.). The U.S. plants pay $6.50 to $8.50 an hour. He describes his visits to these plants as a trip through a time warp. The company's Kentucky employees get one week's holiday after one full year of service, and two weeks after five years. There are no pension plans, medical and life insurance are minimal, working hours are substantially longer, safety practices are almost non-existent, and the working conditions are far poorer. "Where do you think we will be sourcing our Canadian requirements five years from now?" he asks.

Every previous government in the history of this country has attempted to find the balance between private interest and the public good that characterizes our system. This government has joined that of the United States in abandoning the struggle for social justice and sacrificing the needs of the many to the demands of the few.

# 5.
# WAR GAMES: RUNNING WITH THE PENTAGON

"Canada and the United States should eliminate national boundaries with respect to defence production. The orientation of decision makers in both countries should be continental rather than state-centric."

*Leaked Canadian government task force document, 1987*

MARY ADELA ANDREW WAS BORN AND RAISED IN THE wild country of Nitassinan (Labrador, as most Canadians know it). In her lifetime, she travelled many thousands of miles on foot and by canoe. "We have travelled from Uashat [Seven Islands] to Kantshekakamat, a lake in between Knob Lake, Schefferville and Fort Chimo, and from there to Utshimassits [Davis Inlet] where we spent the summer. And from Utshimassits back to Michikamau Lake, where we spent the whole winter with minimum supplies. The rest our parents provided for us with what they killed." She and her parents, and later her own family of fifteen children, lived the life-style that her ancestors had lived for nine thousand years. Their land, a pristine wilderness, is home to immense caribou herds and rich with many varieties of wildlife. Says Rose Gregoire, a friend of Mary's, "Our life as hunters was not easy — but we had control. It was hard, but we were rich in our culture."

Then, one day in the fall of 1983, German Phantom F–4s screamed across the countryside into Mary Adela Andrew's life. From the Canadian Forces' military base at Goose Bay, Canada's NATO allies now fly more than 9,000 low-level training flights a

year. Government officials say that the number of flights could double in the next several years, to 18,000. The invasion of these fighter planes has created enormous stress for the Innu of the area. The noise produced by the low-level flights is often above the threshold of human pain. The jets arrive without warning, howling just above tree level, terrifying children, disturbing sleep patterns, and scattering the caribou. The people — mere troublesome nomads to the Canadian government — call it genocide. As Greg Penashue, president of the Innu in Labrador and Quebec, says, "The government of Canada plans to destroy the Innu."

The flight testing is being moved to Canada from Germany and other populated areas because studies show that the long-term consequences of these simulated war games are serious, and massive public reaction in Europe and the United States has rendered them politically unacceptable there. A German pediatrician says studies in his country prove that flight tests cause enormous stress, fear, and hearing impairment in children, and warns us of serious fall-out in Labrador. "This experience for children is a life-threatening experience; they react with massive fear and panic."

The Department of National Defence suffered a set-back early in 1990, when its environmental impact report on the test flights was ruled inadequate by a federal environmental review panel and loudly criticized as a fraud by groups all over the country. The decision not to place a $500-million tactical fighter base in Labrador was largely a result of the persistent demonstrations by the Innu. The Canadian government had lobbied hard for the base to be built in Canada. But, while the fighter base has not materialized, the regular flights continue, part of Canada's preparation for the Third World War.

For Mary, Rose, and their friends and children, the days are now filled with protest, the courts, and jail. "You need not ask me if I feel betrayed because I do," said Mary Adela Andrew at one of her trials. "I tell you today to set my people free and my children. Over 40 years of forced settlement has been prison enough for me and my family. If you do not set my people and children free, then you will have to incarcerate me as well and my other children. . . . I have told you about the destruction of our land and these are more criminal than what we are doing, fighting back peacefully. . . . That is what I call a crime." Mary signed her court statement with an "x."

Canada's allies see our "uninhabited" open spaces as ideal testing grounds. While a steady build-up took place under the former Liberal regime, there has been a dramatic escalation of such testing in recent years. It is enthusiastically welcomed by this government, which is committed ideologically to an aggressive military future for Canada and to actively furthering a single North American defence posture. Lethal weapons, mostly American, are being tested over Canadian land, and on and under Canadian waters. Air-launched cruise missiles are flown in the Canadian North, where the terrain is said to resemble that of the Soviet Union. Testing of the deadly "stealth" cruise missile was granted permission in spite of its clearly offensive nature. Five special bomber-testing corridors exist now — up from two in 1986. U.S. FB –111, B–52, and B–1B bombers fly in increasing numbers from the Quebec–Labrador border to the British Columbia interior. Military air bases are being built in Inuvik, Yellowknife, Rankin Inlet, Iqualit, and Kuujjuak in northern Quebec; they will serve both U.S. and Canadian jet fighters. The government recently approved mass training flights of U.S. bombers over remote regions of Canada, and a global nuclear-war game known as GLOBAL SHIELD now thunders up the B.C corridor, in preparation for testing that the *New York Times* says will eventually include 200 B–52 bombers carrying nuclear cruise missiles.

Cold Lake, Alberta, and other Canadian bases are increasingly being used to train American and NATO troops. The conclusion of a U.S.–Soviet strategic-arms reduction agreement is cause for great concern in Canada. Progress on some fronts still means a growing reliance on other strategies. It will result in a major increase in Soviet air-launched cruise-missile and strategic-bomber forces, and Canada is coming under heavy pressure from Washington to do more weapons testing in the North and to build up its air defences. Canada is also host to more than eighty military sites related to the nuclear weapons testing of our allies. This places Canada, as a non-nuclear power, second only to West Germany in the number of nuclear weapons–related facilities on our soil. American nuclear warships are making increasing use of our harbours, placing our sea-coast communities at grave risk. The Tomahawk, the sea-launched version of the cruise missile, carries a nuclear warhead whose destructive power is ten times greater than that of the Hiroshima bomb. One U.S. sub that spends time in Canadian waters, the u.s.s. *Benjamin Franklin*, carries nearly four times the fire power used in all of the Second World War. In the spirit of U.S.–Canada co-operation, however, Canada does not have to give permission for American warships carrying nuclear weapons to use our ports.

The U.S. government does not recognize Canada's sovereignty over our North West Passage, which it claims is international waters. Neither, apparently, does the Canadian government; it signed an agreement in 1988 that requires only that the United States notify Canada that it will be making use of these straits. The United States will soon be ready to launch its first Seawolf stealth submarine — the most sophisticated and secretive submarine ever built — and the Pentagon has informed Ottawa that it wishes to test it in Canada's Arctic. MP Jim Fulton warns that U.S. nuclear submarines will soon be using Canadian waters to get to a new underwater sound-testing facility in Alaska. And the United States has recently announced that fifty multi-warhead MX missiles will be dug out of their silos in Wyoming and sent by train to new sites, three of which are very close to the Canadian border. At their new sites, they will be kept in a constant state of alert, awaiting deployment orders from the president. The Canadian government was not consulted or notified of this decision, nor did it protest this treatment. Successive Tory defence ministers subservient to U.S. political, industrial, and military might have abdicated responsibility for a Canadian defence policy.

This trend is taking place against another development about which most Canadians are unaware. During the last several years, while our country held a public and passionate debate over the economic and social aspects of free trade, a parallel and very quiet integration of industrial defence production between Canada and the United States was taking place. No one who monitored this disquieting situation could be surprised at the growth in U.S. weapons-testing in Canada, given the deepening ties between the two countries in the production of war materials and the shared planning for their deployment.

Canadian defence policy has long been based on the assumption that we are not capable of totally financing the defence of our country. We have, therefore, sought security within collective military arrangements. It has also been clear that the United States considers North America to be one military zone and would never permit Canada its own defence policies. Geographically placed between the USSR and the American heartland, Canada is too strategically important to be left without guardianship. As one senior Pentagon official explained, "Defence of Canada is virtually defence of the American homeland."

Canada had three options. It could attempt to secure the continent's northern territory on its own, a possibility discounted by most as unrealistic. It could accept the virtual imposition of a bilateral defence arrangement with the United States, in which Canada would have little authority. Or it could attempt to influence the United States in its foreign policy by joining multilateral and bilateral arrangements. The third option, it was felt, would ensure that Canada's needs and point of view would have to be considered if Canada was "at the table." In order to remain relevant to the defence of the continent, Canada would have to have a presence in Washington.

Thus, paradoxically, Canada relinquished key areas of control in territory, deployment of armed forces, and defence policy, while arguing that it was done to retain some sovereign control over its destiny. The ever-present Canadian struggle between those who wanted a more independent foreign policy for Canada and those who argued that our best defence lay in trusting the United States was present throughout the decades after the Second World War, years when defence policy was being established, and governments vacillated between the two. A senior official at National Defence explained that Canada had to adopt a posture that would make it important to the Americans. If Canada did not remain important to the United States, he explained, access to information vital to its own fate would become restricted. Ironically, however, one of Canada's primary considerations in joining NATO — to offset the dominance of the United States by the presence of other allies — was defeated as it became clear that the organization itself was largely under American influence. Moreover, Canada and the United States were seen as a single NATO region, and Canada was considered an American satellite by the other nations in the Western alliance and in Moscow as well.

In return for "shelter," Canada has had to accommodate itself to American strategic doctrine. As Canadian defence analyst, David Cox, explains: "What is important to Canadians is not what we think the Russians will do; it is what we think the Americans think the Russians will do." As well, leaders in Canadian defence circles advanced a North American strategy, as a partnership with a superpower lent genuine credibility to what would otherwise be the largely civilian defence forces of a middle power. Many of these leaders have worked very closely with the Pentagon, in the role of junior player. The relationship between the two countries has been sealed by more than 70 agreements and at least 2,500 documents covering bilateral defence matters. However, Canada was always expected to toe the U.S. line, and in emergencies, permission for an action that affected Canada was sometimes not even sought.

The Cuban missile crisis of 1962 was a sobering lesson for anyone who thought Canada was in equal partnership with the United States. The Pentagon placed all of North America on war alert, without advising Prime Minister John Diefenbaker. When he did find out, Diefenbaker resisted giving permission for Canadian compliance as he wished first to verify the location of Soviet missiles. He was undermined by his defence minister, who ordered the armed forces on full alert, without informing Diefenbaker. In turn, the defence minister was undermined by his own forces, who had already placed their members on alert with those of the United States.

To insiders, this situation was not new. American security interests had become North American security interests, and Canada was not to dissent. Twenty-seven years later, Douglas Roche, newly retired as Canada's disarmament ambassador, would echo this truth: "I suppose the biggest shock that I got was to learn the influence, the pressure, that the United States government has on the Canadian government on the issues of disarmament and security. . . . it operates at every level, and it operates in varying degrees, from subtlety and politesse to crude threats."

A primary reason for Canadian subservience to American military actions was the growth of a substantial Canadian defence industry dependent on American contracts and co-operation for survival. The Defence Production Sharing Agreement of 1958 was a kind of sectoral free-trade agreement with a political price, much like the 1988 deal. Canadian companies can compete as equals for American military contracts, and vice versa. The United States designs and produces major weapons systems, while Canada develops and produces components for these systems. The two countries must maintain a "rough balance" in trade, Canada buying the finished "off the shelf" U.S.-built weapons in dollar numbers that roughly equal what the American manufacturers have spent on Canadian components.

This arrangement has had two direct results. First, the Americans came to expect subservient co-operation in defence policy as a result of co-operation in defence production. Second, the growing military-production industry in Canada would cause the government to ask, "Is a Canadian position on this particular foreign policy item important enough to risk losing a major contract? Can we afford to offend our defence head office?" For the single biggest feature of Canada's defence-production industry was that it is export-driven, dependent on one country. Therefore, U.S. views are a crucial consideration in defining Canadian policy. A symbiotic relationship has developed between the industry's reliance on American military production and on Canada's formation of policy regarding our security requirements.

As well, this relationship has prevented Canada from developing our own manufacturing base for our own defence needs. Canada's military production became dependent on what wars the United States was involved in and what protectionist sentiments it was espousing. After the Second World War, the Korean War, Vietnam, and the Reagan years — times of greatly increased defence production in Canada to supply U.S. needs — Canada had to make political concessions to find a market for what was suddenly, in peacetime, our excess arms capacity. It became increasingly difficult to cut back our defence production, even if we wanted to, as in order to ensure export growth, Canada had to continue to increase defence spending for the U.S. half of the equation. Canadian military production thus became less and less related to national needs and more and more directed to and by those of the United States.

The current government is not the first in Canada to abandon the national interest under coercive pressure from the American military and government. Canada submerged our industry needs to a "North American perspective" when it scrapped the famous Avro Arrow. American aircraft manufacturers did not want to compete with a major weapons system in Canada, and the American government made it clear that Canada would not find a buyer for it. Although controversy still rages around this plane and its engineering capabilities, a recently declassified U.S. Defense Department memorandum, dated June 1, 1960, makes it clear that the American government was involved in the decision to scrap it: "Prior to the National Security Council paper (December 1958) and following a visit of the President to Canada in July 1958, Canada took the following actions with the understanding that her defense industry depended largely upon the U.S. channelling defense business into Canada; cancelled the CF–105 and related systems contracts; decided to make maximum use of U.S. developed weapons, integrated into NORAD; worked with U.S. toward a fully integrated continental defense." Says John Orr, then director of engineering research with the federal Defence Research Board, "The U.S. aircraft industry had become alarmed by the prospect that they might lose a major USAF procurement contract to Avro Canada." Canada could be allowed to manufacture components, but only the United States could manufacture the complete systems.

A similar agenda affected the decision of a major aircraft purchase. After the Vietnam War, during which Canada had developed a trade surplus in defence goods, American purchases in Canada dropped sharply. In order to continue to have an American market for our products, Canada scrapped plans to buy Canadian-made de Havilland Dash-7 aircraft for maritime patrol. The U.S. government helped Canada to "select" an American product from the troubled Lougheed Corporation, which was inappropriate for Canada's needs. However, as defence analyst Ernie Regehr says, Canada "was not simply buying a plane: it was buying a military market for its aerospace and electronics industry."

A succession of previous Canadian governments have made choices for both business and security reasons that diminished Canada's sovereign control over its foreign policy. Yet, there have been significant traditional differences in the way Canadians and Americans approached the concept of war. Ideologically, the United States is committed to its self-appointed role as the world's police. It has sustained for several decades a permanent war economy that has done irreparable damage to its economic power. Gore Vidal says that ideology and profit came together to form an invincible argument for maintaining this war economy, and to do so, it was vital to have a "fearsome enemy." The result, he says, has been the collapse of the U.S. economy because too many of its resources have been spent on the military: "The Pentagon is like a black hole; what goes in is forever lost and no new wealth is created."

When Reagan was president, he oversaw a $2.5-trillion build-up of the American armed forces. Indeed, the Pentagon now pays the salaries of around one-third of all U.S. engineers and scientists and spends about $300 billion a year on defence. Canada, on the other hand, has not had a military economy outside of wartime. Victor Suthren, director of Canada's War Museum, says that Canadians maintain peaceful ways when not compelled to fight. "Forced to take up arms, they have done so to put an end to war or fighting; having matched and beaten armed bullies, they put weapons away with little ostentatious crowing and get on with the nation's life. They do not, ever, play at war, nor do they see the gun as a solution to social injustice or personal failure."

The main objective of traditional Canadian military policy has been to attempt to avoid a superpower nuclear struggle, knowing that it would be fought over our territory. Since the development of the atomic bomb, the possibility of a protracted nuclear war was unthinkable. So Canada operated on the premise of war avoidance, and we did not gear our armed services for a protracted struggle. The Defence White Paper of 1971 promoted political solutions to world problems. There was, as might be expected, some consternation about the resulting decline in power of the Canadian Armed Forces inside the forces themselves. But Canadians remained largely men and women of peaceable nature.

However, the next Canadian Defence White Paper, released by the Mulroney government in 1987, signalled a significant change in direction for Canadian defence policy. It called for the militarization of the Canadian economy, committed the country to a massive acceleration in defence spending, and foreshadowed renewed government assistance to private military production. It enthusiastically endorsed the American preparation for a protracted nuclear and conventional war.

Canada's defence budget increased by about 50 percent during the 1980s — Canada is now the fifteenth largest military spender in the world. Approximately 10 percent of the current federal budget (almost $12 billion) is allocated to defence, and the government has committed itself to another $50 billion in new equipment during the next decade. The cancellation of the nuclear-powered submarines and the announcement of other defence cutbacks affect these numbers very little. Military spending had been growing at 6 percent a year, making it the fastest-growing area of government expenses apart from servicing our debt — and the cutting of 1 percent a year only knocks out the more exotic parts of the government's "wish list." The budgets of 1989 and 1990 slowed only the rate of growth, not actual growth in defence spending. Canada will spend just under $12-billion in this area in 1990.

The Reagan years were an enormous boon to Canadian arms exporters. Sales to the United States more than tripled in these years, and private companies now produce well over $5-billion worth of armaments a year. Having built this powerful industry, Canadian arms manufacturers are now concerned about the levelling off of American defence spending, and the protectionist mood in the U.S. Congress to preserve the Pentagon market for American firms. Although our sharing arrangement with the United States is supposed to guarantee rough parity in defence trade, Canada has accumulated a military trade deficit with the United States of almost $3 billion. To protect this now substantial industry, there is increased emphasis on the need to secure American contracts and increased pressure by the corporate leaders in this industry for the government to continue our "special" relationship with the United States. The price is our political sovereignty.

It became quite clear from a number of recent key government documents that our two countries have entered a new era of joint production, planning, and deployment of military weapons, and the Canadian government has been calling for extraordinary measures to encourage the growth of a domestic defence industry as a source of high technology and job creation. A 1987 review of Canada's industrial defence base heralded the government's intention to increase government funding of military research and touted the "subordinate" role Canada would take in this joint system. Another report recognized that many U.S. practices are designed to protect the competitive position of U.S. industries around the world and, therefore, a willingness on the part of the U.S. to open business opportunities to Canadian sources would require a corresponding and visible return to the American government and business sector in the form of Canadian co-operation.

A charter was signed in 1987 formalizing co-operation between the two countries, and defence minister Perrin Beatty introduced the Defence Industrial Preparedness Advisory Committee, to be co-chaired by him and a prominent member of the Business Council on National Issues. In April 1988, the government announced a major program to transfer military research to the private sector with large infusions of federal funds, and promised to work with the industry to help it shift to "long war" production runs. The superpower talks on nuclear-arms reduction didn't cool its enthusiasm: one defence contractor explained that there would now be an increased need for conventional weapons.

An internal government task force report, written by senior officials of national defence, external affairs, and international trade, was leaked to the press almost a year after its completion in June 1987. The strongly worded document recommended that Canada and the United States create a "common defence economic market." Explaining that what the two countries had shared in the past were simply defence agreements, the report said that what was now called for was greater continental integration of defence production and collaboration in industrial preparedness. It advised making "joint industrial planning by national defence and the Pentagon an integral part of continental defence," declaring that the two countries should "eliminate national boundaries" in the area of defence.

The report also recommended incorporating a military perspective when considering industrial planning. And, most troubling, it promoted a forum for consultation and resolution of problems "without elevating them to a political level." That these events were taking place at the time Canada was negotiating a free-trade agreement with the United States was no coincidence. In a major speech outlining Canada–U.S. co-operation in defence production, Minister Beatty clearly linked the two: "Though this agreement was reached quite separately from the Free Trade agreement with the United States, the arguments in favour of it are the same. ... We will conclude a Free Trade deal with the United States, and we will develop a North American Defence Industrial Base for one reason and that is that it's good for Canada."

Indeed, says lawyer and defence critic Jack Coop, "The Free Trade Agreement is the means by which the White Paper is implemented." The free-trade agreement establishes a continental energy policy that guarantees the United States secure access to Canadian energy, and thus guarantees the United States energy security, well into the next century (see Chapter 6). "With the U.S enjoying equal access to Canada's energy supplies, those resources will assume strategic importance for the American military. Alberta oil and gas, Quebec hydro, or Saskatchewan uranium, for example, will not only become objects of American political manipulation, they'll become certain military targets of America's enemies," says Marion Mathieson of Veterans Against Nuclear Arms.

The free-trade agreement assures implementation of the Defence White Paper by eliminating all forms of subsidies to manufacturing and resource industries not related to military production. For, apart from energy, the second and only form of government subsidy allowed under the free-trade agreement is for the private production of defence materials. Article 2003 of the free-trade agreement exempts military-production industries from the government subsidies that can be attacked and disallowed as unfair trading distortions.

The United States does not directly subsidize its non-military productions. Instead, the massive Pentagon spending supports a huge military-industrial complex. This is not considered to be a subsidy to business, but a crucial aspect of American security. Therefore, it was not considered hypocritical to permit continued massive subsidies to the American military industry while establishing the illegitimacy of Canadian subsidies. For U.S. non-military industries, therefore, a deal that does away with aid to Canadian business was essential.

In Canada, subsidies have been used as a form of regional development, to promote the growth of Canadian business, and to develop indigenous research capabilities. That Canada has already started to alter this policy cannot be doubted when we watch the government's treatment of Atlantic Canadians as they struggle with the worst crisis of this century. The Canadian defence-production industry will almost be guaranteed large subsidies in return for job creation — and will thrive. This year, the government is subsidizing military contractors in Canada by about $251-million. It is for this reason that the Business Council on National Issues supported the military-production exemption in the agreement, at the same time complaining bitterly about the negative effects of public "dole."

Under the free-trade agreement, Canada's regions will become increasingly dependent on energy megaprojects and military production. Says Coop, "As the regional development programs and subsidies which have nurtured and supported these industries over the years are rendered ineffective or withdrawn by our government in the face of U.S countervailing duties, where will the private capital go? It will follow the subsidies. And the only effective and permissible subsidies will be military industries. . . . In short, over the next seven-year period at least, the FTA will have the effect of facilitating a massive transfusion of private capital into Canadian military industry — thereby accomplishing one of the primary requirements of the White Paper, the militarization of the Canadian economy."

The tragedy of this development is that it will pit people who are fighting increased militarism against those who have lost jobs in manufacturing or primary industry and who have no other employment alternatives than those offered by private armaments makers. Such development will change the very nature of regions such as Atlantic Canada, bringing conflict and confrontation. The federal government made locating in the Maritimes a condition of awarding Litton a contract for radar components for the Air Defence Anti-Tank System. Nova Scotia has announced that the West German arms manufacturer Thyssen will build a $58-million plant in Cape Breton. Its purpose? To manufacture weapons for sale to the Middle East. Says the Canada–Israel Committee: "The sale of Canadian-made arms to Saudi Arabia would escalate the Middle East arms race."

Federal tax incentives given through Enterprise Cape Breton played a large role in attracting Magnus Aerospace Corporation to Sydney. The government of Premier Buchanan has recently given

over $30 million to Pratt & Whitney to manufacture engine parts
for civilian and military aircraft at the aerotech industrial site at the
Halifax airport. This and other private activity comes hard on the
heels of the decision to close down a number of defence bases; but
there are no profits to be made from search-and-rescue work or
from maintaining the bases. Their closing may signal not a decline
in defence commitment in Canada, but a shift from the support of a
public defence system to encouragement of a private arms
industry.

The vice-chief of Defence, Lt.-Gen. John de Chastelain, explained that closing the bases will allow the military to use the
money to buy new equipment. It will also mean that a larger share
of the defence budget is available for private-sector projects. Already, the government has indicated that the closing of the Armed
Forces pilot-training centre in Portage la Prairie will likely result in
the privatizing of this training, and CAE Industries of Toronto has
formed a team made up of its subsidiaries in Canada and the
United States to bid on the contract. The government has called for
private tenders for surveillance of the Atlantic fishery, formerly
carried out by Tracker airplanes from the Summerside Air Base. In
1986, it sold the Crown corporation Canadian Arsenals to a private
arms manufacturer. As well, in the last five years, there has been a
steady stream of senior defence officials and military professionals
leaving the government for careers in the private sector. In fact, the
highest-ranking Canadian military officer, Lt.-Gen. Paul Manson,
recently accepted a job with Unisys Corp., a leading U.S. arms
manufacturer.

This development mirrors the trend to privatization seen in so
many other sectors of Canadian life. Defence is a matter for public
government policy. A responsible government provides a defence
that is adequate to the country's needs. Once the decision-making
leaves government hands, the mandate changes and becomes more
aggressive. When large-scale private interests become involved,
other considerations, such as profit, become relevant.
The privatization of Canadian defence is not taking place in a
vacuum. Chief among the lobby groups is the organization that had

so much success in its efforts to bring about the free-trade agreement, the Business Council on National Issues. In 1981, the BCNI launched its Task Force on Foreign Policy and Defence. This task force, which has six leading arms manufacturers on its eleven-member executive, grew as a major shift of transnational capital was being diverted to Western military industries, and coincided with the extraordinary growth in Canadian government subsidies to the defence industry. Said the defence minister, "In the last ten years, the expansion has been almost sevenfold."

The task force hired former brigadier-general Dr. George Bell to write its position papers, published in 1984 and 1987. That the second report bore a striking resemblance to the government's White Paper should come as no surprise, as Dr. Bell was simultaneously serving as a consultant to the government in its preparation of the White Paper. David Culver, then chairman of the BCNI, openly boasted about the closeness of the relationship: "It is not an accident that we had a lot of help from Defence Department people in making our Task Force report. . . . the same experts were working both sides of the street." The BCNI laid the groundwork for government-industry co-operation in planning Canada's "defence" needs.

Thomas d'Aquino, president of the BCNI, said, "Canadians will need to be convinced that greater sacrifices in the bolstering of our defences will contribute to maintaining peace, and ultimately to reducing the chances of war. If we fail in communicating this idea, do not be surprised if the support the government is seeking for its new defence policy does not materialize. . . . You [the arms industry] have a stake, we have a stake, in making sure the momentum continues." A senior executive of Marconi adds: "It is vital to Canada that the defence industrial base survives and grows, and it is vital to the defence industry that it retains access to the U.S. defence market and continues to be considered as part of the U.S. defence industrial base."

The ethical questions for the BCNI were reduced to: Is it good for business? Does it increase profit? Their non-ideological support of a private weapons industry coincided with a deep conservative strain within certain government and defence circles to augment the influence of the military in Canada. It was a powerful alliance that served both agendas. David Langille has documented the intense lobbying that took place between the BCNI and the Canadian and American governments. BCNI executives received high-level briefings at NORAD and NATO headquarters and they worked closely with the defence establishment to undertake an "education" program for the Canadian public. The Canadian Institute of Strategic Studies was hired by the Department of National Defence to train officers in public speaking so that they could make presentations on the Soviet "threat" and the new military agenda.

This deep collusion between the corporate lobby and the defence department is all the more disturbing in light of the fact that so much of the defence industry in Canada is now controlled from head offices in the United States. Eighteen of Canada's top twenty-five military contractors are branch plants of American multinational corporations. When these corporate leaders confer with government officials, they represent the views of their American bosses. In the early 1980s, the director of operations for the Conference of Defence Associations (an organization representing various branches of the Canadian Armed Forces, as well as individual Service members) went to Washington to drum up support for a more aggressive Canadian defence policy.

The American Defence Preparedness Association (a corporate defence-related lobby group) organized a Canadian chapter called the Canadian Defence Preparedness Association, whose mandate is to improve communication within the Canadian-American defence community and to increase opportunities for Canadian defence exports. These groups all worked closely to strengthen ties between the Canadian and U.S. governments and industry on both sides of the border. The emergence of a military-industrial complex in Canada throughout the 1980s, one so inextricably linked to the American industry, leaves Canada with very little room for autonomy in foreign policy. Our access to the American market under free trade will only heighten dependence on our "special" relationship.

It is crucial to examine the motivation behind the BCNI's support of free trade in defence production. Why would this organization so deeply concerned about the budget deficit in Canada, a strong voice in the call for lowered social spending and less reliance on government, advocate massive infusions of funding into defence? It is hard not to be cynical. It is hard not to believe that the BCNI and its allies underwrote the trade agreement because its members will benefit both from a more "competitive" climate in which they can call (and are calling) for reduced social programs and from increased access to lucrative Canadian and American defence contracts. In this, corporate Canada is joined by corporate America.

Consider: General Motors belonged to the U.S. Coalition for Trade Expansion with Canada; it gave an undisclosed amount of money to the Alliance for Trade and Job Opportunities in Canada; and its Canadian division is a top Pentagon contractor. Litton Industries was a member of the U.S. coalition; it receives huge Canadian government contracts; and its Canadian arm is a top Pentagon contractor. Imperial Oil gave $200,000 to the alliance and $46,000 to the Tories, and is a major Pentagon contractor. Control Data was a member of the U.S. coalition; its Canadian arm is a major Pentagon contractor; it is a member of the BCNI defence task force; and it contributed $5,000 to the alliance. Garrett was a member of the U.S. coalition; its Canadian arm is a top Pentagon contractor; and it is a major recipient of Canadian government defence subsidies "for the purpose of defence export sales."

CAE Industries is on the BCNI defence task force; it has received major Canadian government defence subsidies; it is a major Pentagon contractor; it contributed $6,000 to the alliance. AT&T was an important player in the U.S. coalition; its Canadian branch is a major recipient of Canadian government subsidies; it is a member of the BCNI task force; and it gave $20,000 to the alliance. Honeywell was in the U.S. coalition; its Canadian arm is a member of the BCNI task force; and it gave money to both the Tories and the alliance. SCN Manufacturing, the company that bought Canadian Arsenals, was a U.S. coalition member, and on the BCNI task force.

Bombardier gave $69,000 to the alliance and $30,000 to the Tories; is a major recipient of Canadian government subsidies; and recently received a large contract to build cars for Amtrak, the American rail system that received a $100-million interest-free loan from the Canadian government.

And Boeing Corporation, the Seattle-based U.S. aerospace giant that took over de Havilland Aircraft of Canada in 1985, is eligible for Canadian defence grants. The Toronto subsidiary may receive as much as $51-million to develop a new version of the Dash-7. This subsidy comes on top of a $161-million settlement that the Canadian government paid to Boeing after the sale was made — in essence, the Canadian people were given the bill for a foreign take-over — and the company is now eligible for further government funds. Not surprising, Boeing was a charter member of the American Coalition for Trade Expansion with Canada. The virtues of the "free market" can be bent a little when so much money is at stake.

Clearly, free trade in defence is good for business on both sides of the border. The largest contractual supplier to the Canadian government in 1988–89 was the U.S. Navy. The largest federal government customer was the defence department, including private arms-production firms such as Canadian Arsenals, Bristol Aerospace, Spar Aerospace, and Canadian Marconi. Canadian companies are making increased direct presentations to U.S. defence companies, and the Canadian government is stepping up trade shows and missions to the United States to help Canadian companies acquire contracts. About 133 Canadian companies — many of them key members of the BCNI — hold the status of "Planned Producer" with the Pentagon. Viewed for all intents and purposes as domestic, these companies receive special consideration for contracts in return for willingness to produce for the U.S. government on an emergency or "mobilization" basis. Ken Epps of Project Ploughshares says: "Canadian membership in the Planned Producer Program contributes to, and is part of, the integration of the Canadian and U.S. military industries. In an emergency or during a conflict, the Pentagon would call upon Canadian suppliers at the same time as American ones — under the program no distinctions are made."

Says a senior official with external affairs, "There are lots of dollars of opportunity out there." In its first defence task force report, the BCNI called for an 80 percent real increase in military spending by 1994. Then chairman David Culver said before the 1988 election that his group had been too busy selling free trade to adequately sell their belief in the White Paper, but that "as soon as the trade deal is out of the way, I think our number one effort in 1989 will be on the defence side." Sure enough, a new lobby group has been formed to "shift public opinion about defence purchases." Called the Defence Industry Association of Canada, the group is planning to spend $1 million in 1990 to counter the work of the Canadian Peace Alliance.

And the industry is seeking new business opportunities. In spite of "peace dividend" rhetoric in the United States, the 1990 Pentagon budget has not been reduced in real-growth terms. U.S. Defense Secretary Dick Cheney says that, in spite of changes in the Soviet bloc, the Soviet Union is the only country that could still destroy the United States. He added that now is not the time to become soft on American defence capabilities.

As well, there are about a hundred persistent armed conflicts either currently active or potentially explosive in the world today. Canada, to its shame, is an arms supplier to many countries that regularly abuse human rights: Argentina, Chile, Colombia, El Salvador, Indonesia, the Philippines, South Korea, and Iran. Our military exports to the Third World grew steadily through the last decade, and the prospects for the 1990s are unlimited. Canada is loosening export controls on military goods, and places no content controls on any arms exports to the United States, thus forfeiting any authority to limit their final destination.

The government is participating in a vigorous campaign to promote Canadian arms at armaments fairs all over the world, including those in countries that practise torture. Trade minister John Crosbie travelled to South Korea and Hong Kong recently on a trade mission that included trade in arms. The trade commissions in these countries have identified "defence" as an area of business growth with potential for Canada, and accompanying the minister were senior executives of several Canadian arms manufacturers.

The world is at a turning-point; but Canada remains frozen in time, waiting, it seems, for direction from a country whose values, policies, and rhetoric our government has embraced. Our official response to the powerful changes rocking Eastern Europe is inadequate, cowardly, and, worst of all, greedy. Can it be that our government cannot respond positively to the changes in Europe because peace is bad for business?

The only winners so far are the corporate leaders who masterminded this deal. The only allegiance multinational arms manufacturers have is to the proliferation of wars — and there are still plenty of those to go around.

# 6.
# ENERGY BETRAYAL: THE LAST RESOURCE

"If we can make a fair deal with Canadians, we'll sell it [back] to them."

*Neil Camarta of Shell Oil, speaking about the purchase of Canadian gas exports.*

THE UNITED STATES IS RUNNING OUT OF ENERGY. ITS growing shortfall of oil has been widely reported, and its gas supplies are diminishing quickly. The American Gas Association says supplies in the lower forty-eight states are virtually gone. It is also running short of electricity. Recent studies show that the United States will need new generating capacity roughly equal to Canada's entire electricity system by the year 2000. The United States is casting hungry eyes northward.

When future generations of Canadians look back on this period of their country's history, one provision of the free-trade agreement will stand out. The sell-out of our energy heritage will rightly symbolize the Mulroney government's deliberate betrayal of Canada's national interest. The single largest fight looming on the free-trade horizon is the struggle for control of Canada's energy reserves and the profound environmental consequences of the outcome of this struggle.

For the United States, the energy provisions of the agreement were crucial. A 1985 U.S. report on natural gas warned that the country was quickly running out of this key resource and that Canada would play an increasingly important role in providing it. The congressional study stated that the American government should make it a point of national security to ensure access to

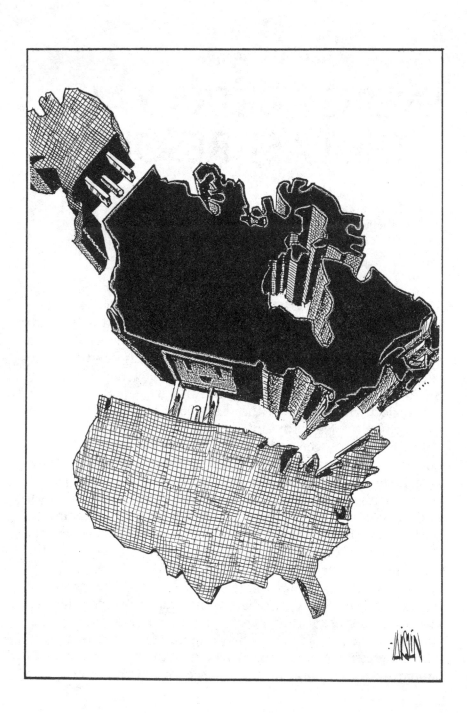

Canadian sources, slamming the then more-heavily regulated export structure as being a direct restriction of American rights to Canadian gas. Republican senator John Chafee favoured the free-trade agreement because it would provide New England with secure supplies of hydro-electricity and natural gas, while Democrat Lloyd Bentsen argued that it would give the United States "almost unlimited access to invest in Canadian energy."

Ann Hughes, now the chief U.S. trade negotiator with Canada, was quite forthright about her country's wasteful energy habits and admitted that Canada's energy, secured by the deal, would forestall conservation practices in the United States. And Edward Ney, the U.S. ambassador to Canada, said recently that Canada's energy reserves were a prime motivation for the free-trade agreement: "The U.S. got access to the great resources which we need." For years, American oil and gas companies, supported by the foreign-dominated Canadian industry, had been pressuring the government to remove access barriers to Canada's energy, seeking unrestricted security of supply and a continental approach to energy use. For years, Canadian governments insisted on controls and restrictions on energy exports, attempting, although often without success, to manage these resources in the long-term interest of the Canadian people.

But this is a whole new era in Canadian resource management. Our water, forests, natural gas, and minerals are for sale — cheap. They are the irresistible bribe our government used to lure the Americans to the table, and they are the pay-off for American favours, real or imagined. Barriers to foreign exploitation of our energy are falling like dominoes; and, more than any other issue, the abandonment of Canada's energy heritage is the metaphor for our conscious surrender of nationhood.

It was no coincidence that it was in the United States that Brian Mulroney announced the demise of the National Energy Program. There were genuine differences of opinion within Canada about the fairness of the NEP. Western provinces, particularly Alberta, had long felt resentful of federal involvement in what many saw as their heritage, which they alone should manage. But these were Canadian disputes and should have been decided in Canada. The fact that the prime minister made public the demise of the program to an American business audience is a strong indication of whose interest he and the energy industry in Canada really serve. The practice of reserving certain portions of all energy discoveries for Canadians was "odious," Mulroney said, and he promised more tax breaks to the oil companies, the same multinational corporations that have received billions of dollars in tax breaks and exploration grants from the Canadian people.

Robert Bourassa also made dazzling appearances in the United States with promises of unlimited Northern Quebec power, and Simon Reisman told a Canadian corporate audience that Canada needed a powerful lure to get the Americans to the free-trade bargaining table. He suggested our water would do nicely. When she was energy minister, Pat Carney boasted to the Canadian Petroleum Association that the energy chapter of the agreement was insurance that no future Canadian government would be able to dismantle the Tories' free-market energy policies. Said the prime minister in a welcoming letter to delegates of a Canadian-hosted energy conference: "From the Arctic oil riches to the vast hydraulic developments of Quebec and the high technology of our nuclear power plants, we have both the expertise and the resources for a secure energy future. It is a future that we are eager to share with other nations."

To "share" these energy sources with the United States, the government dismantled Canadian control of them. The Western Energy Accord deregulated oil and gas exports, turning the system over to the free play of the unfettered market. The National Energy Board was stripped of its powers: NEB approval for short-term export sales was dropped. The vital-supply safeguard, the requirement that there always be a twenty-five-year surplus of natural gas before export applications could be granted, was first reduced to fifteen years, and then abandoned. Today the board can merely monitor vague standards of "net public benefit." A complaints mechanism was established; but it's not for Canadian consumers, it is for the industry.

The practice of charging Canadian consumers less than American consumers for our energy was abandoned. The NEB announced that it no longer required export applicants to file an export impact assessment. Moreover, the requirement that eastern Canadian gas distributors rely on supplies carried by TransCanada PipeLines was dropped. Major gas companies in central Canada wanted to profit from deregulation and successfully lobbied to be allowed to buy gas from U.S. distributors. The government sacrificed an all-Canadian system for gas distribution so its industry friends can buy reimported gas shipped through American pipelines.

The Mulroney government destroyed the National Energy Board's once extensive powers protecting the rights of the Canadian owners of these resources and future energy supplies. The free-trade agreement put in place, forever, a deregulated, first-come, first-served energy future. In good times and in bad, multinational corporations have virtually unfettered right to export Canadian gas, oil, and hydro-electricity.

The free-trade agreement rules out a policy of guaranteeing sufficient supplies for Canadians before exporting energy, as such protection would contradict the fundamental concept of "free trade." There is no government or industry agency now empowered to ensure that Canadians will have adequate supplies even ten years from now. The free-trade agreement has removed the ability of government to act as steward of these resources on behalf of the Canadian people. As well, under the terms of the agreement, minimum export prices cannot be set, nor can Canada place an export tax on energy exports. Canadians hit by the new Goods and Services Tax will pay a tax on Canadian energy we will not be able to match with a U.S. export tax.

Most serious, however, Article 904 of the deal places strict limits on the ability of our government to intervene in energy exports in times of Canadian need. To restrict exports, the government would have to declare a critical need in Canada; Canadian consumption and exports would then have to be cut back proportionally to ensure that the United States receives the share of energy exports that it has been receiving.

In an astonishing surrender of sovereignty, our government signed an agreement that explicitly denies the NEB the right to "refuse to issue a licence ... or revoke or change a licence for the exportation to the United States of energy goods." Not only are energy supplies more critical to Canada because of our harsh climate, but equal cut-backs would have a far greater effect on Canada. For instance, a 10 percent decline in gas production would result in a 10 percent decline in gas availability in Canada and a 10 percent decline in gas exports to the United States. However, Canadian gas is still a relatively small percentage of total American gas consumption; a 10 percent cut-back would result in a less than 1 percent decline in gas availability in the United States. Canada would bear the brunt of the shortage.

Perhaps the most significant result of the free-trade agreement is that it has set in motion an unprecedented assault by powerful economic and political forces on what remains of Canada's energy protection. Deregulation and free trade have made it easier than ever to export energy to the United States, and the Canadian government and its corporate allies have committed the country to an energy policy driven by massive, guaranteed exports, corporate control of supplies, and an economic policy more dependent than ever on the exploitation of primary resources.

The battle to regain control of these resources is being met with stiff opposition, as it is in the interests of many players that this not happen. The U.S. government needs the energy security of friendly Canada and would not take kindly to a reassertion of Canadian authority in this jurisdiction. In fact, former U.S. trade negotiator Peter Murphy has made it clear that the only conditions under which the United States would consider renegotiating the free-trade deal would be to remove all remaining Canadian protections in key sectors such as investment and energy.

The Alberta government has gained the right to sell its energy to the highest bidder. Alberta energy minister Rick Orman believes that any national legislation that might derogate from his province's jurisdiction over these resources is an infringement of provincial rights. Industry leaders call proposed federal standards to protect the environment the "son of NEP," and Orman, on their behalf, declared he would fight to keep the federal presence out of his province. He also warned that Ottawa should scrap its remaining restrictions on foreigners taking over healthy oil and gas companies and let the market settle ownership issues. The Canadian oil industry was built on foreign money and should be left to operate on its own, he added. Apparently the people of Canada or of Alberta who have paid with their taxes for the exploration and production of this energy have no prior claim to the use and profit from it. His government's stand pleases the industry, and so it should. Foreign control of the energy sector is on the rise again, and potential profits from these energy fields are massive.

Canada has never had much control in the industry. American money discovered the first great fields of Alberta oil in the late 1940s. By the end of the 1950s, the huge reserves of oil and gas were largely in the hands of American multinationals. The companies tied up control of much of the best acreage in Canada. They received exploration permits from the Alberta government on Crown land, and they were given most favoured treatment from the Canadian government in the form of tax breaks, exploration grants, and depletion allowances and other subsidies. By 1960, these companies had found the cheapest, biggest oil fields in Canada and had sewn up the rights to them. Virtually all the major finds were made by foreign-controlled companies, who consequently dominated the Canadian Petroleum Association, formed to fight government attempts to take some control. By 1980, foreigners owned 75 percent of Canada's oil and gas industry.

Enormous profits from these resources go to the companies' head offices in the United States. For instance, Amoco, which recently bought Dome Petroleum, invested just over $300 million in Canada in its first twenty years here. During that same time, it sent $2 billion back to its parent firm in the United States. Every year, foreign-controlled firms reap large profits from Canada.

About 65 percent of the oil and gas profits earned in Canada each year leave the country, and the amount has been increasing steadily during the past five years. (The percentage may be higher, in fact, as according to the federal Petroleum Monitoring Agency, some foreign-based companies have used dummy shareholders residing in Canada to inflate their paper levels of Canadian control.) Dividend payments to foreign parent firms jumped 36 percent in 1988.

Had Canada developed its own energy industry, the profits could have been used to build secondary manufacturing companies, which are going to be most needed in the energy-producing provinces when the energy supplies are depleted. But attempts to Canadianize the industry always met with hostility and threats from the U.S.-dominated petroleum companies. The irony of American outrage over Canadian attempts to control at least some portions of its resource sector is, of course, that Americans would never permit foreign domination of any sector of their economy, let alone a sector as vital to national security as energy.

Knuckling under to intense political pressure from the United States, the Tory government dismantled the restrictions on foreign investment in the energy industry that had been put in place earlier in the decade to halt the high foreign domination. (Canadian control had risen to almost 50 percent by 1984.) Once again, foreign companies have snapped up both financially distressed and healthy Canadian petroleum companies, and Canadian control of the industry has fallen to just one-third.

At the same time that Canadians are losing jurisdiction over our most basic resources — Canada is unique among developed countries in permitting such a high level of foreign control in this strategic sector — the foreign corporations are becoming increasingly concentrated. Thus the vast majority of our oil and gas reserves are falling under the control of an ever-smaller, ever-more-powerful group of multinational corporations. As we allow this, we entrench the power of these foreign energy corporations over our entire economy, and create an integrated North American energy regime in which Canadians will find it increasingly difficult to win back access to our own dwindling energy resources.

And dwindling they are. Since 1969, light crude reserves have fallen by 60 percent, particularly after deregulation in 1985 opened up rapid-fire, short-term exports. Canada has only a seven-year supply of conventional crude oil left in the ground at the current rate of production; to replace it, we are developing more costly and environmentally risky sources, such as the Athabasca Tar Sands. During the summer of 1989, for example, only 132 of the country's 522 oil rigs were in operation, and many of those were operating at a loss.

The multinationals are moving their development funds to greener pastures, lured by "elephant" finds in Libya, Pakistan, Malaysia, and other developing countries. Gulf has "gone international"; it estimates that 90 percent of Canada's oil reserves have been spoken for. It is virtually certain that Canada will have to import oil fairly soon, and Gulf intends to supply that need. Indeed, the Canadian Energy Research Institute has forecast that Canada will be importing one million barrels a day of light crude by the turn of the century. And the prices will rise sharply.

Canadian tax-payers invested enormous sums in the companies that are now pulling up stakes. The Petroleum Incentives Program alone gave more than $6 billion to the industry before it was cancelled in 1984. Immediately upon elimination of this grant, frontier exploration all but dried up as the talk about getting the government off the backs of business evaporated in a puff of hypocrisy. Now, the companies are moving out, leaving us to deal with oil shortages, job loss, higher energy prices, and a dying oil industry. It would seem, however, that we haven't learned much from the experience.

We are setting out to repeat the story in natural gas. American gas companies have told the National Energy Board that U.S. consumers will "desperately" need our natural gas by the next century. In many American states, clean-air legislation is fuelling the search for alternatives to oil and coal, and the green movement is a strong selling point in the marketing of Canadian gas. "We're seeing a tremendous amount of foreign interest in Canada," says a natural-resource specialist with an American mergers and acquisitions company. Experts talk of a gas "feeding frenzy" in Alberta, British Columbia, and Saskatchewan.

Major petroleum companies not leaving Canada are shifting their Canadian operations over to gas. They see the gas-export boom as the answer to their prayers. BP Canada, for example, which is controlled by multinational giant British Petroleum, expects to spend 90 percent of its exploration budget on natural gas in 1990.

There has been a spectacular increase in the sale of this resource to American markets. Natural-gas exports have grown by 70 percent since the deregulation of the industry; under the free-trade agreement, that means that 40 percent of our gas production is now guaranteed to the United States. The National Energy Board predicts that there will be another 30 percent increase by the end of 1992, and that at that time our exports to the United States will equal our total domestic demand.

These exports must be accompanied by a dramatic increase in pipeline capacity. This has brought forth an unprecedented burst of proposals for new natural-gas pipelines from Canadian gas fields to American markets stretching from California to the Atlantic Ocean. The competition is fierce. "The temperature is nearing flashpoint in a battle between competing pipeline promoters backing multi-billion-dollar projects to ship Canadian gas to the U.S.," the *Financial Post* says. A map of the routes under construction resembles a snakes-and-ladders game board, the dozens of gas-transportation connections all leading south, strong visual evidence of the weakening of east-west links in Canada. Once these pipelines are on-stream, the pressure to keep them operating at full capacity will be relentless.

Of all the projects underway, the most controversial involves a huge natural-gas field in the Mackenzie Delta region of the Northwest Territories. The NEB has granted three companies — Esso, Gulf, and Shell — the right to export 90 percent of the proven gas reserves in this area. The sheer size of these reserves is staggering — 260 billion cubic metres (9.2 trillion cubic feet) of gas, to be exported over a twenty-year period. So large is this project that it could increase the proportion of our gas production exported to the United States to 60 percent.

Under the free-trade agreement, Canada could be forced to continue to supply 90 percent of these Arctic reserves to the United States. If new gas sources are found, Canada would owe the United States 60 percent of them, forever. The United States would thus acquire a legal, binding claim to well over half of Canada's gas reserves. The free-trade agreement confers on the United States a permanent entitlement to an increasing share of all future Canadian gas discoveries. If there are not other large pockets of this energy source, Canadians will have to do without, for the rights to our own natural-gas reserves have been signed away under the deal.

Canadians will also bear an unfair financial burden. The real price that Canada receives for a cubic metre of gas in the U.S. market is only one-third the price we received in the early 1980s. So, although we are exporting record amounts of natural gas, our export revenues have fallen sharply. The drastic collapse in gas prices, especially for export markets, means that Canada's gas reserves are being sold not only quickly, but cheaply.

Most Canadian consumers, however, will miss the benefits from this cheap gas. That is because gas companies in the consuming provinces, serving the smaller Canadian population, are negotiating shorter-term contracts. When prices rise, and the NEB predicts that they will, Canadian consumers will be forced to outbid American customers for the gas, and will consequently pay higher prices. American companies, facing a much greater need for gas, are buying our gas under long-term contracts, ensuring rock-bottom prices even when our gas prices rise. Free trade means that Canadians will have to compete for our own energy against an economy that is ten times our size, is the most wasteful energy addict in the world (although per capita, Canada is worse), has rapidly dwindling reserves and accelerating demand. It will be very expensive for Canadians to do so.

As we have seen, under the terms of the free-trade agreement, government subsidies are permitted for defence-industry production. The only other subsidy allowed is the search for new energy sources. Canadian tax-payers will continue to subsidize the exploration for frontier development, so that we can continue to assure American consumers a steady supply of cheap natural gas, even as our conventional reserves dwindle. Canadian tax-payers are subsidizing American consumers in the sell-off of our energy.

That this cannot work to Canada's advantage is illustrated in two recent controversies involving pipeline construction. A practice called "tolling" would force Canadian consumers to subsidize the building of the major gas pipelines into the United States to carry Canadian natural-gas exports. The TransCanada PipeLine expansion, which will benefit American consumers and the big exporting companies, could cost Canadian consumers about $100 million a year.

However, the minister of energy admits that the same free-trade agreement that allows this practice prevents the Canadian government from subsidizing construction of a pipeline from Sarnia to Montreal. The company in question, Polysar, asked the U.S. Department of Commerce what it would do if the construction was assisted by Ottawa, and was told that the Americans would lay a charge. "They also assured us all other exports including ours would be affected," said a company official. The government has once again penalized Canadians by forcing us to subsidize gas pipelines for U.S. consumers, but forbidding us to do so for our own system. As a result, the partners in this project are seriously considering abandoning the Canadian route for this pipeline, building it instead through a cheaper U.S. route.

Canadians could be forgiven for asking, "Whose gas is it, anyway?" One of the country's largest distributors says that the NEB's export licensing procedures are "fundamentally unworkable" in holding back reserves for Canada's future needs. Says Art Duloff of Trans-Canada PipeLines, "Under the pact, it's first come, first served, regardless of nationality." Well, clearly, if the first to arrive calling on these resources is bigger and richer and can use the gas right away, and if the first to come is the senior partner in an unbalanced trading arrangement, first come will indeed be first served, with the lion's share, no questions asked. It is now North American gas, and Canada will have to bid on it like any American state.

If there were unlimited supplies of this resource, the issue wouldn't be so pressing. While it is true that, compared with many countries, Canada has been endowed with a wealth of natural-gas reserves, according to NEB studies, known reserves in western Canada peaked in the early 1980s, and it has been downhill ever since. Based on the current rate of production, including the Beaufort Sea project, Canada now has only a twenty-five-year supply of gas left. But, we must remember, we will have to share 60 percent of it with American consumers. Forty percent — a ten- to fifteen-year gas supply — is Canada's share.

The government and the gas companies argue that there are vast gas reserves under the Beaufort Sea and that development of the Mackenzie project will bring in the necessary finances to develop them. But Gordon Taylor, senior petroleum geologist at the federal department of the environment, contradicted Jake Epp, the energy minister, when the latter assured the House of Commons that there are untold amounts of gas for the taking in Canada's North. The estimates of gas are "meaningless," said Taylor, because much of the gas in that area is located in deep water and may well not be reachable, economically or environmentally. And, reachable or not, the United States will have an iron-clad, free-trade right to well over half of whatever is found. As Roland Priddle, chairman of the NEB, explains, the gas no longer has a flag.

Foreign control of vulnerable energy stocks diminishes Canada's sovereign claim to the North, which has come under much pressure in recent years. The American government has not always recognized our legal claims to our Arctic waters and has repeatedly violated our territorial integrity. The development and production of natural gas from Canada's Arctic is relevant to this concern of sovereignty in broad, geopolitical terms. Development of this gas will spark the greatest short-term boom of economic growth that the North has ever seen — a development that will be undertaken by a consortium dominated by foreign multinationals, with the sole purpose of delivering natural gas to a foreign nation.

This chain of events will further undermine our political authority in the Arctic, since it would be increasingly apparent to the rest of the world that Canadians are not exercising sovereign control over our resources there. By licensing the long-term export of Arctic gas to the United States, Canada is abdicating our sovereign power to utilize the resources of the North for the best interests of Canadians.

Just how seriously American energy corporations and the U.S. government take any infringement on their new-found unfettered access to Canadian energy sources was evident in a nasty little showdown that occurred when the National Energy Board turned down a few relatively minor applications for gas exports in 1989. One of the few powers left the board after deregulation and free trade was a test called "cost-benefit" — a requirement that the board be satisfied that an export application was of net benefit to Canada. The test lacked the strength of the standards it replaced but it was virtually all that kept government abdication of its responsibility from being total.

These applications were denied because the board felt the exports being sought would not bring a net return to Canada. The amount of gas represented only 1 percent of all outstanding NEB export licences, but the companies involved, all American, were dismayed at the precedent; crying foul, they took the board to the Canadian Federal Court to have the decisions reversed. They charged that, under free trade, the Canadian government had no right to ask if an export is in Canada's interest. American companies must be accorded "national treatment," they argued, and that means that they must be treated as if they are Canadian.

The president of one of the companies, Indek of Chicago, said that this test in effect treats U.S. companies in a different manner from Canadian companies, and therefore violates the free-trade agreement: "This does not fit with the free-trade agreement or a plain free-trade approach. The whole goal of the agreement was to remove regulatory barriers." Another said that, by applying this test to exports, the board was discriminating against sales to the United States: "All contracts involving the sale of natural gas, whether for export or not, should be subject to identical criteria." Translation: It's our gas as much as it is Canada's. The companies were joined by the government of Alberta, whose energy minister, Rick Orman, warned that the NEB actions could damage Canada–U.S. relations, and said that the market alone, not Canadian needs, should determine energy sales. A fuming Orman reminded Canadians that free trade essentially did away with government "distortions" of the market-place. "The agreement gives us a new environment for doing business in the U.S. and it's been very, very fruitful."

But, the U.S. government wasn't willing to wait for a Canadian court decision, and warned the government that a formal complaint under the free-trade agreement would be launched if the NEB did not dispose of this problem itself. "We've made it abundantly clear" that the U.S. is unhappy with the board's decision, said a U.S. energy official. Loath to have the Americans lay a free-trade complaint that the government would likely lose, and fearing the public back-lash if the court found in favour of the American complainants, the Canadian government and the NEB decided to "review" the whole procedure. The American government let it be known that it would not lay a complaint if the board voluntarily fixed the problem, and the companies indicated that they would be happy to drop their cases as well.

In its terms of the reference for the "review," the NEB questioned only whether the board should apply such a test "as part of the Market-Based Procedure," not whether it had the right to do so, which was the real issue.

The review attracted little attention in Canada outside the industry; after all, it was a very technical review of an obscure procedure by a government agency many Canadians have never heard of. The NEB did not give much notice time, nor did it attempt to find widespread representation from Canadian interest groups. But it attracted amazing interest south of the border. The U.S. Department of Energy, the New York State Energy Office, twenty-three U.S. gas importers, and a number of major American gas producers registered their intention to intervene. At the last minute, the U.S. Department of Energy sensed that its public intervention would be tactically unwise. Instead, it worked behind the scenes, government to government, to secure its desired outcome.

Not surprisingly, the overwhelming bulk of energy-industry submissions called for the test to be scrapped. "The spirit of the free-trade agreement was that nationalistic barriers on both sides of the border would be reduced such that the flow of goods would be less restricted than in the past," said a Canadian company, arguing that Americans were now feeling "uneasy" again about access to Canadian energy. "Our company agrees with the Canadian Petroleum Association's position on the benefit-cost test and want it eliminated" was the curt submission of a number of U.S.-based companies, indicating a well-organized lobby by the association dominated by foreign-owned subsidiaries. The government of Saskatchewan prefaced its submission, in which it said that the test was inconsistent with the free-trade agreement, with the statement that in its view, the only mandate that the board has is to "review and approve applications for export of natural gas from Canada."

Predictably, the NEB announced early in 1990 that the cost-benefit test was no longer necessary and was being dropped. Shortly thereafter, it approved resubmitted licence applications for the companies that had been denied exports. In so doing, the government surrendered its last remaining tool to manage Canada's energy exports for future use. It was a major capitulation of Canadian sovereignty and directly tied to the free-trade agreement.

In other energy sectors, the federal government is also abdicating authority, through neglect, the transfer of these powers to the provinces, or by acquiescing to the economic strait-jacket its free-trade agreement has wrapped around government authority. One such sector is the export of hydro-electricity. Canada has sold power to the United States for many years, but exports mush-roomed during the last decade. Massive new projects are under way in British Columbia, Manitoba, and, of course, Quebec. As indi-vidual projects, each is immense, but as a group, they represent an astounding build-up that would effectively sacrifice control over close to 10 percent of our total electricity supply.

Both Quebec and Ontario have experienced serious black-outs and brown-outs during the past several winters. Hydro-Québec's customers suffer an average of 20,000 black-outs annually. Studies have linked this problem to the neglectful maintenance practices of a utility more interested in pursuing high-profile export contracts than in servicing its own customers. Hydro officials have admitted they have neglected domestic maintenance, says the *Montreal Gazette*, adding, "Hydro has the reputation of a corporate mono-lith, more concerned with peddling electricity to the United States than with the plight of domestic customers."

Hydro-Québec needs the sales to the United States because of its massive borrowing; its debt represents 40 percent of all money owed in the province. Almost half of the Hydro debt is owed to U.S. investors who were strongly in favour of free trade. Canadian customers are paying: electricity rates have been steadily rising, and hydro supplies are tight right across the country as demand soars. The president of the Quebec farmers' union, Jacques Proulx, says that electricity price increases of 111 percent since 1985 will wipe out 1,200 greenhouses in the province. They were encouraged to invest $300 million in the projects by the provincial government with promises of cheap electricity, but the prices jumped right away. Proulx points out that Quebec customers are paying 3.8 cents an hour while New England customers of Hydro-Québec pay 2 cents, and won't be facing a price increase in 1990.

Manitoba, worried about recent decreases in exports to the United States as a result of low water levels, has increased prices for its own consumers as one method of building up supplies for export. As in the case of natural gas, American contractors are seeking long-term security of supply, and the current, ominous trend is towards firm power contracts for twenty years or longer. Canadians will wind up paying higher prices, as domestic supplies become more scarce and expensive, especially if Canada will not be able to charge American customers more for hydro-electricity, as we have been able to do in the past, to cover our increased costs.

There is another concern lurking behind the current spate of power-export proposals — a trend towards the privatization of electrical utilities. Saskatchewan is privatizing part of Sask. Power; British Columbia plans to turn over the export side of the electricity industry to private subcontractors. Once these utilities are privatized, they can be sold to foreign interests. British Columbia had the distinction of overseeing the very first foreign take-over of an electric utility in Canadian history, dams, water rights, and all, when it sold West Kootenay Power & Light to a foreign-owned private company, Utilicorp United of Missouri. B.C. Hydro has created five wholly owned subsidiaries that are to become completely self-sufficient. The subsidiaries expose the company to market pressures, says Larry Bell, B.C. Hydro's CEO, who, when asked if privatization was down the road, responded enthusiastically, "Oh, sure. There's a prospect of spinning these off, particularly if the employees express an interest."

It is not so far-fetched to fear that this unprecedented orientation towards American power sales could ultimately lead to the demise of the public electricity system in many parts of Canada. Moreover, because of the proportionality clause of the free-trade agreement, a province with long-term American export contracts might be obliged to meet rising domestic demand for electricity through the construction of expensive new generating facilities, as the province will not be permitted to cut back on exports.

At the very time that the National Energy Board should be strengthened to deal with the new realities resulting from the government's policies, the government has truncated its powers by cancelling the requirements for public hearings on hydro-electric exports in order to make it easier for the provinces to sell power to the United States. This change will further erode the public's access to decision-making, diminishing the democratic right of Canadian citizens to influence energy decisions. This is a dangerous precedent that could easily be extended to gas and oil. Crucial is the fact that the free-trade agreement promises that Canada, as a whole, will honour energy contracts negotiated by any province. If several provinces, not monitored by any national body, commit to massive exports to the United States, all provinces will have to guarantee that supply, jeopardizing the energy security of all Canadians.

There are a number of larger issues related to this surrender that should be addressed. The growing U.S. need for our raw resources, particularly energy, is distorting the structure of our economy. Big new investments are almost exclusively oriented to the primary sectors, as our manufacturing and high-technology industries shut down, move away, or are taken over. We have a negative balance of payments as a result of exports of interest and dividends. Economic growth is unstable, dependent on fluctuating commodity prices. The spiralling exploitation of our raw resources is a shaky foundation for a stable economy, even for the producing provinces.

Furthermore, we are dismantling our energy-regulating institutions, even when not explicitly required by the free-trade agreement. This is a perfect example of Canada–U.S. harmonization at work. For the effects of the free-trade agreement go far beyond its mere wording. What happened to the National Energy Board should serve as a warning to other sectors of Canadian society where domestic corporate interests coincide with American goals. When those opposed to the deal talked about a threat to the Canadian way of life and Canadian institutions, it was exactly this form of harmonization they had in mind.

As well, the sell-out of our energy interests was made easier by several historic and regional tensions, all exacerbated by the free-trade agreement. Quebec nationalists openly touted the agreement as a nail in the coffin of confederation. If Quebec ever separates from Canada, it will need the wealth generated from Quebec hydro exports to enable it to exist as a financially viable country. Alberta's alienation abetted the process and was, in turn, furthered by it. In fact, much as American negotiators wanted the energy provisions of the deal, they were taken aback by the Canadian delegation's enthusiasm to include them. The free-trade agreement feeds on, and is fed by, regional tensions and this works against national solutions to our problems.

When the terrible facts of this energy betrayal are told, the angry question remains: Why? Why would Canada allow this to happen? Obviously, there is a confluence of interests that came together at a time when the country was very vulnerable.

Once again, the hand of the Business Council on National Issues can be seen in the shadows. Back in the early 1980s, the BCNI, concerned with the loss of revenue to the multinational energy companies from current government energy policy, set out to engineer a new energy accord. Just as it had written the government's defence position by setting up a task force whose recommendations were lifted wholesale, the group set up the Business Council Task Force on Energy Policy. It was chaired by the president of Imperial Oil and worked with members of the energy industry, Conservative provincial governments, the banking community, and the federal government. It developed the private-sector, producer-consumer consensus that became the government's deregulation blueprint and later, the energy provisions of the free-trade agreement.

The companies that make up the energy industry, most of whom are also members of the BCNI, generously contributed to the free trade fight. Many — BP Canada, Shell ($250,000), Amoco, Imperial Oil ($200,000), Texaco ($100,000), and TransCanada PipeLines among others — gave to the Alliance for Trade and Job Opportunities. The industry was also very well represented in the American Coalition for Trade Expansion with Canada. The American Gas Association, the Interstate Natural Gas Association of America, Mobil Oil, Exxon, BP, Shell, and Amoco were influential members of the group that was so helpful in shaping the final version of the free-trade agreement.

Their work paid off in dividends, but not for Canadians. There is money yet to be made in Canada's wilderness. And some other old friends are very busy helping the energy industry to cash in. Former U.S. energy secretary Donald Hodel and former Alberta energy minister Neil Webber have been hired as special advisers to a pipeline company planning major expansion into the American Northeast. Former Alberta premier Peter Lougheed has been hired by a rival firm, the Iroquois pipeline. Their job is to sell the projects to the Canadian people, because the exports are likely to drive now-record gas exports even higher, providing Canadian consumers with greater competition for the gas.

On election night, 1988, a group of American trade officials and businessmen joyously watched the results high atop the Canadian embassy building in Washington. With a broad grin of satisfaction, one American trade official quipped, "We could have gone for their water, too."

# 7.
# ENVIRONMENT AT RISK

"The fact is that countries look after their national interests to the extent that they are capable of doing so and when the devil drives, watch out. Sooner or later the U.S. is going to go after our water."

*Simon Reisman*

"Every waste of energy is an act of murder in the Third World."

*René Dumont*

SEVERAL YEARS AGO, A U.S. COALITION CALLED THE Alliance to Save Energy was formed to try to find some common ground between energy-industry leaders and the country's environmentalists. In January 1988, it held a well-publicized conference in Washington, Preparing for the Energy Challenge, 1990, which was chaired by Senator Daniel J. Evans and addressed by the secretary of the U.S. Department of Energy, John Harrington. The truce between the conservative industry lobby and those who have long opposed them was tentative at best, and both sides were uneasy and suspicious during the conference.

Canadian environmentalist and energy consultant Ralph Torrie attended. During the speech, John Harrington referred to the upcoming Canada–U.S. Free Trade Agreement favourably, citing its beneficial (to the U.S.) energy provisions. Right, said an environmentalist sitting behind Torrie, "It's called drain Canada dry."

Little New Zealand, reeling from a failing political course of free trade with Australia, a debilitating sales tax, and massive privatization, has put its entire stock of plantation forests — over half of the country's forest cover — up for sale. The forests are to be marketed internationally to the highest bidder in order to cover the country's mounting debt; most of the wood will be exported before being processed. New Zealand has chosen a course that many of the world's nations have forced on them: the sale of their resources in exchange for foreign currency. The dilemma is obvious. While these sales may bring some temporary economic relief, the foreign corporations have very little interest in the country once the products have been extracted, and their legacy is usually one of stripped forests, flooded lands, gaping mine holes, dirty air, and fouled water.

The Brundtland Commission, a United Nations–sponsored report on the state of the world's ecology, identified this practice as one of the most serious impediments to ecological survival. "Developing countries face the dilemma of having to use commodities as exports, in order to break foreign exchange constraints on growth, while also having to minimize damage to the environmental resource base supporting growth." The essence of free trade, which is really the essence of deregulation, is that it becomes impossible for a country to place safeguards and curbs on exportable products, including — perhaps especially — raw materials. Developed countries and the transnational corporations want unrestricted access to these resources.

Their success in doing so is astounding. Transnational corporations control 80 percent of the world's land cultivated for export-oriented crops. "Eighty to ninety percent of the trade in tea, coffee, cocoa, cotton, forest products, tobacco, jute, copper, iron ore, and bauxite is controlled in the case of each commodity by the three to six largest transnationals," says the United Nations. A study by the Canadian Environmental Law Association states that, under a free-trade regime, the market is given pre-emptive rights to determine the course of resource development, placing these decisions beyond the democratic reach and control of the people. Speaking of the Canada–U.S. free trade-deal, the group says, "By limiting the right of governments to regulate the development of natural re-

sources or to control that development to accomplish environmental objectives, the trade deal has undermined critical opportunities to accomplish goals that are necessary to abate global warming."

Large-scale resource extraction and the misuse of the world's resources have hastened the global environmental crisis; yet, the multinationals continue their agenda of unlimited economic expansion and the pursuit of profit at the expense of all else. They can and do use their international position to bully individual countries: if environmental standards are too strict in one country, they move to a more "business-friendly" locale. Therefore, many countries swallow the environmental consequences in order to prevent the companies from leaving. In a free, *i.e.*, unregulated, trade arrangement, environmental standards can actually be considered an unfair trading barrier, and government assistance for environmental protection can be disputed as a subsidy.

Canadians don't think of Canada as a "developing" country. Proud of our gleaming office towers and state-of-the-art telecommunications technology, we see ourselves as being on the leading edge of First World economics. But just beneath the wealth and glitter are resource practices not much more enlightened or independent than those found in many Third World countries. Canada is growing more dependent on the exploitation of our natural resources because deregulation and free trade are hastening the decline of manufacturing and high technology. To create wealth and jobs, governments in many provinces are relying more and more on their natural-resource sector for job growth and to attract investment.

This exploitation is going to have profound effects on our environment, particularly in the North; the 1990s are witnessing an unprecedented assault on our northern wilderness. The Science Council of Canada says that an environmental disaster is looming, one far exceeding any met by earlier generations: "A threat more fundamental than total nuclear destruction is the accelerating pressure of human activities on the natural resources and ecosystems on which life depends."

Up in the vast Alberta north, there is a struggle being waged over one of Canada's last unspoiled boreal forests, and the majestic Athabasca and Peace rivers. The struggle pits the insatiable appetite of several large multinationals against the stubborn notion of democracy held by a handful of residents and environmentalists who believe that these forests belong to the Canadian people. At stake is the environmental health of the mighty river system, and the right of governments to impose ecological standards on the use of these trees.

The Alberta government, anxious to wean the province off its dependence on its declining oil reserves, has set out to triple the size of its pulp-mill industry by the turn of the century. Without proper public consultation or environmental assessment, it has signed leases to develop northern lands the size of Great Britain to a handful of mostly foreign pulp companies. Lured with billions of dollars of provincial grants and loans, eight major projects are under negotiation, including a $450-million expansion to the existing mill in Grande Prairie by Cincinnati-based Procter & Gamble, construction of the world's largest chemical pulp mill, a $1.3-billion mega-project on the Athabasca, by Japanese-owned Crestbrook, and a $500-million mill to be built by Japanese Daishowa Paper on the Peace River. One plant, Japanese-owned Alberta Pacific Forest Industries, has been granted timber rights to an area more than nine times the size of Ontario's Algonquin Park. Alberta's forest-products industry is in the midst of a virtual explosion, spurred on by generous government incentive packages, dubbed by some as "the great forest sell-off."

The contracts were negotiated in haste and secrecy. Says former U.S. Environmental Protection Agency official John Bonine, "In 17 years of practising and teaching environmental law, and lecturing in countries around the world, I have never seen an environmental impact-assessment as deficient with regard to toxic effects as the one that the Mitsubishi Alberta project issued for its planned pulp mill on the Athabasca." The Alberta Medical Association has said that the projects could seriously jeopardize the prospects of a healthy future for the children of the province. "The

AMA is appalled at the material tendered by Alberta-Pacific camouflaged as a health impact assessment." A member of Friends of the Athabasca, an organization of people who live near the planned site, charges: "We are going to murder a forest before we even know what's in there. This is a Third World operation."

Several of the projects, including Alberta-Pacific, are now on hold, pending environmental assessments forced on the province by a review panel of Environment Canada. But a struggle is ensuing over provincial control of the projects. Alberta premier Don Getty says that Alberta, not Ottawa, will decide their fate and the province has joined with Ontario, Quebec, British Columbia, Manitoba, and Nova Scotia to lobby for severe restrictions on the federal ability to impose national standards for environmental assessments. The provinces want to exempt projects under way from federal assessments and want legislation to clarify that federal interests will be considered secondary to provincial interests.

The Mulroney government's response has been weak, yet again abandoning the traditional power and responsibility of the federal level. It did not renew reforestation agreements with the provinces, instead turning the responsibility over to provincial jurisdiction. As a result, forest harvests will be in serious shortage by the next decade, says the B.C. Council of Foresters. And, the federal government's recently announced environmental assessment legislation has been hailed by environmental groups as a backward step, and more flawed than the legislation it will replace. Important sections of the bill have been left to regulations yet to be drafted, and which statutes will be affected is left indefinitely to future regulations. Furthermore, the bill must get agreement from the provinces, several of whom are opposed to this process, to go ahead. And, perhaps most disturbingly, cabinet will still maintain the right to accept or not environmental assessments regarding politically sensitive projects. None of the current projects in dispute will be subject to this legislation, giving the green light to Alberta's forest projects and other sensitive undertakings in Canada. It appears that the government knows that a strong federal assessment policy would interfere with the interests of the corporate and provincial free-trade allies of the federal government, and has back-tracked on yet another crucial promise.

Alberta is not alone in its forestry plan. Ontario is clear-cutting large areas of its North. Saskatchewan is building a major mill in the northern community of Meadow Lake. Manitoba has privatized its pulp-and-paper industry; the company that bought it, Repap, is planning a $1-billion expansion of its mill at The Pas, and the eventual exploitation of forests covering 20 percent of Manitoba. The project will require intensive clear-cutting of the North.

In British Columbia, massive clear-cutting of forests continues; 60 percent of the B.C. Pacific forest has been destroyed in the last forty years. China's showcase multinational corporation is involved in a large expansion in the southeast, with its partners Power Corp. and Consolidated-Bathurst of Chicago. A Portland, Oregon, forest products giant, Louisiana-Pacific, is opening a huge mill near Chetwynd. Fights are underway to save the remaining trees of the Carmanah Valley on the west coast of Vancouver Island. And public anger is mounting over the environmental impact of Crestbrook's parent company in Skookumchuck, whose mill leaks so much effluent into the Kootenay River that ground water beneath the plant, including drinking water, is chemically polluted. Private companies are licensed to log public forests in perpetuity, and there is no limit on the size of clear-cuts.

In all, there are $13.3-billion worth of proposed pulp mega-projects in Canada. Canada is now losing one acre of forest every five seconds, most of it to foreign corporate interests. European environmentalists are seriously considering a boycott of Canadian forest products to sound a world alarm over our mismanagement of this resource.

Corporate concentration and foreign take-overs are the driving trend in this industry, as in so many others. Companies like Fletcher Challenge of New Zealand and Stone Container of Chicago now count among the largest half-dozen forest-products giants in the country. Japanese and Korean investment is also on the rise. Canadian control in the industry has dropped to 60 percent from 72 percent just five years ago, and the decline will continue as the new projects come on stream. As well, since the free-trade agreement was signed, U.S. investors have returned to make a big push into the industry, and analysts predict growing American interest in Canada's forests.

It has been said that the best corporate citizens must breathe the same air and drink the same water that we do. The more our forests are put in the hands of foreign private interests, the more environmental danger there is. Environmentalists charge that Alberta's projects, for example, rival the destruction of the rain forests in Brazil. They also point out that the Athabasca venture alone will dump tons of dioxin into the river every day. The industry is responsible for half the waste water dumped in Canada every year.

Many of these companies now operating in Canada have a poor environmental record. Japan, in particular, has a reputation of impeccable environmental standards at home and wanton disregard for ecological safeguards everywhere else. Japanese industrialists have emptied the forests of Southeast Asia, leaving enormous environmental damage in their wake. They are major players in the destruction of Brazil's rain forests, and Mitsubishi, one of the companies involved in the Athabaska project, has a "reprehensible" toxic-waste record, according to Cultural Survival Canada. Mitsubishi's subsidiary in Malaysia, Asian Rare Earth, has been accused of dumping radioactive waste around its site, close to large populations.

Yet, Stuart Lang, chairman of Alberta-Pacific, the project in which Mitsubishi is a central investor, reacted angrily at having to "lower" himself to an environmental review. Daishowa spokespersons have said that further delays for environmental reasons could affect the financial viability of the project. Adam Zimmerman, chairman of Noranda, who states that dioxins, one of the most deadly substances on earth, haven't yet been proven harmful, admired the way Alberta sped the process along. When his company pulled out of a project in Tasmania because of environmental guidelines, Zimmerman told the Australian government that it could learn from Alberta where "they kiss [the pulp companies] on both cheeks and give them grants."

Slowly, but relentlessly, Canada's forests are being removed from the public domain and sold to the first — not even highest — bidder. And the free-trade agreement adds another danger. Canadian forests are in serious trouble because of overcutting and inadequate reforestation practices. Since 1950, Canadian annual wood harvests have increased by 50 percent. Environment Canada has confirmed that present harvests are often in excess of allowable maximum cuts. What little reforestation is carried out in Canada has been heavily subsidized by the federal government. The U.S. lumber industry regards reforestation grants as an unfair trade practice and a subsidy to our lumber exports. In accordance with the free-trade agreement, the government of British Columbia ended replanting subsidies to the forest industry. Thus, under the free-trade agreement, the right of Canadian governments to establish environmental assistance programs was successfully challenged, greatly reducing public control of corporate behaviour and its treatment of the environment.

The more forest resources are turned over to private and foreign interests, the less likely will be the chance of environmentally sound logging and reforestation practices. We are now poised to strip our northern boreal forest, destroying vast tracts of wilderness that take fifty to seventy years to regenerate. To add insult to injury, we are selling the trees dirt-cheap and sending 90 percent of the mulch to be processed out of the country, creating jobs elsewhere by their destruction.

Perhaps instead we should be trying to understand the special role of these trees in the ecosystem. The boreal forest holds a significant portion of the world's carbon supply and may well qualify with Brazil's rain forests as the other lung of the earth. But, the transnationals seeking control of these forests are not interested in the ecological impact of their destruction. The president of foreign-owned Fletcher Challenge stated in a recent speech that the industry needs guaranteed access to steady supplies of timber, and governments must choose between the industry and environmentalists who are "loose with the facts." Calling for a "prompt solution" to the "disruptive issue of Indian land claims," he admonished governments against the preservation of "decadent wilderness."

Canada is committing itself to a resource policy of deregulation, privatization, and massive exports just when we should be developing environmental and economic policies that promote conservation and responsible resource management. We should be strengthening, not weakening, our capacity to allocate Canadian natural resources, and to establish environmental standards to protect our fragile ecosystem. But we are moving in the opposite direction, abdicating forever, as we have in the free-trade deal, our right to use regulatory tools to manage our resources in the Canadian public interest. In fact, we are under increased pressure for the market-driven, continental exploitation of our resources to accelerate. With free trade, corporations have been given the pre-emptive rights to determine the allocation of Canada's resources as long as they last. The decadent wilderness is theirs.

Nowhere is this government's willingness to protect the environment for big business more obvious than the continued push, at great ecological risk, for the construction of frontier energy mega-projects. The government has maintained its commitment to Hibernia off Newfoundland, and the heavy-oil upgrader at Lloydminster, B.C., at a cost of billions of dollars to Canadian tax-payers. As our conventional reserves decline, Canada will be forced to seek out these frontier supplies, relying on mega-project development to honour our free-trade commitment of a guaranteed level of energy exports to the United States. A study by the Canadian Energy Research Institute draws a clear link between the free-trade agreement and the development of economically risky mega-projects. Deregulation is hastening the day when we will need these resources, and undertakings that the oil produced can be exported to the United States is central to agreements launching the projects. Moreover, in the Beaufort Sea, companies finding significant oil and gas reserves will be allowed permanent entitlement to further gas discoveries. As the government backs out of the energy sector, abandoning its responsibility to safeguard the fragile eco-system of Canada's North, crucial decisions regarding these giant energy projects will be made almost exclusively by the industry. And the industry has a poor environmental record. A recent U.S. government report says that the oil industry has left a legacy of pollution in the wake of exploration in the Alaskan tundra, seriously damaging the environment in the Prudoe Bay area and in the Arctic National Wildlife Refuge. The report documents areas of tundra blackened by chemical spill, oil wastes seeping from drilling pads, stacks of leaking chemical drums, and careless handling of hazardous materials. Contractors who worked in the Canadian Arctic in the 1960s and 1970s sent their hazardous wastes out to sea on ice-floes or merely left them behind when they left, to save transportation costs. PCBS were left at old construction sites, including many American air force bases, now abandoned, and are now in the food chain of the North.

In spite of this record, the Mackenzie Delta gas project was endorsed by the NEB, even though no environmental assessment had been undertaken. In fact, an NEB report assumed that, by the year 2015, there will be no fewer than six huge pipeline projects out of the frontier, each carrying an average of 1.3 billion cubic feet of gas per day. This is a dangerous assumption for it has not yet been determined that even one pipeline is technically achievable or environmentally safe. The Canadian Environmental Law Association points out that natural-gas drilling, transportation, and combustion result in the emission of large amounts of greenhouse gases, fuelling what a United Nations conference called the most important environmental problem facing the world. We know next to nothing about the potential dangers of blow-outs in this icy world, nor how we would cap them in the dead of winter. We know little about the long-term damage of transporting the gas to the United States.

In a rare win against the federal government, the association recently forced it to agree to seek environmental assessments from companies prior to large energy exports, but the companies have vowed to fight this ruling and have been joined by the energy-producing provinces in a jurisdictional struggle.

Should pipelines to carry this gas be constructed, they will become the largest fuel transporter in North America. Therefore, the decisions made concerning pipeline routes are critical. Why, for instance, do the Americans not use their own abundant gas supplies in Alaska first? This would give Canada an opportunity to assess our need for our own gas. In fact, Canada has already approved the Canadian portion for a pipeline along the Alaska Highway. If this pipeline were built first, and Canada wanted to export some of the Mackenzie gas, it could be linked relatively cheaply to this route following the Dempster Highway. However, if the Canadian gas and pipeline are developed first, there will be an overwhelming pressure for the Alaska gas to be piped across the sensitive Arctic National Wildlife Preserve to link up with this existing system. There is a sound environmental argument for developing the Alaska gas first; however, the United States would prefer to lock up Canadian gas now while it is politically secure and cheap. Once our gas is gone, American consumers will still be guaranteed an Alaskan energy supply. We will not.

There is another environmental imperative regarding these gas reserves. The global environmental crisis will soon necessitate radical action by the world's governments. A former official with the United Nations Commission on Environment and Development warns that Canada should scrap its ambitious oil megaprojects and adopt targets for fossil-fuel reduction. James MacNeill says that the threat of global warming is second only to nuclear war; Canada, which has the highest energy use in the industrialized world, must fundamentally change its ways as part of the solution.

Of all the fossil fuels, natural gas emits the least carbon dioxide per unit of energy produced, and virtually no sulphur or nitrogen oxides, the causes of acid rain. Canada is in the process of developing a strategy for achieving a reduction of greenhouse-gas emissions. As Canadians decide to reduce these emissions or as Canada is forced by international standards to do so, an aggressive program of substituting this natural gas for oil should be undertaken. The role of Canada's gas reserves must be assessed thoroughly before decisions are made. Under free trade, however, this is not possible. Our government is aggressively promoting resource exports while cutting back on conservation projects. The free-trade agreement, by allowing the subsidization of mega-projects while disallowing similar assistance for the development of alternative energy sources, is undermining our country's ability to develop sustainable resource management.

The James Bay hydro-electric development in Northern Quebec is another struggle of wills and jurisdiction whose outcome will have enormous ecological implications. For Quebec premier Robert Bourassa, exporting the immense electrical power of northern waters to the U.S. has been a long-time dream; his right to do so, unhampered by federal interference, was a major factor in his support of the free-trade agreement. He wrote in *Power from the North*: "Quebec is a vast hydro-electric plant in the bud, and every day, millions of potential kilowatt hours flow downhill and out to sea. What a waste!"

James Bay II is a $40-billion project of powerhouses, transmission lines, dikes, roads, towns, and airports; together with James Bay I and III, it will harness the power of twenty rivers flowing into Hudson and James bays and forever change the fundamental geography of one-fifth of Canada's largest province. But environmentalists say that the project will cause massive flooding, destroy many species of wildlife, and devastate the Cree, who have lived and hunted in the area for centuries. When the reservoir for the first stage of the project was diverted from the Caniapiscau River, so great was the volume of water involved, that the earth's crust shifted, causing a tremor.

The Quebec government has targeted James Bay II as key to its economic success and has strongly resisted attempts to force public environmental assessments of it. It has passed legislation that exempts northern projects from the environmental scrutiny and public hearings that are required in the south of the province. Native leaders call this "environmental racism." The province simply granted applications to proceed with development. Enraged Cree leaders were forced to take their case to the New England states for a hearing.

Alan Penn, a geographer working with the Cree, says the review process that has been established between the Quebec government and the developers is not designed to focus on problems, but to "provide general reassurance." He adds that this is what happens when the developer designs the system of environmental monitoring for a project from which it will benefit. The current Grand Chief of the Cree, Matthew Coon-Come, calls the process a "farce and a sham."

How did the province of Quebec get direct authority over a project of this size? The federal government made it possible through its evisceration of the National Energy Board, in order to leave energy development to the play of the market. The NEB removed hydro-electricity export hearings from the national jurisdiction. Recently, the federal government has reluctantly ordered an environmental review of the project, but only after being forced by a Federal Court order, a result of actions taken by environmental groups. Quebec's environment minister, Pierre Paradis, has made it clear that he sees this as intolerable federal interference in the business of his province and has insisted on limiting the scope and duration of the hearings. The free-trade agreement was supposed to free the province of this type of federal interference.

The Cree Council fought the first stage of James Bay, for which no government conducted an environmental assessment. "Only the beavers" have a right to build dams in their homeland, they declared. This is a region rich in birds, fish, and thirty-nine species of animals, including moose, caribou, beaver, muskrat, and lynx. As well, the coastal waters are an internationally renowned resting and breeding ground for millions of migratory birds. The Cree were promised in their final settlement that any further development would include an environmental review process, and they are now determined to see the Quebec government honour this commitment. They now have first-hand knowledge of the destruction that massive projects of this kind can wreak on the land and its inhabitants.

Some rivers have been reduced to creeks as a result of phase I of James Bay; others have become flooded, destroying vegetation, eliminating breeding grounds for waterfowl, and submerging vast tracts of forest. Spawning grounds have been destroyed, and the temperatures of water systems are being altered, creating fresh-water lakes, which don't freeze even in winter, where none existed before. "Normally, rivers run highest during the spring melt; levels are lowest in winter. The James Bay development will reverse this natural pattern," says journalist Peter Gorrie. The long-term impact is not known; but, scientists warn it could be catastrophic.

The Audubon Society warns that millions of migratory birds are endangered by these changes in temperature and salinity. Many species are severely threatened, possibly even to extinction. If ice patterns are affected, it says, beluga whales, a staple of the diet of the northern Cree, could be at risk. As well, the group fears that a rare population of fresh-water seals whose presence in the Quebec north has long puzzled scientists could be threatened. And a Vermont commission studying the effects of the project was told by two American energy specialists that the damming of rivers in northern Quebec contributes directly to global warming. Deforestation is another possible result: to open an area this big, the province will have to cut down 12 to 18 million cubic metres of marketable trees, most of which will be exported. Says Brian Craik, a consultant to the Cree, "The environment would be subsidizing not only the sale of hydro but also lumber to the United States."

Of one terrible consequence, there can be no doubt. Flooding of La Grande River in the first phase of the project dissolved large quantities of naturally occurring mercury in the water, contaminated fish, and put the native people of James Bay at grave risk. A 1984 survey of Cree in one village found that 64 percent of the villagers had unsafe levels of mercury in their bodies. A Hydro-Québec study of the problem could only lamely suggest that the Indian people stop eating the tainted fish. One Cree elder scoffs at government enthusiasm over the "clean power" that this project generates. It may be clean for the Americans who buy it, he says, and it may be clean for the sellers in Montreal; but it leaves an awful mess of human and wilderness destruction behind. He warns Canadians that the consequences of this development will not stay in the North, but will affect us all one day.

The Quebec government appears to be willing to sustain whatever the long-term consequences, to satisfy growing markets in the United States and its economic independence. It is not alone. British Columbia is planning to build the third massive dam on the Peace River, a multibillion-dollar project that will necessitate the flooding of a magnificent valley, home to eighty farm families and a rich abundance of wildlife. The province has already negotiated access to U.S. transmission lines, and the site will be used to export up to three decades' worth of power to the United States. The federal government, in yielding its powers to regulate these projects, is forfeiting the right of the Canadian people to protect and preserve the wilderness.

Hydro-electricity is only one of the benefits of Canada's northern rivers that appeal to resource-anxious Americans. Canada is seen as having unlimited supplies of the most important natural gift of all — water. Demand for water in the United States has been growing rapidly since the 1950s. In the last thirty years, total water withdrawals grew at a rate 66 percent greater than the population. In some states, water is "mined," withdrawn at rates faster than it can be replenished. A presidential task force predicted that one-fifth of the United States will face a chronic water shortage by the year 2000, when obtaining adequate water will become critical to Americans. Simon Reisman has said that U.S. politicians, including former U.S. trade representative Clayton Yeutter and former Speaker of the House of Representatives James Wright, are desperate for our water. Corporate interests have long been planning for its diversion. Statements by U.S. politicians have ranged from polite requests to outright threats.

In 1971, a resource adviser to president Nixon, Henry Gablinger, said that the fresh-water situation would be so serious by the end of the century, that the United States would have to "take over Canada, through either economic pressure or force." In 1980, at the eighth annual conference of New England governors and premiers of eastern Canada, Governor Richard Snelling of Vermont proposed that U.S. utilities provide 100 percent of the financing for new hydro-electric projects in Canada that could export power. He suggested that an international commission be established to oversee the use of Canada's water and power resources.

Over the past twenty years, there have been nine multibillion-dollar proposals to divert Canadian water to the United States. U.S. Senator Moss called for major western Canadian river diversions to the United States during the 1988 drought, and in the same year, thirteen American senators and the governor of Illinois called for the diversion of water from the Great Lakes to supplement the flow of the Mississippi River.

Months before the Canadian election, Congressman Fred Grandy, an Iowa Republican and a member of the Agriculture Committee of the U.S. Congress, was questioned on the Cable News Network about the U.S. drought and whether it was connected to the greenhouse effect. He said, "I think one of the reasons the United States wants to negotiate a Free Trade Agreement with Canada is because Canada has the water resources that this country is eventually going to need. And the marriage of these two nations is to take a resource-rich country like Canada and merge it with a capital- rich country like America, and that I think is something we are looking at down the line."

Such sentiments, while not widely reported in Canada, have met with a great deal of interest from some members of Canada's business community. Large-scale water diversions are not new. Canada diverts more water, mostly for hydro-electric projects, than any other nation on earth, with more than six hundred dams and sixty large domestic interbasin diversions. But, until recently, very few political or corporate leaders in Canada would discuss exports of this resource. In 1985, the leading U.S. business magazine *Fortune* published an article based on an interview with Prime Minister Mulroney that claimed he was enthusiastic about water sales: "Mulroney is so ready for the leap that he is prepared to sell some of his country's abundant fresh water — a shocking thought in Canada, and one most previous Canadian political leaders wouldn't have entertained for a moment. . . . But Mulroney seems to invite offers. If a proposition makes economic sense and would help relations between the countries, he says 'Why not?' "

It is not surprising that Mulroney was the politician to speak the unspeakable. His definition of "helping relations" between Canada and the United States is removing barriers to the flow of whatever "goods" U.S. corporate interests want.

The most ambitious water diversion scheme is called the GRAND Canal and would involve the unprecedented transfer of water between watersheds and from one oceanic basin to another. Developed by engineer Tom Kierans, the Great Recycling and Northern Development Canal scheme called for the construction of a dike between Hudson Bay and James Bay that would transform the latter into a fresh-water lake. The flow of many rivers would be diverted into canals, dams, power plants, and locks, to deliver this recycled water to the United States. The $100-billion plan would siphon off Canadian waters and send them to the thirsty American Southwest at the rate of 62,000 gallons a second. Its backers, not surprisingly, were a number of powerful companies, including Bechtel, the U.S.-based engineering giant that actively supported the pro–free trade Canadian Alliance for Trade and Job Opportunities.

Robert Bourassa endorsed the plan: "Water is a good like any other, and can be bought and sold. . . . There is little doubt that Quebec and Canada, to their great benefit, could be a source of water for North America for years to come." Simon Reisman, who had a financial stake in the GRAND scheme, said that water "could provide the key to a free trade agreement with the United States. . . . I have personally suggested these ideas to leaders in government and business on both sides of the border, and I have been greatly heartened by the initial response."

By the time of the election, however, the Canadian government, in spite of the evidence of intense interest in water sales to the United States, vehemently denied that water was a part of the trade deal or was more vulnerable because of it. But many experts, including the influential Rawson Academy of Aquatic Science, believe that the agreement includes all natural water and substantially reduces Canada's freedom to meet its own water needs. Even those who dispute this interpretation, however, agree that the free-trade deal would force Canada to continue to supply this resource if we did start exporting it to the United States in large quantities. Moreover, the continental economic planning that drives this government will make North American water planning increasingly likely.

The consequences for our environment and our sovereignty are profound. The water-diversion schemes would require a massive reversal of the natural direction of Canada's water flow. The only major early environmental assessment of the GRAND Canal darkly warns of the "irreversible detrimental changes" that could result from a project involving massive flooding and climate changes.

If this project were ever implemented, it would establish a lifeline to the American Southwest from Canada's heartland. Irrespective of any environmental damage, under the free-trade agreement, major water exports would be impossible to turn off once American businesses and consumers became dependent on them.

While public talk of large-scale water diversion has died down in the last several years, met by a solid wall of protest from the Canadian public, many water experts believe that the resolute manner in which Quebec is forging ahead with the James Bay project is an indication that Mr. Bourassa still dreams of the GRAND Canal, with its promise of financial independence for the province, and its future construction fits very well into long-term plans for Quebec's north.

Quebec is not alone. Some opponents of the Rafferty-Alameda dam project in Saskatchewan believe it is a water-diversion scheme in disguise. They charge that this mega-project, along with the Oldman River dam under construction in Alberta, fits in with a long-standing U.S. corporate plan to divert the Peace and Athabaska rivers to the Missouri River in the United States. American proponents of the Rafferty-Alameda testified before the Saskatchewan enquiry; North Dakota senator Quentin Burdick is on record calling for the dam to be built on the Canadian side, so that the financial and environmental costs to the United States would be substantially reduced.

Richard Bocking, in his disturbing book *Canada's Water: For Sale?*, said that, if we convert our great rivers into engineered canals, we will destroy the country as we know it: "Its diversity and beauty and promise will have been submerged by the dams and diversions that have resulted from an attitude that is alien to Canadians. Without her great wild rivers and magnificent silent lakes, there will be much less reason for an independent Canada to exist, and probably much less will to keep it so on the part of her people."

The wanton exploitation of Canada's resources, to feed North American appetites, could spell devastation for Canada's aboriginal people. Say the Dene of the Northwest Territories, "Somehow the North always seems to be on the receiving end of everyone else's garbage." Referring to the Alberta forest projects, the group points out that the concerns of native people living in the area seem irrelevant. "We have Toxaphene in our fish, radiation in our caribou. Bureaucrats come to us and tell us not to worry about it. They say we don't eat enough country food for the chemicals to affect us. They say the reports of toxics in the ecosystem are exaggerated. They tell us that they are good people and they don't want to pollute our environment. Mostly they don't even want to listen to our concerns, let alone believe them." Says Cree leader Coon-Come, "We are being asked to accept the end of our way of life, the destruction of our land, the extinction of our rivers. Why? To export electricity to the Americans."

The government's course of free trade, deregulation, cut-backs to social programs, and massive resource exports could be on a collision course with the well-being and self-government of aboriginal people. Future land claims may well be subject to energy deals and weapons-testing arrangements Canada has made with the United States. The National Energy Board approved the Mackenzie gas exports with a curt dismissal of the relevance of land-claim concerns of the native groups involved. In the free-trade agreement, the government has a powerful new tool to use against native access to land, resources, preferential treatment in hiring, and independence.

Constitutional lawyer Tony Hall says that we are harmonizing the treatment of Canadian aboriginal people with the U.S. system by diminishing the federal role in protecting land treaties. In its 1990 budget, the Mulroney government viciously punished native groups that have been critical of it and cut operating grants completely to the most important group, the Assembly of First Nations. In a further assault on the democratic process, Mulroney's Conservatives have attacked the communication lifeline of the aboriginal movement for self-reliance by cutting $1.6 million in grants to native communications systems.

The tragedy of moving backward in this fight does not solely affect the native people themselves. Other Canadians have much to learn about living in harmony with our environment and would do well to listen to Canada's first people. Joe Bearskin of Fort George describes his origins simply: "I have come from what I have survived on." When we tamper with nature, we all pay the price.

The Mulroney government, in its haste to make a deal with the corporate power élite of North America, sold out the birthright of every Canadian. Unquestionably, our own environmental legacy is unacceptable: we have permitted intolerable levels of pollution of our lakes, land, and air. And in a number of areas, the United States has superior environmental regulation. But the new philosophy, entrenched in the free-trade agreement and driven by corporate control, dramatically limits our ability to alter our ways. And it places a downward pressure on regulators on both sides of the border to seek the lowest common standards.

We have agreed, for instance, to harmonize our standards to those of the United States in a whole host of agricultural areas, including the registration and use of pesticides. Only in recent years have scientists started to understand the cumulative damage to our environment and to the productive capacity of agricultural lands that pesticides pose. Since 1945, 35,000 different pesticide formulations have entered the global market. Pesticide use has risen to more than four billion pounds used world-wide every year — almost one pound for every person on earth. According to Greenpeace, "the pesticide revolution, rather than improving living conditions in the world, is making them worse." The World Health Organization estimates that 500,000 to 1 million people are injured by pesticides annually; 5,000 to 10,000 of these people die. The United States has an abysmal record under its pesticide-control law. A U.S. congressional study found that the vast majority of pesticides on the market in that country have not been adequately tested for their propensity to cause cancer, genetic damage, or birth defects.

Furthermore, weak as the laws are for the sale of pesticides in the United States, American manufacturers are allowed to export pesticides that are unregistered, banned, or severely restricted in the United States. Many international chemical companies locate their factories in developing countries, where costs are lower and environmental and safety regulations are few. Free trade provides a safe passage for unsafe goods to be manufactured in the United States and sold internationally.

Pesticide use in Canada has grown in recent years, as in other countries; but successive Canadian governments have developed a very different set of standards for pesticide certification. Our emphasis is put on the safety of the product; in the United States, the legislation requires a balancing of the risks of the product with the benefit it might create. For example, in spite of the fact that the U.S. Environmental Protection Agency has identified sixty-six cancer-causing pesticides currently in use on food, it recently announced that it was adopting a "negligible risk" policy to set "acceptable" levels of these carcinogens. The policy is a victory for the American pesticide industry as it ensures that economic considerations will be protected in defining safety standards.

In the United States there are 20 percent more active pesticide ingredients registered for use and more than seven times as many pesticide products as there are in Canada. For example, the cancer-causing herbicide alachlor is banned in Canada but licensed in the United States. The differences between the Canadian and American approaches were important, but they are about to change. The Tory government has established a pesticide-review committee; one of its mandates is to harmonize our pesticide-control system to conform with that of the United States as Canada is obliged to do under the free-trade agreement. As well, the two countries have established technical working groups in the agriculture sector to oversee the process. One of the mandates of the pesticide team is to "identify tolerance differences seen as trade irritants." Simply put, the American chemical industry doesn't want to bump into higher pesticide standards at the Canadian border, and we are going to make sure they are not inconvenienced.

The Americans know that the smaller country will conform to the larger, and the U.S. committee has been very slow to organize. It is in no hurry, as they know no changes will be required of the U.S. side. In spite of the obvious environmental consequences to Canada of harmonizing to the inferior standards of the United States, no environmental representatives were asked to sit on either the technical teams or the Agriculture Advisory Committee. However, the food industry is well represented, and Cargill, the international farm and chemical giant that was such a key player in writing the agriculture sector of the free trade deal, continues to be a prominent member of the negotiations. As in the United States, market values, determined by the interests of the chemical industry, will soon dictate the standards of potentially dangerous substances in Canada.

But what happens in an area where Canada has much lower standards than the United States? Take the disposal of toxic and nuclear waste. The United States produces a great deal of the world's toxic waste. When it wants to dispose of it, the United States looks north. Four-fifths of all the toxic waste it dumps ends up Canada. In recent years, applications by American firms wishing to dispose of waste in Canada have increased tenfold. The hard granite of the Canadian Shield is currently being studied for its suitability for the disposal of nuclear wastes. American firms are also interested in the incineration of wastes in Canadian maritime waters. Quebec, in particular, has been inundated with shipments of hazardous garbage, including soiled diapers, bandages, sanitary napkins, and liquid and medical waste, illegally dumped, usually at night, in landfill sites or farm fields.

The government's policies of free trade and deregulation exacerbate this dangerous situation in two ways. First, keeping or making our standards lower are seen as a profit incentive by many Canadian businesses. The Quebec vice-president of the Canadian Manufacturers' Association, Richard Le Hir, says that Canada should open its borders to American hazardous waste. Both he and former federal environment minister Lucien Bouchard have cited the economic benefits to Canada of waste dumping. Canada is using its willingness to take the environmental rap as a lure for new business. The same sentiments are heard in hearings on James Bay II. Hydro-Québec makes its sales pitch to the United States based on "avoided costs" — that is, the savings to American consumers if Canada builds the nuclear plants or burns the coal.

Second, the free-trade agreement will work to the advantage of corporate-driven governments on both sides of the border. New Canadian initiatives to clean up the environment will have to satisfy American as well as Canadian business interests. Corporations in both countries, aided by their governments, are striving for the lowest common denominator in setting environmental standards; and attempts to establish controls are seen as a trade irritant.

For example, attempts in Washington to place some standards on the disposal of American toxic-waste exports in Canada are being fought by the Canadian industry. The proposed legislation would be a progressive move for the United States to make. The American government has set tough new waste disposal standards for the country (which is why so much is dumped in Canada), and some Americans believe that to export to countries with lower standards would be environmentally irresponsible.

Tricil of Sarnia disposes between 80 percent and 90 percent of all U.S. toxic wastes dumped in Canada; the company has hired a Washington lobbyist to fight the bill in Congress. Canadian ambassador Derek Burney sides with Tricil. He is asking the U.S. government to make an "exemption" for its special trading partner, Canada. He says that if Canada does not get an exemption, it will consider this an "infringement on Canadian sovereignty." An exemption, of course, would lead to more toxic-waste dumping in Canada.

Similarly, when a U.S. senator tried to establish the same tough standards for Canadian electricity imports that are produced by dirty coal-fired power plants as have just been passed for American electricity plants, Burney argued against the proposed legislation. He said that such a move would run counter to the "open border objective of the Canada–United States free-trade agreement regarding trade in energy."

It can come as no surprise, then, that American corporate lobbies are using the free-trade agreement to force the Canadian government to end industrial environmental subsidies. The powerful non-ferrous metals industry in the United States is urging the American trade office to launch an action against Canada because the Canadian government assists its industry with plant-modernization grants for environmental protection. The association has met with some early success in Washington, and it is very likely that stepped-up monitoring by the Americans will lead to countervail duties on Canadian metal exports to the United States or to the increased involvement by the U.S. industry in setting Canadian environmental standards. The U.S. non-ferrous metals industry believes that employee "sacrifices," in the form of lower pay, should subsidize environmental regulation. And, not surprisingly, it has some very definite ideas about what those standards should be and who should set them.

President Bush recently publicly warned against costly economic solutions to global warming: "Wherever possible, we believe that market mechanisms should be applied — and that our policies must be consistent with economic growth and free market principles in all countries." He has failed to commit his government to international measures for reduction of carbon-dioxide emissions. Such thinking resonates into Canadian corporate and political circles. The oil companies in Canada say that calls for cleaner-burning gasoline would seriously jeopardize the industry's ability to do business. Said Claude Brouillard of the Canadian Petroleum Association, "We don't have the smog problems [of California] . . . for the most part we don't have a problem."

Industry in Canada recognizes the inevitable collision between deregulation and environmental damage and is jumping to offer market-based solutions. Thomas d'Aquino, BCNI president, says business must pre-empt government before government is forced to take action. Industry would like to set the terms of this debate rather than have it open to some public process it cannot control. One industry leader in the United States calls for tradeable pollution permits for industry. The CEO of Canadian Forest Products urges politicians to be wary of "emotional, often orchestrated, highly organized, anti-everything movements" that he says characterize environmental groups. And the Fraser Institute, an influential right-wing Canadian think-tank, says that the only way to save the environment is to sell it — lakes, forests, oceans, and all — to private corporations. "Most people have this notion that the ocean is the heritage of all mankind," scoffs Walter Block, a director of the institute. He labels anyone who has such thoughts as a "pinko-greeno," "radical tree-hugger," or "naive."

This statement would be dismissable if it were not finding such a receptive ear in influential media and government circles. The *Globe and Mail*'s Terence Corcoran welcomed the departure of Lucien Bouchard as environment minister because of his potential for "interventionist" environmental policies. He says that Block's analysis, in his new book, *Economics and the Environment: A Reconciliation*, is a "solid launching pad," a "manifesto" to be read by all Canadians. The environment, he informs us, is simply part of the economy and the faster we all understand that, the sooner we'll establish "market-oriented economic solutions" to environmental problems. Terence Corcoran is the intellectual embodiment of free trade. It is little wonder that most environmental news reported by the *Globe and Mail* is found in the business section.

This thinking is not lost on the government. The Mulroney government has a deplorable environmental record. The federal budget for conservation and renewable-energy programs will have fallen by 93 percent between 1984 and 1993. Five hundred jobs have been slashed from Environment Canada, and in the 1989 budget, $10 million was cut from the department's alternative-energy research program; the 1990 budget slashed another 20 percent off the funds from the environmental assessment office. In October 1989, the government abruptly cancelled a major international government/university clean-up project of the Great Lakes. (The International Joint Commission's 1990 report on the Great Lakes was highly critical of the lack of progress by both Canada and the United States.) As well, the federal parks service had its 1990 budget decreased, just as some provinces, like Saskatchewan, have cut expenditures by privatizing their parks.

Paralysed by the financial deals it made with the corporate sector, the Mulroney government increased defence spending by $1 billion during the last six years; during the same time period, the environment budget fell by a million dollars. In 1989, the defence budget was fourteen times larger than that of environment. These numbers exactly mirror the proportions in the United States during the same years.

A recent memo was leaked to a member of Parliament by a twenty-year veteran of the federal Department of Oceans and Fisheries in British Columbia. It detailed how the department was giving immunity to large corporate polluters while harassing "little" guys. The big companies, said O.E. Langer, were permitted to discharge toxic effluent "and not be in fear of prosecution," even when the company had not been complying with regulations for years. "Alcan and their contractors, without any approvals, largely destroyed a salmon stream at Kemano. Due to our 'special relationship' with Alcan, it has been determined that the violation will probably not be prosecuted." Langer said that the continuation of this unfair policy "will result in a wholesale loss of fish habitat and a continued degradation of water quality."

Crab fisherman Bruce Adams fished for years in Howe Sound, British Columbia, "the best, most beautiful crabs, and I mean anywhere." But because of poisons in the water, Howe Sound and eight other shell-fishing zones have been closed, and the fishermen are now crowding into a smaller number of non-contaminated areas. "Adams's livelihood literally went out with the tide," says journalist Alan Hardy. The men and women working the shore have known for years about the conditions described in the fisheries memo. The pulp mills and smelters control their own standards, they say, and if you have friends in high places, you can get away with murder. Says the head of the B.C. Wildlife Federation, "Because of this, we are looking at the imminent death of the Strait of Georgia."

Yet, former fisheries minister Tom Siddon rejected a call for a review. Instead, he called in the RCMP — not to charge the polluters or to investigate why they hadn't been charged. The Mounties' job was to find out who leaked the memo.

The environmental agenda in Canada today is set by a handful of power-brokers who have sold out their country's environmental heritage for private profit. Alcan the favoured gave $250,000 to the pro–free trade alliance — a small price to pay for Tory friendship — thus indeed winning for itself a "special" place in the history of Canada's fight for clean air and water.

# 8.
# THE CHOICE

"Cultures, like families, teach their children by the examples of their actions, not by their declarations of intentions. Never before have young Canadians had so many public role models demonstrating so clearly that great profit and applause accrue to those well practised in the ancient arts of theft and brutality."

*Kevin McMahon*

THE MULRONEY GOVERNMENT HAS EMBARKED ON A social and economic agenda that becomes more difficult to alter with each passing day. Corporate political control has grown so strong that public policy is in its thrall. The fallout is apparent already: growing social anger, alienation, and intolerance. There is a gnawing suspicion that there isn't enough money to go around; there aren't enough jobs for everyone. Out of that suspicion grows the attitude that rights are scarce and finite — rights given to one group must somehow be taken from another. The English resent the French; men resent women; everyone seems to resent visible minorities.

Compassion and tolerance are being sorely tested in Canada as our society daily grows to resemble America's: a survivor's society — weakest to the wall; the fittest on top. Our belief in linguistic and regional equality is being submerged. We speak uncaringly about Canada's survival. "Let Quebec go," say too many non-Quebeckers, sounding, for all the world, like a weary spouse in a marriage depleted of passion, empty even of anger. The provinces grab what they can. "Stay out of our business," they tell the federal government and each other.

This government has disenfranchised whole groups of Canadians. Democracy itself is threatened when the government shuts down the voice of dissent within national and regional groups struggling to speak for native rights, women's equality, or environmental responsibility. Those who criticize it are punished in a swift and brutal way. This is the government that sends task forces across the country to discuss its regressive policies, such as the GST, warning that it will not change a word of the policy regardless of their findings and insulting its critics. Yet, as it closes down dissent, it spends millions of dollars of our money to tell us that these policies are good for us.

Democracy in Canada is fragile. This government, backed by the most powerful alliance of foreign and domestic corporations that has ever existed in Canada, has, in effect, declared war on democracy, and has served notice that if you are not a part of the élite of Canada, you are not welcome at the feast.

Canadians could learn a lesson from the great democratic experiment to the south of us. America is in decline, not because of the Pacific Rim or an emerging Europe, but because, in its ideological pursuit of world dominance, it directed its wealth and resources into the biggest arms build-up in the history of the world, submerging social concerns to this overarching goal. The dream of equality died on the streets of Harlem and the back alleys of Los Angeles. American democracy lost its central goal, that the dream must be for everyone. A society that has given up the quest for social justice has lost its way. A country that has abandoned its weakest members is no longer a vibrant democracy. When the Donald Trumps speak of freedom, it is of freedom *from* democracy.

Is this what Canadians want? It has become fashionable to decry the nation-state and to submit to the inevitability of the global transformation of the economy: none of this is our fault, we say, nor can we do anything about it. The "market" is hard, but fair, and it disciplines as it needs to. Perhaps the first question Canadians must ask is: If the global economy is moving inexorably to one system, why should Canada, or any other country, for that matter, exist?

The single most powerful argument for nationhood is democracy itself. In a world without nations or borders, there is, as yet, no democratic way to force transnational corporations to abide by any standards. It is through the formation of democracies that people determine standards of living, access to the resources and wealth of a country, and the conditions under which business will be conducted. A nation is made up of the history, customs, traditions, and laws of the families and communities who live in it and is more than an economic unit. To surrender that history and that common heritage to economic forces is to define Canada only in terms of the bottom line, the corporate vision.

For Canadians who have a wider and deeper vision, the urgent matter is to wrest Canada back, while there is still time. Democratic institutions must have the power to legislate on behalf of their populations. For Canadians to play the role on the world stage that is essential to nationhood, we must ensure that we are managing a fully functional democracy.

Such assurance cannot be had until we curb the anti-democratic, lop-sided power that multinational corporations, foreign and domestic, have come to have on the politicians of Canada and the decisions they make that affect our lives. The influence they exert is symptomatic of the deeper, more pervasive problems we face that will require fundamental restructuring. The first thing we must do is reform our electoral system to reinstitute the processes of democracy. Politics in Canada has become a rich person's game. Those without access to money have almost no way of reaching positions of political power. There are few rules governing the choice of candidates or leaders for political parties, and abuses of all kinds, especially financial ones, abound.

The amount of money permitted in the leadership contests of the Liberal and Conservative parties gives an unfair advantage to wealthy candidates, and forces those who are not personally wealthy to seek sponsorship. By and large, corporations are the only sources with sufficient financial clout to fund a leadership, so the candidates become beholden to these sponsors. The candidates then are likely to conform to the political views of these interests, and it is very difficult for them to take political positions not approved by big business. Big money can also buy party memberships and people to attend meetings. To prevent such abuses, leadership contests should come under the control of the Canada Elections Act. Ceilings should be put on the expenditures, and full disclosure of contributions should be made mandatory.

The corporate agenda will dominate our policies until we curtail other financial abuses of the election process as well. The 1988 federal election demonstrated conclusively that uncontrolled activities by third parties are a clear and present negation of Canadian social values and the democratic process. They defeat the purpose of election rules, which impose spending limits and disclosure of donations to candidates and parties, but permit interest groups to spend unlimited amounts of money to support partisan positions. If big-business interests are free to spend, money will flow to and through them in order to circumvent the rules. Direct collusion is created between politicians and these third-party lobbies.

Limits are needed on third-party spending and advertising during a campaign, and contributions to political parties and candidates should be restricted to individuals. Openly partisan financial contributions should not be deductible as business expenses. During the 1988 election, the corporate members wrote off their contributions to the Alliance for Trade and Job Opportunities as a business expense, thereby saddling the Canadian tax-payer with the bill for the self-serving activities of its members. The amount was in the millions. The financial clout of these corporations, much of it routed through Canadian subsidiaries of American parent companies, bought the election and imposed a corporate agenda on Canada.

But, perhaps the most pressing need is to attack the Canadian electoral system itself, which now consistently fails to return governments that reflect the democratic will of the population as a whole. In 1988, the majority of Canadians voted for parties clearly opposing the free-trade agreement. But the country was obliged to accept the deal, as, under the existing system, the Tories had won the right to impose it, even without majority approval. The election of members of Parliament on the basis of pluralities in single-member constituencies was appropriate in the two-party system of the nineteenth century. With a third party firmly established for some sixty years, it has been clear in a number of elections that split votes have had marked effects on the outcome in many cases. Moreover, within regions, the absence of representation in Ottawa of substantial interests has led to serious regional polarization, expressed in a sense of alienation from the power centre.

Canada remains one of the few parliamentary democracies that has not moved to a form of proportional voting. It is true that proportional voting carried to an extreme can lead to paralysis, as it has in Israel over the past few years. But proportional voting could introduce a very helpful element in the governance of a difficult state. A good model for Canada to consider is West Germany, which has had successes in government over the past several decades. The difficulty in bringing about an improvement in our electoral system will be in the reluctance of elected politicians to make any change from the process by which they were themselves elected. It would be a shame if Canada had to wait for a crisis before deciding to reform a system evidently flawed.

The next major task towards restoring democracy in Canada is to remove the single most important tool used to impose this flawed system on Canadians. As long as the Canada–U.S. Free Trade Agreement is in effect, no future government will be able to determine the fate of this country. As one Conservative politician and economist after another has maintained, the real force of this deal is to lock future generations of Canadians into the economic strait-jacket of the deregulated, privately controlled market-place. Self-serving corporate interests have nearly destroyed the way of life Canadians have built up over many years and are now dictating our future.

Opposition politicians who try to protect their "alternative" vision without openly discussing the shackles the agreement places on their ability to put that vision into practice either don't understand the deal or are prevented from criticizing it by their own close ties to the corporate élite of this country. There can be no realistic talk of renegotiating or "fixing" the free-trade agreement when we have no bargaining position left. The reality of free trade is that, for example, it has removed the ability of this or any future government to implement a national day-care program, create a strong federal environmental-protection policy, or build home-grown Canadian industry to serve Canadian needs.

To the fair question "Won't we be too far in to back out?" the answer depends on our collective will to survive as a country. There will be difficulties, and probably retaliation, if Canada abrogates the free-trade agreement. The alternative, however, is the slow decline of Canada as a sovereign nation. The price of abrogation may seem high in the short run. The price of remaining on this course will be infinitely higher.

Canadians outside of Quebec have much to learn from the way the province responded to the exodus of anglophone corporations in the early 1980s. Many predicted economic devastation for Quebec. In spite of, or perhaps because of, the hardship this exodus created, Quebeckers themselves worked together to forge a powerful domestic industry that, ironically, forms the basis of the new financial confidence young Quebeckers have in their province.

The argument put forward by boosters of free trade is that it will provide the economic prosperity to maintain our standard of living. To date the agreement has not brought prosperity to any but a handful of wealthy corporate leaders. Give us an alternative, they challenge. There are ways for Canadians to prosper and maintain our sovereignty.

First, Canada must regain control of its economy and stop selling off our resources, remaining enterprises, and Crown corporations in the name of deficit reduction. No nation can sell off the ownership and control of its key resources and remain competitive in the modern world. It is like the homeowner who sells the house to get rid of the mortgage. We are selling our house, the roof over our heads, the energy in the ground, the land we stand on.

Understandably, American and other foreign-controlled parent companies make decisions about their Canadian subsidiaries based on what is good for head office. It is economically irresponsible to ship billions of dollars out of the country every year as dividends, interest payments, and licence and management fees to these transnationals. Canada needs an investment policy based on an understanding of the distinction between investment and foreign control. The current threshold of review under the free-trade deal of $150 million is senseless. It is the small- and medium-sized businesses in Canada that create the jobs. To allow them to be picked off, one by one, as they become viable is economic suicide.

As political scientist Stephen Clarkson has noted, in order to get better access to the American market, Canada has given up the very policies needed to help us successfully compete there. Our continued reliance on non-renewable resources and the lack of sufficient research and development in Canada are both long-recognized, deep-seated barriers to a healthy, diversified economy. Canada needs to regain the tools to ensure that business operating in this country gives something back to it. An industrial strategy, long debated, but never really tried in this country, could include requirements regarding employment and research, and would allow Canadian governments to give preference to domestic firms over foreign ones. All successful economies emerging in Asia, for example, have established an industrial strategy. Economist Mel Watkins explains: "Governments in successful economies don't just sit by idly watching the market spew out losers; they help create winners." There is simply no way that Canada can regain economic sovereignty and stability while it does not have the means to favour the growth of home-grown, technologically advanced industry.

To achieve this independence, there are many creative options open to us. The tax system could provide incentives for companies that manufacture Canadian products and that reinvest profits in Canada. We could require that a certain percentage of all research and development be done in Canada and that, in lieu of this requirement, companies could pay a special tax to help build a science and high-tech base in Canada. We could ensure minimum levels of domestic processing to create and expand employment. We have to create a climate favourable to Canadians buying and creating businesses, and successfully operating them. Otherwise, many Canadian companies are going to find themselves in a life-and-death struggle against international giants and will have no option but to sell.

Western business leader Bill Loewen says that Canadians have never been afraid to invest but have been encouraged to disinvest. Canadian banks lend great amounts of money to American companies to buy Canadian resources. The claim that Canada continues to need foreign investment is a false one in that our savings rate has always been higher than that in the United States. Our own money should be building a Canadian business infrastructure. Again there is a lesson for non-Quebeckers in Quebec's nationalist pension fund, Caisse de dépôt et placement du Québec, which has become a major player in the economic life of the province. This strategy of using pension funds to form a partnership between business and government to protect the interests of Quebeckers has great potential as a role model. But in the 1990 budget, Michael Wilson increased the portion of pension funds that may be invested outside Canada. This is a backward step.

Some forward-thinking observers are calling for a national employee and stock savings plan, modelled on the Caisse. Companies eligible for the plan would be required to have a Canadian head office. Such a plan could provide the backbone for a needed "national policy" to encourage Canadians to invest in their own country, and could include encouraging employee ownership participation in their company of employment. We badly need strategies for democratizing access to wealth creation, as the concentration of capital and the resulting poverty continues to grow. A strong country requires an economic system that is widely supported and fairly distributed. The current corporate "spin" that defends unemployment and large income gaps as a necessary consequence of a healthy economy is a cavalier and wrong-headed notion. Social justice is good business.

Above all, Canada must reorder its priorities. Jim Laxer writes: "Economic policy should give expression to the social goals of Canadians; and trade policy should be an aspect of economic policy. With the free trade deal, this has all been reversed so that economic and social policy have become adjuncts to a trade agreement." The corporate élite who dictate public policy now, and who are deeply influencing educators all over Canada, say that we must sacrifice social goals on the altar of competitiveness. Living under the constant threat that these companies will move elsewhere, governments in Canada are held captive to their agenda, and are asking Canadians to accept higher taxes, a lower standard of living, lower wages, and reduced input into public policy. This is the corporate meaning of globalization, and why corporate leaders belittle nationalists as being regressive and old-fashioned, when they continue to talk about the quaint notion of democracy.

Neil Brooks and Linda McQuaig wrote in *This Magazine* a brilliant challenge for tax reform in Canada based on the principles of democracy and progressivity, as an alternative to the Conservative system that so strongly favours the rich. They would abolish the existing sales tax and raise revenues through a combination of income, corporate, and wealth taxes. Broaden the tax base by eliminating many tax breaks, they suggest, such as the business entertainment deduction, the capital-gains exemption, and the special treatment accorded real-estate developers. Eliminate tax breaks for corporate mergers and acquisitions, and tighten the rules for multinationals. For example, among many other transfer-payment devices, these companies have long gouged the Canadian taxpayer by borrowing money in Canada to finance overseas subsidiaries and then deducting the cost of interest from their Canadian income.

Restoring the progressive rate structure to the income-tax system, they add, could ease the concern of many that we need to target our income support to those in need rather than the principle of universality. Place a tax on inheritance, which one economist says has cost Canada $12 billion since it was abolished in 1971, and clamp down on the business friends of the government that don't get audited like they used to. Finally, they say, raise corporate taxes so that the big companies are paying their fair share. Their proposed changes would generate more than $13 billion a year.

Another device, not mentioned as part of this proposal, would be to increase the withholding tax on corporate dividends leaving the country. This would require amendment of the U.S./Canada Tax Agreement, one Canada is unlikely to get.

The most significant factor about these alternatives is that they put to rest the Tory refrain that there are only two options to the deficit: the GST or lowered social spending. So persistently has the government put this message out, and used so much of our money to do it, that many Canadians have stopped asking if there are other options. There are clear alternatives, but they are not those advocated by the multinationals. Canadians can have a decent standard of living, good social programs, and economic independence.

Canadians must once again assert our fundamental belief in universal social programs. Perhaps more than any other aspect of Canadian society except Canada's bilingual nature, our core belief in the justice of distributing our resources in this way differentiates us from U.S. society. And universal social programs strengthen national identity. To weaken them is to further weaken the country.

Many Canadians depend on these programs but, because women still carry the major responsibility for child-rearing and live to an older age, they are more in need of them. One crucial program remains to be established, however, before equality for women can be attained in Canada.

The lack of adequate child care in Canada makes a mockery of the recent gains women have made in securing legal rights. It is impossible to take advantage of newly opened doors when women have no access to decent care for their children. The government says that it cannot afford to provide child care for working families, yet it continues to permit its corporate friends to pay no taxes, and gives its foreign corporate friends millions of dollars to take Canadian companies off our hands. Canadian women have been sacrificed to make this agenda work, and the hard-won gains of the last twenty years could be lost in an orgy of budget cuts, slashed funding to women's centres, and a reversal of the commitment to fight violence against women. Women are poorer than men, and are more dependent on a strong and committed national system to safeguard their entitlements, but Brian Mulroney's new Canada is being built on the ruin of women's equality. Any economic reforms put forward must incorporate a commitment to this principle.

As well, Canada must commit to a long-term goal of self-government for aboriginal peoples. Their cycle of poverty and dependence will not be broken until native Canadians are making decisions for themselves. They have been locked out of the halls of power for too long and their time has come. Canada cannot speak with authority in the international arena of human rights until its own house is put in order.

Another fundamental principle for our future is our responsibility for, our stewardship over, the abundant resources Canada has been given. Our role is twofold: to use these resources carefully so that they will be there for future generations of Canadians, and to preserve a Canadian wilderness for all time.This means that we must develop these resources in a far more responsible way than we have in the past.

First, we must reassert a strong Canadian presence in the resource sector, particularly energy, and halt the sharp decline in Canadian control over our resources. Countless studies have shown that foreign-based energy companies do little research in Canada and are not committed to processing their product before it leaves the country. The profits from these energy sources should be staying in Canadian hands, to create jobs here and to advance the environmental technology needed to fight global warming. Giving up control of our primary resources is tantamount to national surrender. Economic recovery depends on the wise use of these key resources.

Second, we need to reassert Canadian public control over the conditions under which companies develop these resources. The National Energy Board must have the powers restored that were taken away in the implementation of the free-trade agreement so that it may act as guardian to ensure an adequate supply of energy for Canadian needs. We should legislate to ensure that access to resources is contingent on the developer creating local jobs (including native employment for northern projects), undertaking research, and buying supplies from Canadian suppliers.

Our use of these resources must be measured against strong national environmental legislation and the long-term assurance that they will be replenished where possible, wisely utilized where non-renewable. We must adopt a policy of no net loss of renewable resources, including fish stocks, agricultural lands, parks, and forests. Every government department and program must be subject to rigorous environmental standards, and every opportunity must be taken to find creative alternatives to ecologically damaging practices now in place.

For example, Finland has found ways to use its forests in balance, maintaining a large number of woodlot owners, and has used government-backed marketing boards or consortiums of producers to allow smaller units to survive in a world market-place. B.C. forester Patricia Marchak says that Finland has proved that a thriving forest industry can develop in a northern latitude without multinationals at the helm, and suggests granting licenses to small communities in that province — native groups, for example — who would then be charged with the responsibility for replanting and selective harvesting. Finland has also developed a close relationship between foresters and engineers, to develop secondary industry, she points out, and has established forestry schools to teach young people about the importance of woods and wilderness.

Enough public money has been wasted on the big multinationals whose uncontrolled practices have depleted our East Coast fisheries. Anthropologist Anthony Davis suggests converting government subsidies that now go to corporations like National Sea to the communities that depend on marine resources for their livelihoods. Fish-plant workers, the fishermen themselves, and local entrepreneurs must be given control of the system, to manage for themselves and their communities. This would allow them to survive while putting an end to the mass, non-selective harvesting practices that have proved to be so harmful.

Canadians care very much about their environment and the health of their country and need ways to express their concerns and ideas. Missing in Canada are processes by which citizens can participate in the resource and environmental decisions being made. The situation is largely confrontational, and people who have concerns about projects use demonstrations or the courts to try to force governments to listen to them. There should be national and regional citizens' advisory boards to debate publicly the difficult issues of development versus preservation of our resources. When citizens have no input, when they see that decisions are made by foreign-based multinationals, and when they also see companies leave widespread environmental damage in their wake, they become rightly suspicious of the motivations of developers. The secretive, conspiratorial atmosphere of the government's current practices, which include looking the other way when corporate friends get out of line, merely increases public suspicion of, and antagonism towards, a government from which it is shut out. This is the antithesis of the open, honest, public debate that is needed.

Similarly, government must retake the right to create standards for environmental clean-up. We need an independent forest service to plant and nurture the future forests of Canada. Government will also have to lead in the search for energy alternatives to our high-use, intensive dependence on fossil fuels. The principle characteristic of this alternative is the use of energy sources that are always there, whether we use them or not — *i.e.*, sun, wind, and vegetation — rather than using non-renewable resources, such as oil and coal. Our natural gas could be developed to be a part of this trend, as it is a safer fossil fuel than the others. The added benefit to Canadians of seeking out these alternatives, apart from the ecological value, is that it relies on diverse, flexible, decentralized energy sources that could help wean us from our dependence on huge, foreign-dominated energy interests.

A singular economic advantage to Canada of our resources is that we are in a unique situation to lead the world in the development of environmental clean-up technology. The folly of the free-trade agreement was that it allowed for a national strategy to find and exploit finite fossil fuels, but disallowed government leadership in promoting ecologically safe alternatives. A labour- and research-intensive strategy to build a Canadian industry that the Brundtland Commission report identified as one of the world's key sunrise industries could be a critical element in reviving the Canadian economy.

None of this, of course, would take place in a vacuum, nor should it. For the other half of the answer to the question — Why nationhood? — lies in the international realm. The world's population is growing at the rate of a quarter of a million people every day. By the turn of the century, there will be more than six billion of us on the earth. We are crowding out wildlife; every year, 20,000 species of plants and animals disappear. The wrecks of nuclear submarines leak radiation into the oceans. Forests are razed and grasslands converted to desert, bringing drought and hunger to vast areas on several continents. Reports out of East Germany say that 90 percent of the trees are dead or dying. Coastal communities in Southeast Asia are being submerged as global warming takes its inevitable and tragic toll. The French agronomist René Dumont says that we are on the verge of the greatest famine in the history of the world.

The Worldwatch Institute warns that if we don't reverse the trend towards ecological destruction of our planet in the next ten years, it may be too late. Like-minded countries must come together to find the solutions to what are truly international problems. For Canada to attack the crucial questions of environmental destruction alone would be wholly inadequate. Just as Canada's answer to bilateral trade with the United States must be through international organizations, like the General Agreement on Tariffs and Trade (GATT), United Nations Environment Program (UNEP), and the Organization of Economic Cooperation and Development (OECD), so must our commitment to environmental well-being. Canada should play a leadership role in working with other middle powers to seek long-term changes in international institutions that could work to eliminate, or at least reduce, ecological devastation.

As the Brundtland report so strongly underlined, it is not possible to separate economic development from its environmental consequences. Yet, most trade agreements, including the Canada–U.S. Free Trade Agreement and the GATT, do not concern themselves with environmental issues. As the Canadian Environmental Law Association points out, the GATT is now being renegotiated, with virtually no consideration of its environmental implications. Environmental organizations are not a part of the process, which is made up of trade experts in governments and large corporate and private trade interests. These interests believe that bigger is better, and faster is smarter, and they work towards a never-ending cycle of competition, resource depletion, higher corporate concentration, and higher profits.

In a study on the environmental impact of international trade, the GATT admitted that, without rules, companies would favour the countries with the lowest environmental standards. Thus it concluded that it would not be "desirable" for any country to adopt environmental measures that would drive away investment.

Trade negotiations that take place in the shadowed world of boardrooms and trade offices undermine other international attempts to combat ecological destruction by refusing to deal with this issue. They are about as far away as one can get from the democratic processes that people in our country and others are struggling to establish, and serve the private interests of those who want to pursue their own profit without accounting for their actions.

Canada, as a strong supporter of the OECD and GATT in the past, and a major contributor to the launching of the Brundtland Commission, could show leadership by introducing the concept of environmental stewardship into its international relations. Countries should be permitted and encouraged to establish strong environmental legislation and should be guaranteed that opening trade will not diminish their right to do so. We should strive to establish international environmental conventions. Special efforts would have to be made to win the support of the developing countries, no doubt at some cost to the industrialized world.

More specifically, within GATT, Canada should work towards the recognition of optimal environmental standards, codes of ethics, and impact-assessment procedures. To this end, Canada should initiate action to help co-ordinate the environmental initiatives of the other international agencies (including UNEP, the IMF, the World Bank, and regional-development banks) to ensure their acceptance within the GATT.

A pro–free trade argument cited often is that the world is breaking up into trading blocs, and Canada has no choice but to enter into one of them. While some trading blocs, like Europe, may make historic and geographical sense, the trend to world trade blocs will undermine the international GATT system Canada has worked so hard to build. Sylvia Ostry said, in a recent study for the U.S. Council on Foreign Relations, that the world trading system is at risk. If the trend continues, trade wars loom large: "If the United States can achieve most of its trade policy objectives more efficiently and effectively with a combination of section 301 investigations and bilateral free trade agreements, how long will it continue to uphold the rule of law of multilateralism rather than deploy the enormous power of its large market?"

As well, trading blocs generally work only for the biggest player. Canada is already on the losing end of the free-trade agreement we signed. Eighty-five percent of our trade was already with the United States. Instead of tying ourselves to an economy in decline, thus diminishing our competitive position, what Canada needs is to seek more world markets. And Canada's interests are better protected in the multilateral forum.

The move to these trading blocs is also hurting the countries of the Third World because no one wants them as partners. In spite of years of development aid, the Third World is sliding into pervasive poverty. It is being dropped out of the international economy. The irony of this trend is that free trade is touted as being the opposite of protectionism, a chance for all to compete openly so that the best may win. But these huge trading blocs are nothing more than closed clubs for wealthy countries and those who would serve them without question, and "Do Not Disturb" signs have been erected around them.

The answers to the inequalities and poverty in the world need fresh and creative solutions. Canada has generally followed the U.S. perspective on world problems, which rejects the need for real structural change. It is time Canada stepped out from under the policy thumb of the United States and worked with like-minded nations towards new world trading systems that would be less dominated by a few superpowers and more committed to the north-south dialogue.

Canada could call for an international forum to deal with new rules of trade and Third World debt, and establish long-term stabilizing influences to help poor countries to self-reliance. Canada needs to help build international alternatives to the system being put in place by the increasingly powerful transnational corporations of the world. Eventually, through the United Nations and other such organizations, all nations will have to devise ways of making these corporate giants accountable.

And what of the greatest test of our time — the chance to convert the tools of war to the service of peace? Canada has an opportunity here as well, if we can see our way to an independent foreign policy. For forty years, the United States has led world events by the sheer weight of its power. Now, followed meekly by Canada, it has fallen behind, and is marching to a tired and increasingly irrelevant drummer. The United States is becoming peripheral to events unfolding in the world because it refuses to recognize the great breakthroughs in easing international tensions.

Unable psychologically or economically to convert its massive military infrastructure, the United States will continue to find ways to justify this drain on the national treasury, and will not be able to lead in this arena. Canada, however, is in a position to link the process of disarmament to development, and to help the world to redefine security, nationally and internationally. One definition will be in terms of ecological degradation. The new enemy is the nightmare conditions that we have created in so many parts of the planet.

Canada cannot take its rightful place in the search for international solutions to world problems until it puts its own house in order. To effect change in this arena, Canada must start at home. The Defence White Paper should be relegated to the obscurity it deserves, and a whole new policy, based on a new definition of security, introduced. Ernie Regehr has called on the government to place defence policy in the service of an overall security blueprint that encompasses economic, environmental, and other non-military elements of security. Security should be defined as the preservation of life on the planet and the need to extend the rule of law from the nation-state to the world community. A fundamental tenet of Canadian security must be that all military activity in this country on and under its waters and in its air space come under the exclusive control of the Canadian government.

Canada's defence forces can be trained to play a leading role in a policy defined by national and international security interests, and should clearly project a defensive character in keeping with international changes. Peace-keeping and border defence against polluters, drug-traffickers, and terrorists are key functions of a new force. Enforcement of offshore fishing rights will have to be ensured. And whole new challenges in the defence of the environment from ecological damage are arising. MP Charles Caccia has suggested developing a centre for research and development of new technologies to protect the ecosystem through the Department of National Defence, linking the issues of security with our environmental well-being.

When we are no longer constrained by the free-trade agreement, Ottawa should shift its grants and subsidies from the production of armaments to the production of environmental clean-up technology. Now subject to countervail attack under the agreement, a government/industry collaboration on this project would be in keeping with the emerging role of the armed services.The Canadian Centre for Arms Control and Disarmament calls for the establishment of an advisory commission on economic conversion that would help arms manufacturers convert their production to minimize dislocations and take advantage of the possibility of a true "peace dividend."

Perhaps, most importantly, Canada has always isolated defence policy from foreign policy, considering them to be different areas of policy and jurisdiction. Thus, the larger goals of a Canadian foreign policy have been submerged by the more immediate demands of defence. Because our defence policy is so closely linked with the Pentagon, our foreign policy has also tended to reflect American direction and decisions. It should be the other way around. Foreign policy should be the foundation for a defence policy, not vice versa. Then, our foreign policy could reflect the values of Canadians and the kind of world we would like to see. Defence would serve these values and goals, not the values and goals of Washington.

Internationally, Canada can have persuasive force in working towards converting arms spending and helping the world grow away from equating peace with power. Canada should immediately start phasing out our forces stationed in Europe. The $6-billion saving is badly needed elsewhere. We should recognize that our territory, lying as it does between the two superpowers, is a major political and diplomatic asset in negotiating world disarmament.We should be playing a very different role in NATO, supporting the non-military provisions that are part of its purpose. It is a common error to think that NATO is just a military alliance. In fact, six out of eight of its founding obligations relate to peace-keeping and the requirement to find non-military solutions to conflict wherever possible. Article 2 on economic co-operation was included in 1948 on Canada's insistence. It has been largely ignored, and it would be singularly appropriate for Canada now to champion its revival.

Another common misconception about NATO is that its member countries are required to support the foreign policies of their allies. In fact, loyalty to the alliance might well mean the opposite. As Escott Reid has pointed out, if a member country believes that a policy of one of its allies increases the risk of war, it is bound to oppose that policy. Canada should urge NATO to provide the forum for the process needed to ease the United States into lasting non-military relations with the Soviet Union. As well, Canadians who were opposed to a NATO base in Labrador may be relieved that the base will not be going ahead. Canada should stand four-square against building such a base anywhere as well as against the current flight testing. Its purpose is aggressive, and in light of recent world events, obsolete.

The money earmarked for such a base could go into international monitoring and verification of military movements and supporting the growth of a world system of law to govern disputes, through the United Nations and other international agencies. Canada should be a leader in promoting the United Nations as a guarantor of the world's security, including the creation of international policing mechanisms under the Security Council. For example, Canada could develop an International Satellite Monitoring Agency that could work with the United Nations, and warn the world instantly of any military provocation.

Finally, Canada has a special role in forging a circumpolar community organized to protect all northern territories from environmental damage and military interventions. We should negotiate with other northern nations a demilitarized circumpolar zone, and work together to protect northern wilderness as the common heritage of all humanity. The added benefit to Canada would be a way to maintain close ties to a number of countries, and offset the overreliance we now have on continental security.

Canadians have always acknowledged, with some pride, that we are not a superpower. Any authority on the world stage has come from a moral presence. When we are heard, it is as a middle power that has strived to give real meaning to the struggle for human rights and the search for non-violent answers to conflict. The challenges of the decade — common security, ecological stewardship, and international human rights — are daunting. But they are also the areas in which Canada has earned respect and in which we have some authority. As the cold war ends, the superpowers are losing the supremacy based on weapons superiority. Power in the emerging world will be measured in different ways, and countries such as Canada could take the ascendancy. A new day and new realities call for new answers.

In recent years, however, Canada is being seen more as a satellite of the United States and less as an autonomous nation. To play a real role in confronting these issues, nationally and internationally, will require sacrifice and courage on the part of Canadians. It will require reclaiming our own voice in the community of nations. It will also require financial hardships while we reclaim our economic independence. But we have a future full of hope. In essence, Canadians now must decide what kind of society we want. Indeed, we must decide if we want to exist as a nation at all.

The pain of our recent constitutional struggles has caused many Canadians to wonder if the country called Canada is about to die. Intolerance eats away within. Foreign intervention intrudes from without. Is there a national dream worth fighting for? For many of us, recent events have proven a catalyst for action. Suddenly, something taken for granted must be fought for. A Welsh poet once wrote of his pain as he witnessed his own country in a similar conflict: "This is the experience of knowing that your country is leaving you, being sucked away from you as it were by a consuming, swallowing wind, into the hands and possession of another country and civilization."

Canadians must find again our shared values, and, as uncomfortable as it might be for us given our reticence for self-examination, we must seek to give expression to them. We have a proud and unique heritage, and traditions worth fighting for. Our most enduring legacy is our love of the land, harsh and unrelenting as it can be. Survival, not dominance, is central to our definition of self.

We honour the generations that have gone before us. We cherish the survival of traditional values in the established customs of our country. We are an evolutionary, not revolutionary people. Our strong historical will to exist, and to resist the more commercially natural lines of north-south trade, led to the creation of national institutions, whose role was to deliver services equal in quality to every part of the country. A national railway, an airline, a broadcasting service that gave us a way to speak to each other in a common voice — these were developed to link us, from coastal fishing villages in the outports of Newfoundland, across prairie farmhouses, to the northern reaches of our country.

We believe that individual freedom can be attained only within public order, and we invest in our government the responsibility to safeguard our freedom. Our collective rights to safety outweigh our individual right to bear arms, a remarkable difference between Canadians and Americans. We attempt to find balance between the often-conflicting rights of individuals and rights of groups, such as minorities, and it renders us a more tolerant society. Although we have our own shameful stories of bigotry, racism, and abuse, we are attempting to establish an experiment — the belief that people can come from all over the world to settle here and still retain their own heritage. Except for Canada's first people, we are all immigrants to Canada and so we have great potential in living a model for peaceful co-existence for peoples all over the world.

We are a people seeking justice. We have been ashamed of poverty in our midst. We are a people with a tradition of compassion. We are also a peaceful people, proud of our international peace-keeping role. Our capital city is filled not with symbols of war, but of peace and human rights. Canadians can face the future with pride and hope.

We developed a belief in regional equality, and, although it has not always worked as we might wish, Canadians accept as a fundamental value the inherent worth of each part of our country. Unlike the United States, where people must move to find work, we believe that Canadians have the right to live, love, and work in the place of their birth. Our commitment to two founding cultures has created a nation rich in linguistic and cultural duality, and given us a deep appreciation of diversity. More than any other factor, this part of our make-up distinguishes us from American culture.

A Canada without Quebec would be unalterably diminished. French Canadians explored and opened up this country. In fact, the term "Canadian" originally referred to the hardy people who settled the St. Lawrence and tamed the Quebec wilderness. French and English fought side by side in two world wars. Canada has been a living example that two cultures can live and work together for a stronger whole.

Canadians outside of Quebec cannot force the province to remain in Confederation. Only mutual trust and shared goals can do that. English and French Canada have shared a dream. Our histories are irrevocably intertwined. We are each other, even as we recognize fundamental differences. A recommitment to each other and the country must be born out of a shared task. It is not too late.

Our shared task must be the reinstatement of these cherished traditional Canadian values as we face the challenges that lie ahead. Canada must rediscover its national purpose. The United Church says, "We believe that the test of our civilization is how we treat the poor, the powerless, the marginalized — those people who are least competitive in the survival-of-the-fittest gladiatorial contest in which we seem to be engaged. From our point of view, the economy is the way we love each other publicly." We have taken steps that lead to "very selective loving," and increasing injustice for the powerless in Canada.

Canada must reassert its commitment to equality, or we will not be recognizable in ten years. We must preserve what is of value to us even as we prepare to meet the high-technology demands of the twenty-first century. Rural life is a part of our past and our future. It must be safeguarded by government. We must retain the right to establish conditions of work and of social life, because we don't measure everything, including standard of living, against other columns in a ledgerbook kept in a New York boardroom. We must be free to determine our own fate and our own priorities, because we have a common heritage based on human values.

These are the fundamental principles upon which this country was built. We must call them ours again, not only for the next generation of Canadians, but for the role we might play in the new global order. Canadians must build upon our traditional tolerance to reclaim our future. If we fail, we will lose not only those characteristics that most truly define us, but the values vital to the survival of humanity. In the emerging global reality of the twenty-first century, these values could be Canada's finest gift to the world.

# AFTERWORD

The shape of Canada changed profoundly and forever when the Meech Lake Accord died on June 23, 1990. For the better or not, Canada as we have known it is gone. Whether a new Canada can rise from the old depends on the reaction of non-Quebecers ("English Canada" is simply not an accurate description of non-Francophones) to the aspirations and assertions of the new generation in Quebec. Quebec now is not an equal province, one among ten. It is a unique and distinct society with its own culture, language, legal tradition and history.

In our future deliberations, we must acknowledge that Canada is composed of three founding nations: English, French and Aboriginal. Each has rights and entitlements. Each must be accorded certain basic powers. If non-Quebecers insist that everything remain the same, and refuse to recognize these basic rights, Quebec will be forced to leave Confederation. It is not inconsistent for a Canadian nationalist to understand and support the yearning for self-determination of the people of Quebec.

At the same time, it is imperative that Quebecers look long and hard at a future totally independent of Canada. It is most unlikely that the United States would have much tolerance for Quebec's distinctive features. The *Wall Street Journal* says that Quebec's language laws are "meddlesome." Although the economy of the province is much more dynamic and independent than it was a decade ago, it continues to suffer from the same hardships as the rest of the country. Ironically, the free trade agreement, which was supposed to lead to greater economic opportunities, has created even higher unemployment and more lay-offs in Quebec than in most other provinces. In 1989, the province lost 51,000 manufacturing jobs. Flawed as it may have been, and in transition as it is,

Canada is still a safer place for Quebec than the world outside its borders.

Canada needs constitutional reform. The Meech Lake process was deeply flawed. The negotiations were conducted with far too much secrecy. It was wrong simply to present the agreement to the Canadian people in its final form. The process was poisoned by precisely the same conditions that disenfranchised Canadians during the free trade debate. Once again, average citizens were given no opportunity to voice their thoughts and feelings.

What was worse, Brian Mulroney characterized the debate as an English-French conflict. He went into Quebec immediately after the Accord was drafted and provocatively told Quebecers that any concern about Meech Lake on the part of Anglophones should be interpreted as a rejection of Quebec. The legitimate concerns of many thoughtful Canadians about the potential balkanization of the country that the Accord might produce were dismissed as the ranting of bigots. There are enough bigots to go around without the Prime Minister manufacturing more.

The people of Canada claimed the Constitution as their own in 1982 and will never again allow governments to shut them out of the process of constitutional reform. Canadians have a deep love of our country, our whole country, and are capable of working together to find solutions based on mutual tolerance, respect and goodwill.

# Appendix: Job Loss Register

The following list of plants closed down and jobs lost in the after-math of the free-trade deal has been compiled by, and is published courtesy of, the Canadian Labour Congress. It is a partial listing only, reflecting reports available at the time of going to press, in June 1990.

| Company/Ownership | Location(s) | Product(s) | Date | Job Loss |
|---|---|---|---|---|
| Gillette (US) | Montreal, Que. | shaving products | Nov. 1988 | 590 |
| Jarman Inc. | Lachine, Que. | footwear | Nov. 1988 | 50 |
| Ortho Diagnostic Systems (Johnson & Johnson — US) | North York, Ont. | pharmaceuticals | Nov. 1988 | 16 |
| Pittsburgh Paint and Glass (US) | Toronto, Ont. | paints | Nov. 1988 | 139 |
| Weston Foods (Interbake Foods Division) | Longueuil, Que. | food processing | Nov. 1988-Feb. 89 | 360 |
| Northern Telecom | Aylmer, Que. | telecommunications equipment | Dec. 1988 | 680 |
| Northern Telecom | Belleville, Ont. | telecommunications equipment | Dec. 1988 | 240 |
| Molson Breweries of Canada Ltd. (Cdn/Aus) | Across Canada | beer | Dec. 1988 | 140 |
| Chrysler Canada (US) | Ajax, Ont. | automobiles | Dec. 1988 | 400 |
| Bell Northern Research | Toronto and Ottawa, Ont. | telecommunications | Dec. 1988 | 58 |
| Canadian Imperial Bank of Commerce | Across Canada | financial services | Dec. 1988 | 1,000 |
| Taurus Shoes | Contrecoeur, Que. | footwear | Jan. 1989 | 100 |
| Canadian Tire Corp. (Cantire) | Toronto, Ont. | auto parts | Jan. 1989 | 457 |
| Group Saucier | | forest products | Jan. 1989 | 44 |

| Company/Ownership | Location(s) | Product(s) | Date | Job Loss |
|---|---|---|---|---|
| Lawson Margo | Montreal, Que. | printing | Jan. 1989 | 40 |
| Thomas Lipton | Montreal, Que. | food processing | Jan. 1989 | 46 |
| Windsor Hosery Mills | Windsor, Que. | clothing | Jan. 1989 | 36 |
| Council of Furniture Manufacturers | Across Canada | furniture | Jan. 1989 | 3,500[1] |
| Allergan Pharmaceuticals (Smith, Klein & French), US | Montreal, Que. | pharmaceuticals | Dec. 1988 | 62 |
| Kraft (US) | Montreal, Que. | food processing | Jan. 1989 | 290 |
| Trion Canada | Kitchener, Ont. | air cleaners | | 25 |
| J.K. Campbell & Assoc. | Edmonton, Alta. | roofing & sheet metal | Dec. 1988 | 150-200 |
| Northern Telecom Electronics Ltd. | Nepean, Ont. | telecommunications | | 60 |
| Steven's Control System (US) | Renfrew, Ont. | thermostats | | 49 |
| Storwal International | Pembroke, Ont. | office furniture | Jan. 1989 | 100 |
| CNR Inspectors | Fort Erie, Ont. | transportation services | | 124 |
| Warnaco | Montreal, Que. | textiles | Jan. 1989 | 140 |
| Dominion Textile | Sherbrooke, Que. | textiles | Feb. 1989 by Sept.-Dec. 89 | 170 |

[1] The figure of 3,500 does not take effect immediately, but is projected over the next five years.

| Company/Ownership | Location(s) | Product(s) | Date | Job Loss |
|---|---|---|---|---|
| Dominion Textile | Trois-Rivieres, Que. | textiles | Feb. 1989 by Sept.-Dec. 89 | 55 |
| Dominion Textile | Beauharnois, Que. | textiles | Feb. 1989 by Sept.-Dec. 89 | 200 |
| Dominion Textile | Granby, Que. | textiles | Feb. 1989 by Sept.-Dec. 89 | 250 |
| Chasse Inc. | St. Marie, Que. | wood products | Feb. 1989 | 86 |
| Kruger Inc. | Anjou, Que. | paper products | Feb. 1989 | 93 |
| Cie de papiers St. Raymond | St. Raymond, Que. | paper products | Feb. 1989 | 56 |
| Queens Wear International Ltd. | Montreal, Que. | clothing | Feb. 1989 | 113 |
| Celanese Canada (Germany) | Millhaven, Ont. | textiles | Feb. 1989 | 108 |
| Inglis (US) | Toronto, Whitby, Cambridge, Ont.; Montmorency, Que. | washing machines | Feb. 1989 | 870 |
| Albright and Wilson Americas Inc. (US) | Long Harbour, Nfld. | phosphoric acid | Feb. 1989 | 290 |
| Warner-Lambert (US) | Brockville, Ont. | pharmaceuticals | Feb. 1989 | 35 |
| Alcon Canada Inc. (US) | Mississauga, Ont. | pharmaceuticals | Jan. 1989 | 48 |

| Company/Ownership | Location(s) | Product(s) | Date | Job Loss |
|---|---|---|---|---|
| Ivaco Canada Inc. | Dunnville, Ont. | wire cable | | 170 |
| Ivaco Canada Inc. | Ingersoll, Ont. | wire cable | | 125 |
| Sysco Steel | Sydney, N.S. | steel | Feb. 1989 | 500[2] |
| Kelsey Hayes (US) | Windsor, Ont. | auto parts | Feb. 1989 | 231 |
| Westcott Fashions | Winnipeg, Man. | clothing | Nov. 1988 | 470 |
| Lowney (Hershey) Chocolate (US) | Sherbrooke, Que. | confectionery products | Feb.-Oct. 1989 | 466 |
| Freedland Industries | Kingsville, Ont. | auto parts | Jan. 1989 | 235 |
| Echlin Canada (US) | Rexdale, Ont. | auto parts | Jan. 1989 | 125 |
| Fletcher Challenge (NZ) | Lumby and Williams Lake, B.C. | forest products | Dec. 1988, Jan. 1989 | 235 |
| Ogilvie Mills | Winnipeg, Man. | food processing | Feb. 1989 | 90 |
| Canada Packers | Winnipeg, Man. | food processing | Dec. 1988 | 107 |
| Central Guarantee Trust | Halifax, N.S.; Montreal, Que.; Toronto, Ont. | financial services | Feb. 1989 | 91 |
| Simpson's | Montreal & St.-Bruno, Que. | retail services | Jan. 1989 | 1,100 |
| Molson-Carling | Across Canada | beer | 1990–1992 | 1,400[3] |
| Texaco Canada (US) | Across Canada | oil and gas | 1990–1992 | 1,000 |

[2] Job losses could run as high as 700 or 800.    [3] Another 2,600 job losses are projected.

| Company/Ownership | Location(s) | Product(s) | Date | Job Loss |
|---|---|---|---|---|
| Consolidated Bathurst (US) | Across Canada | forest products | 1990–1992 | 1,000 |
| Canadian Printing Industries Assoc. | Across Canada | printing | 1990–1992 | 2,100 |
| Fiberglas Canada (US) | Mission, B.C. | insulation | Mar. 1989 | 180 |
| John Forsyth Shirts | Montreal, Que. | apparel | Feb. 1989 | 50 |
| John Forsyth Shirts | St. Jean, Que. | apparel | Feb. 1989 | 120 |
| Canadian Airlines | Across Canada | airlines | Mar. 1989 | 600 |
| Canadian Marconi (UK) | Mont-Royal, Que. | electronics (semi-conductors) | Mar. 1989 | 300 |
| Aliments Sedor Inc. | Val Belair, Que. | food processing | Mar. 1989 | 100 |
| Woodbridge INOAC | St. Jerome, Que. | auto parts | Mar. 1989 | 270 |
| Southam | Across Canada | printing and publishing | Jan. 1989 | 900 |
| Fletcher Challenge (NZ) | Vancouver Island and Cowichan Valley, B.C. | forest products | Feb. 1989 | 420 |
| Novastran | Saint John, N.B. | rope and industrial yarn (textiles) | Feb. 1989 | 50 |
| Beverage Central and Starlife | Saskatoon, Sask. | bottlers | Jan. 1989 and Mar. 1989 | 46 |
| Various Northern Ontario sawmills | Ontario | forest products | Mar. 1989 | 900[4] |

4 These jobs lost due to the softwood export tax. according to estimate by the Canadian Forestry Institute.

| Company/Ownership | Location(s) | Product(s) | Date | Job Loss |
|---|---|---|---|---|
| Dofasco | Kirkland Lake and Temagami, Ont. | iron ore | Mar. 1989 | 700 |
| Northern Telecom | Bramalea, Ont. | telecommunications equipment | Mar. 1989 | 120 |
| Midas (US) | Toronto, Ont. | auto parts | Mar. 1989 | 140 |
| Geoffrion-Leclerc/Levesque-Beaubien | Montreal, Que. | investment dealers | Mar. 1989 | 300 |
| Arnold Manufacturing | Windsor, Ont. | restaurant furnishings | Feb. 1989 | 100 |
| Duo-Matic/Olsen Inc. | Tilbury, Ont. | heating equipment | Nov. 1988 | 59 |
| John Deere Ltd. (US) | Welland, Ont. | farm equipment | Dec. 1988–Mar. 1989 | 161 |
| Northern Telecom | St-Laurent, Que. | telecommunications | Jan–June 1989 | 250 |
| Campagnie Emballage Sommer-ville Inc. | St-Laurent, Que. | packaging | Feb.–June 1989 | 180 |
| Lear Sieglar Industries Ltd. (US) | Kitchener, Ont. | auto parts | Jan. 1989 | 199 |
| Libby St. Clair | Wallaceburg, Ont. | glassware | Dec. 1988 | 123 |
| Libbey-Owens-Ford of Canada Ltd. (US) | Lindsay, Ont. | auto parts | Jan. 1989 | 187 |
| Trailmobile Group | Brantford, Ont. | truck trailers | Nov. 1988 | 111 |
| Greening Donald Co. Ltd. (US) | Midland and Hamilton, Ont. | wire products | | 40 |

| Company/Ownership | Location(s) | Product(s) | Date | Job Loss |
|---|---|---|---|---|
| Samsonite (US) | Stratford, Ont. | | Nov.-Dec. 1988 | 86 |
| Andrew McNiece Ltd. | Cambridge, Ont. | footwear | Nov.-Dec. 1988 | 56 |
| Atwell Fleming/Young Ltd. | Toronto, Ont. | | Dec. 1988 | 85 |
| UTDC | Thunder Bay and Mill-haven, Ont. | rolling stock | Jan. 1989 | 500 |
| Stelco | | steel pipe unit | | 176 |
| Canron Inc. | St. Thomas, Ont. | foundry | Nov. 1988 | 104 |
| Cecutti's Bakeries Ltd. | Sudbury, Ont. | food processing | Jan. 1989 | 113 |
| Drug Trading Company Ltd. | Hamilton, Ont. | drug wholesaler | Nov. 1988 | 65 |
| Ford Motor Co. of Canada (US) | Windsor, Ont. | automobiles | Dec. 1988 by Dec. 1989 | 180 |
| Freuhauf Canada (US) | Mississauga, Ont. | auto parts | Dec. 1988 | 372 |
| Long Manufacturing Ltd. U.S. | Oakville, Ont. | auto parts | Mar. 1989 | 425 |
| MacMillan Bloedel Ltd. | Thunder Bay, Ont. | forest products | Jan.-Feb. 1989 | 85 |
| Monarch Fine Foods | Scarborough, Ont. | food processing | Mar. 1989 | 66 |
| Nu-Kote Canada Inc. (US) | Scarborough, Ont. | office machines | Nov. 1988 | 119 |
| Square D Canada Electrical Equipment Inc. (US) | Arnprior, Ont. | electrical equipment | Nov. 1988 | 70 |
| The Great A & P Co. Ltd. | North Bay, Ont. | food retailing | Nov. 1988 | 121 |

| Company/Ownership | Location(s) | Product(s) | Date | Job Loss |
|---|---|---|---|---|
| Amway Corporation (US) | London, Ont. | consumer products | Mar. 1989 | 106 |
| Photo Engravers & Electrotypers Printing | Toronto, Ont. | printing | Feb. 1989 | 450[5] |
| Clearwater Fine Foods | Port Mouton, N.S. | fish processing | Mar. 1989 | 150[6] |
| Eureka Coach | Concord, Ont. | auto parts | Feb. 1989 | 130 |
| Dubarry Furniture | Toronto, Ont. | furniture | Mar. 1989 | 43 |
| Control Data (US) | Mississauga, Ont. | systems designers | Jan. 1989 | 182 |
| Scholl-Plough (NS) | Scarborough, Ont. | personal care products | Apr. 1989 | 105 |
| Combustion Engineering | Ottawa, Ont. | engineering | | 104 |
| United Grain Growers | Vancouver, B.C. | grain terminal | | 90 |
| Postech | Toronto, Ont. | computerized payroll | | 60 |
| Union Carbide of Canada (US) | Lindsay, Ont. | plastics | | 85 |
| Great West Life Insurance (US) | Winnipeg, Man. | financial services | | 25 |
| Transcontinental Inc. | Winnipeg, Man. | printing | Mar. 1989 | 47 |
| Phillips Air Distributing (US) | Kitchener, Ont. | fans/exhausts | | 100[7] |
| L-Tec Canada (US) | Mississauga, Ont. | welding torches, etc. | | 60[8] |
| Lady Manhattan (Dylex) | Toronto, Ont. | apparel | May 1989 | 45 |
| Mobil Oil Canada Ltd. (US) | Across Canada | oil and gas | Apr. 1989 | 375[9] |

[5] Jobs lost as a result of a free-trade lockout.   [6] Figure includes 40 full-time and 110 seasonal jobs.   [7] Estimate of probable job loss.
[8] Estimate of possible job loss.   [9] Approximate figure.

| Company/Ownership | Location(s) | Product(s) | Date | Job Loss |
|---|---|---|---|---|
| Microtel | Brockville, Ont. | telecommunications | Apr. 1989 | 145 |
| Cameco | Saskatoon, Sask. | mining/energy | Mar. 1989 | 170 |
| Simpson Timber (Sask.) Ltd. | Hudson Bay, Sask. | forest products | to June 1990 | 600[10] |
| Airlite Glass | Toronto, Ont. | | Fall 1988 | 40 |
| Vulcan Packaging Inc. (US) | Toronto, Ont. | metal cans | Feb. 1989 | 60 |
| G.H. Wood | Toronto, Ont. | sanitation products | Jan. 1989 | 40 |
| Eimco Jarvis Clark | Sudbury, Ont. | hydraulic repair | Dec. 1988 | 20 |
| Giant Yellowknife | Timmins, Ont. | gold mine | Mar. 1989 | 175 |
| Canada Building Systems | Guelph, Ont. | steel bridges | Jan. 1989 | 85 |
| Dayton Walther | Guelph, Ont. | steel foundry | | 50 |
| P & S Water Industries | London, Ont. | pumps | Mar. 1989 | 33 |
| Mitten Vinyl | Cambridge, Ont. | vinyl siding | Dec. 1988 | 88 |
| Ball Packaging | Simcoe, Ont. | | Mar. 1989–Nov. 1989 | 90 |
| Transpersonnel | Sarnia, Ont. | trucking | Mar. 1989 | 9 |
| Nerco Mines | Yellowknife, NWT | gold/silver | Jan. 1989 | 80 |
| Domtar Fine Papers Ltd. | Toronto, Ont. | forest products | Feb. 1989 | 77 |
| Bovie Manufacturing | Lindsay, Ont. | disposable clothing | Feb.-Mar. 1989 | 60 |

[10] Figure includes full-time and seasonal jobs.

| Company/Ownership | Location(s) | Product(s) | Date | Job Loss |
|---|---|---|---|---|
| Hostess, Frito-Lay (US) | various location in Ontario | food processing | Apr. 1989 | 139 |
| Hostess, Frito-Lay (US) | Laval, Que. | food processing | Apr. 1989 | 110 |
| Anova Inc. | Barrie, Ont. | barbeques | | 140 |
| Bailey River Farms | Bradford, Ont. | food processing | | 125 |
| Beaver Foods | Peterborough, Ont. | food processing | | 122 |
| Beaver Foods | Thunder Bay, Ont. | food processing | | 62 |
| Beaver Foods | Mississauga, Ont. | food processing | | 61 |
| Carleton Cards | Mississauga, Ont. | printing/distribution | Feb. 1989 | 80 |
| Lecours Lumber | Calstock, Ont. | forest products | Apr. 1989 | 80 |
| Levesque Lumber | Hearst, Ont. | forest products | Mar. 1989 | 300 |
| G.W. Martin Lumber (Veneer) | Searchmont, Ont. | forest products | Apr. 1989 | 70 |
| United Sawmill | Hearst, Ont. | forest products | Apr. 1989 | 100[11] |
| La Belle Fermiere | Montreal, Que. | food processing | Apr. 1989 | 80 |
| Ben Hokum | Pembroke area, Ont. | sawmill/forest products | Apr. 1989 | 30 |
| Consolidated Bathhurst US | Pembroke area, Ont. | sawmill/forest products | Apr. 1989 | 25 |
| Murray Brothers | Pembroke area, Ont. | sawmill/forest products | Apr. 1989 | 52 |
| Bonar Packaging | Burlington, Ont. | plastics/packaging | Apr. 1989 | 42 |

[11] Temporary job loss.

| Company/Ownership | Location(s) | Product(s) | Date | Job Loss |
|---|---|---|---|---|
| Lloyds Bank | Across Canada | financial services | Apr. 1989 | 175 |
| MTD Products | Kitchener, Ont. | | Apr. 1989 | 199 |
| Marr's Leisure Products Edson Boat Div. (US) | Brandon, Man. | pleasure boats | Apr. 1989 | 40 |
| Circo Craft | Montreal, Que. | electronics | Apr. 1989 | 75 |
| Les Papiers de L'Est Ltee. | Montreal, Que. | paper products | Apr. 1989 | 69 |
| Tend-R-Fresh Poultry | | food processing | Apr. 1989 | 205 |
| Corah PLC | Barrie, Ont. | clothing | Mar. 1989 | 200 |
| Harmonic Home Fashion Inc. | Toronto, Ont. | | Apr. 1989 | 88 |
| Ontario Institute for Farm Machinery | Mississauga, Ont. | farm machinery | Apr. 1989 | 51 |
| Plastic Engine Technology Corp. | Kingston, Ont. | | Apr. 1989 | 175 |
| Progressive Anodizers | Scarborough, Ont. | | Apr. 1989 | 50 |
| Maple Leaf Mills (UK) | Peterborough, Ont. | food processing | Apr. 1989 | 145 |
| Commander Electric (US) | Scarborough, Ont. | electrical products | Apr. 1989 | 70 |
| Ontario Bank Note | Ontario | printing | Apr. 1989 | 59 |
| Carbolide Canada | Ontario | | Apr. 1989 | 41 |
| Chromalux | Toronto, Ont. | air conditioning and heating equipment | Apr. 1989 | 45 |

| Company/Ownership | Location(s) | Product(s) | Date | Job Loss |
|---|---|---|---|---|
| Savage Shoes | Cambridge, Ont. | footwear | Jan. 1989 | 45 |
| Jordan St. Michel Winery | | wine | Apr. 1989 | 27 |
| K.T. Industries | Winnipeg, Man. | fibre optic tape, etc. | Apr. 1989 | 20 |
| Canadian Broadcasting Corporation | Across Canada | broadcasting | May-June 1989 | 500 |
| CNR (truck maintenance) | various | transportation | May-June 1989 | 1,500[12] |
| Chaussures CDR | Montreal, Que. | footwear | May 1989 | 95 |
| Marystown Shipyard | Marystown, Nfld. | shipbuilding | Apr. 1989 | 170 |
| Fisheries Products International | Newfoundland | fish processing | May 1989 | 4,000[13] |
| Department of Energy, Mines and Resources | Ottawa, Ont. | public service | May-June 1989 | 458 |
| Galtaco | Brantford, Ont. | auto parts | May 1989 | 169 |
| Galtaco | Paris, Ont. | auto parts | May 1989 | 131 |
| Galtaco | Orillia, Ont. | auto parts | May 1989 | 141 |
| Toro Co. (US) | Manitoba | lawn mowers | May 1989 | 68[14] |
| National Sea Products | Nova Scotia and Newfoundland | fish processing | May 1989 | 4,000[15] |
| Magna International | Brampton, Ont. | auto parts | May 1989 | 110 |
| J.H. Warsh Ltd. | Toronto, Ont. | clothing | May 1989 | 45 |

[12] Another 700 to 800 job losses are likely.

[13] At time of publication, the number refers to temporary (six-month) layoffs; the number of permanent layoffs has not been announced.

[14] Figure includes 28 permanent and 40 seasonal jobs.

[15] Of the 4,000, 150 are confirmed permanent jobs lost in Lockeport, N.S.; the balance so far are designate 1 as temporary layoffs.

| Company/Ownership | Location(s) | Product(s) | Date | Job Loss |
|---|---|---|---|---|
| de Havilland (US) | Toronto, Ont. | aircraft manufacturing | May 1989 | 700 |
| Scierie Grand Remous | | forest products | May 1989 | 81 |
| Societe de chemises Mylord | Montreal, Que. | clothing | May 1989 | 51 |
| Lipton Inc. (US) | Winnipeg, Man. | food processing | June 1989 | 29 |
| Neepawa Farms | Winnipeg, Man. | meat processing | May–June 1989 | 65-70 |
| VIA Rail | Across Canada | transportation | June 1989 | 3,500[16] |
| Consumers Packaging | St. Pierre, Que. | glass containers | June 1989 | 460 |
| Consumers Packaging | Redcliff, Alta. | glass containers | June 1989 | 500 |
| Brenda Mines | Peachland, B.C. | molybdenum mine | June 1989 | 400 |
| Bendix Safety Restraints Ltd. (US) | Collingwood, Ont. | auto parts | June 1989 | 400 |
| Rothman's Benson & Hedges (US) | Montreal, Que. | tobacco | June 1989 by June 1990 | 239 |
| Pemberton Securities | | investment services | June 1989 | 500 |
| G.W. Martin Lumber Ltd. | Sault Ste. Marie, Mattawa, Harcourt, Alban, Huntsville, Ont. | sawmill/forest products | Apr. 1989 | 300 |
| MIL Vickers | Montreal, Que. | submarines | May 1989 | 380[17] |
| Star Expansion Industries (US) | Toronto, Ont. | fasteners | May 1989 | 36 |

[16] Cuts begin to take effect in Jan. 1990.   [17] Estimate of probable job loss.

| Company/Ownership | Location(s) | Product(s) | Date | Job Loss |
|---|---|---|---|---|
| Progress Co. (Hanson US) | St-Laurent, Que. | lighting products | May 1989 | 75 |
| Textiles Esmond Inc. | Granby, Que. | textiles | June 1989 | 258 |
| Cycles Talisman Inc. | Toronto, Ont. | bicycles | June 1989 | 187 |
| Burlington Carpet (US) | Brampton, Ont. | textiles | July 1989 | 450 |
| International Playing Card Co. (US) | Windsor, Ont. | paper products | July 1989 | 35 |
| Marimac | Sherbrooke, Que. | textiles | May-June 1989 | 237 |
| Mineraux, Noranda Ltd. | Rouyn-Noranda, Que. | copper mine | June 1989 | 170 |
| Texaco Canada (US) | Newfoundland (off-shore drilling) | oil and gas | May 1989 | 250 |
| Johnson & Johnson (US) | Montreal, Que. | pharmaceutical | July-Dec. 1989 | 86 |
| M.A.N. Ashton Inc. | St-Laurent, Que. | printing trades mach. | July-Dec. 1989 | 215 |
| Stone Safety Co. (UK) | Scarborough, Ont. | emer. lighting system, air conditioning | July 1989 | 100[18] |
| Arvin Automotive | Ajax, Ont. | auto parts (exhaust systems) | June 1989 | 32[19] |
| Chrysler Canada (US) | Windsor, Ont. | autos | Aug. 1989 | 120 |
| Design Made Millwork/Dortec Manufacturing | Vancouver, B.C. | custom furniture (cabinets) | June 1988 | 20 |
| Takahashi Industries (Sander Industries) | Vancouver, B.C. | custom doors | June 1989 | 20 |

[18] Plant closed Sept. 1989.     [19] Plant closed July 1989.

| Company/Ownership | Location(s) | Product(s) | Date | Job Loss |
|---|---|---|---|---|
| Sander Industries | Vancouver, B.C. | furniture | | 55 |
| Industries Thundercraft | Lachute, Que. | pleasure boats | July 1989 | 170 |
| Advanced Gibson of Canada Ltd. (US) | Windsor, Ont. | electrical circuit breakers switch parts | | 36 |
| Novalis (Div. of Groupe Media) | Ottawa, Ont. | printing | July 1989 | 41 |
| Le Droit (commercial printing division) Groupe Media Inc. | Ottawa, Ont. | printing | June 1989 | 63[20] |
| Spar Aerospace | Ottawa, Ont. | telecommunications products | July 1989 | 17 |
| Litton (US) | Etobicoke, Ont. | defence electronics | July 1989 | 300 |
| Amoco Canada (US) | 90% Alberta | | Aug. 1989 | 450 |
| Arrowhead Metals Inc. (Ivaco) | Etobicoke, Ont. | wire tubing & other copper products | | 400 |
| R.J. Reynolds Tobacco (US) (Nabisco) | | tobacco | Aug. 1989 | 12% |
| Sunbeam Shoes | Port Colborne, Ont. | shoes | Aug. 1989 | 115 |
| Petro Canada | Across Canada (mainly Alberta) | oil and gas | Aug. 1989 | 1,200 |
| Unisys Canada (US) | Montreal, Que.; Winnipeg, Man.; Toronto, Ont. | electronics (computers) | Aug. 1989 | 250 |

[20] Plant closed Aug. 1989.

| Company/Ownership | Location(s) | Product(s) | Date | Job Loss |
|---|---|---|---|---|
| Sterling Drug Inc. (US) (Kodak) | Aurora, Ont. | pharmaceuticals | Aug. 1989–Sept. 1991 | 220 |
| Simmons Ltd. (US) | Elora, Ont. | furniture | Sept. 1989 | 108 |
| Westmin Resources | Mainly Alberta | oil and gas | July-Aug. 1989 | 36 |
| Oakwood Petroleums (Sceptre Resources) | Mainly Alberta | oil and gas | Spring 1989 | 40 |
| Suncor | Across Canada | oil and gas | Summer 1989 | 250 |
| Gulf Canada | Across Canada | oil and gas | Summer 1989 | n/a |
| Various petroleum service companies | Mainly Alberta | oil and gas | July 1989 | 130 |
| Sklar Pepplar | Hanover, Ont. | furniture | Sept. 1989 | 42 |
| Eastman Kodak (US) | Various | photographic and chemical | Aug. 1989 | 450 |
| Mack Canada (US) | Oakville, Ont. | trucks | July 1989 | 231 |
| Maple Leaf Mills (UK) | Peterborough, Ont. | food processing | July 1989 | 133 |
| Modine of Canada (US) | Toronto, Ont. | auto parts | July 1989 | 46 |
| Caulfield Apparel Group | Downsview, Ont. | clothing | July 1989 | 60 |
| Fedders Inc. (US) | Orangeville, Ont. | | July 1989 | 57 |
| Ford Motor Co. (US) | Windsor, Ont. | autos | July 1989 | 136 |

| Company/Ownership | Location(s) | Product(s) | Date | Job Loss |
|---|---|---|---|---|
| G & B Automated Equipment Ltd. (US) | Downsview, Ont. | machine tools/robots | July 1989 | 100 |
| ITW Shakeproof Div. (US) | Mississauga, Ont. | fasteners | July 1989 | 45 |
| Picker International Canada Inc. (US) | Bramalea, Ont. | x-ray equipment | Mar.-June 1989 | 160 |
| Schlegel Canada Inc. (US) | Burlington, Ont. | rubber products | July 1989 | 104 |
| Star Expansion Industries (US) | Toronto, Ont. | hardware fasteners | July 1989 | 36 |
| Motor Wheel Corp. of Canada (US) | Chatham, Ont. | auto parts | June 1989 | 200 |
| SKD Co. | Amherstburg, Ont. | auto parts | July 1989 | 47 |
| SKD Co. | Amherstburg, Ont. | auto parts | Dec. 1989 | 200 |
| Leviton Manufacturing of Canada (US) | Montreal, Que. | electrical products | by Sept. 1989 | 253 |
| Northern Telecom Ltd. (Laboratories) | Toronto, Ont. | telecommunications | Sept. 1989 | 151 |
| Kendall Canada (US) | Toronto, Ont. | surgical supplies | June 1989 | 311 |
| Les Aliments Catelli | Montreal, Que. | food processing | Aug. 1989 | 52 |
| Maila Candelle (Consultex) | Montreal, Que. | textiles (drapery) | Aug. 1989 | 93 |
| Scierie Aime Gaudreau Inc. | Pohenegamook, Que. | forest products | Aug. 1989 | 125 |
| Vulcan Emballages Inc. | Montreal, Que. | packaging (steel drums) | Aug. 1989 | 71 |

| Company/Ownership | Location(s) | Product(s) | Date | Job Loss |
|---|---|---|---|---|
| Black and Decker Canada (US) | Brockville, Ont. | hardware/consumer products | June 1989 | 45 |
| Garlock of Canada (US) | Toronto, Ont. | rubber, fibreglass and asbestos products | June 1989 | 82 |
| Fiberglas Canada (US) | Guelph, Ont. | fibreglass insulation | Sept. 1989 | 91 |
| Rockwell International Measurement and Flow Central Canada Inc. (US) | Barrie, Ont. | valves/clamps | Aug. 1989 | 45 |
| J.M. Schneider | Kitchener, Ont. | meat processing | Oct. 1989 | 140 |
| Ault Foods Ltd. | Toronto, Ont. | food processing | Sept. 1989 | 50 |
| Ault Foods Ltd. | Weston, Ont. | food processing | Sept. 1989 | 11 |
| Better Blouse Co. | Toronto, Ont. | clothing | by Dec. 1989 | 73 |
| Canadian Coleman (US) | Etobicoke, Ont. | heating systems/camping equipment | by Apr. 1990 | 214 |
| National Grocers Ltd. | Weston, Ont. | food retailers | by Aug. 1989 | 186 |
| Rowntree McIntosh Canada (US) | Toronto, Ont. | confectionery | by Jan. 1991 | 400 |
| International Malleable Iron Co. | Guelph, Ont. | foundry | by Aug. 1989 | 250 |
| Unimatic Industries | Guelph, Ont. | auto parts | Aug. 1989 | 189 |
| Abatoir des Cedres | | meat processing | Aug. 1989 | 125 |

| Company/Ownership | Location(s) | Product(s) | Date | Job Loss |
|---|---|---|---|---|
| Donahue Inc. | Clermont, Que. | forest products | Aug. 1989 | 60 |
| EKCO Canada Inc. | Laval, Que. | kitchen utensils | Aug. 1989 | 87 |
| United Maple Products Inc. (Borden Inc.) (US) | Delta, Ont. | maple syrup processing | July 1989 | 18 |
| Canadian Foremost Drill Systems International | Calgary, Alta. | drill rigs/drill pipes | Sept. 1989 | 110[21] |
| Wang Canada Laboratories (US) | Toronto, Ont. | computer systems | Sept. 1989 | 65 |
| Springhill Colony (Hutterite Brotherhood) | Neepawa, Man. | hog processing | Sept. 1989 | 180 |
| Multiver Ltd. | Hawkesbury, Ont. | glass products | | 50 |
| X-Pert Metal Finishing Ltd. | Burlington, Ont. | platings/coatings | | 50 |
| Furst Manufacturing (Enfield Corp.) | Cambridge, Ont. | plastic products | | 90 |
| Thermetic | Toronto, Ont. | auto parts | | 45 |
| Standard Tube | Toronto, Ont. | auto parts | | 45 |
| Shell Canada Products Ltd. (UK/ Netherlands) | Toronto, Ont. | oil and gas | Sept. 1989 by 1992 | 77 |
| Canron (US) | Etobicoke, Ont. | railroad equipment | Sept. 1989 | 20 |
| Charles Lave Ltd. (US) | Windsor, Ont. | auto parts | July 1989 | 20 |
| Imprimerie Laprairie Inc. | Laprairie, Que. | printing | Aug. 1989 | 37 |

[21] 110 represents maximum number of jobs to be cut.

| Company/Ownership | Location(s) | Product(s) | Date | Job Loss |
|---|---|---|---|---|
| Fibres Textiles Liberty | Montreal, Que. | textiles | Sept. 1989 | 41 |
| Tricots Hallmark Cie. (Kaymar Div.) | Montreal, Que. | clothing | Oct. 1989 | 25 |
| Perma-Flex | Montreal, Que. | rubber products | Oct. 1989 | 47 |
| Camco | Montreal, Que. | major appliances | Sept. 1989 | 200 |
| Computing Devices Co. | Ottawa, Ont. | electronics | Sept. 1989 | 41 |
| Campbell Soup Co. (US) | Portage la Prairie, Man. | food processing | Aug. 1989 | 168 |
| Becker Fashions | Downsview, Ont. | clothing | Sept. 1989 | 40 |
| National Research Council | Ottawa, Ont. | public sector research | Sept. 1989 by 1991 | 250 |
| Outboard Marine Corp. (US) | Peterborough, Ont. | outboard motors lawn mowers, etc. | Sept. 1989 | 290 |
| Lawson Mardon Group (UK) | Laval, Que.; Toronto, Ont. | printing and packaging | Sept. 1989 | 190 |
| BTL Industries | Belleville, Ont. | fine chemicals | Sept. 1989 | 106 |
| Firestone Canada | Stoney Creek, Ont. | tires | Sept. 1989 | 38 |
| Artex Wollens | Hespeler, Ont. | textiles | Oct. 1989 | 130[22] |
| Consolidated Stone Inc. | Braeside, Ont. | softwood lumber | Oct. 1989 | 150 |
| Unisys | St. Laurent, Que. | computer equipment | Oct. 1989 | 230 |

22 Figure could rise to 150.

| Company/Ownership | Location(s) | Product(s) | Date | Job Loss |
|---|---|---|---|---|
| Boeing | Downsview, Ont. | aircraft parts | Oct.-Dec. 1989 | 308 |
| Holiday Knitwear | Toronto, Ont. | clothing | Sept. 1989 | 120 |
| Lindzon | Toronto, Ont. | clothing | Oct. 1989 | 29 |
| Hudson Fashion | Toronto, Ont. | clothing | Oct. 1989 | 37 |
| Stelco-Swansea | Toronto, Ont. | steel | Oct. 1989 by 1990 | 300 |
| AAF Canada (US) | Montreal, Que. | air filters | Oct. 1989 | 97 |
| G.M. Van Plant (US) | Scarborough, Ont. | auto manufacturing | Oct. 1989 by 1991 | 2,700 |
| Lancaster | Mississauga, Ont. | auto parts | Aug. 1989 | 60 |
| Wonderbra (Canadelle Inc.) | Hawkesbury, Ont. | apparel | Oct. 1989 by Feb. 1990 | 93 |
| Canadian Dressed Meats (Burns Foods) | Toronto, Ont. | meat processing | Nov. 1989 | 112 |
| Dominion Securities | Various centres | financial services | Nov. 1989 | 100 |
| CIL Agriculture (UK) | Courtright, Ont. | chemicals (ammonia) | Dec. 1989 | 150 |
| Eddy Match Co. | London, Ont. | paper products | Nov. 1989 | 90 |
| Form Rite | London, Ont. | auto parts | Dec. 1989 | 97 |
| Gold Crest Furniture | Toronto, Ont. | furniture | Dec. 1989 | 125 |

| Company/Ownership | Location(s) | Product(s) | Date | Job Loss |
|---|---|---|---|---|
| Homeware Industries | Tottenham, Ont. | metal products | Dec. 1989 | 113 |
| Plax Inc. | Brampton, Ont. | plastics | Nov. 1989 | 51 |
| Stafford Foods (Multi-Foods Inc.) | Toronto, Ont. | food processing | Nov. 1989 | 74 |
| USARCO Ltd. | Hamilton, Ont. | electrical products | Nov. 1989 | 90 |
| Monroe Auto Equip. (US) | Owen Sound, Ont. | auto parts | Nov. 1989 by Jan. 1990 | 88 |
| Siemens Automotive (US) | Chatham, Ont. | auto parts | Jan. 1990 | 312 |
| Manchester Plastics (US) | London, Ont. | plastics | Oct.-Dec. 1989 | 171 |
| Glidden Co. (UK) | Toronto, Ont. | paints (chemicals) | by Apr. 1990 | 90 |
| Fiberglas Canada (US) | Sarnia, Ont. | fibreglass insulation | Oct. 1989 by Apr. 1990 | 285 |
| Bombardier Inc. | La Pocatiere, Que. | railway cars | Nov. 1989 | 305 |
| Stone Consolidated | Montreal, Que. | forest products | Nov. 1989 | 20 |
| Fiberglas Canada (US) | Guelph, Ont. | fibreglass insulation | Oct. 1989 by Apr. 1990 | 86 |
| Ricwil Ltd. (US) | St. Thomas, Ont. | prefab piping systen s | July 1989 | 30 |
| Butler Metal Products | Cambridge, Ont. | auto parts | Dec. 1989 | 375 |
| Walker Exhausts | Cambridge, Ont. | auto parts | Dec. 1989 | 250 |

| Company/Ownership | Location(s) | Product(s) | Date | Job Loss |
|---|---|---|---|---|
| Electrolux | Montreal, Que. | vacuum cleaners | Nov. 1989 by Mar. 1990 | 68 |
| Libby St. Clair | Wallaceburg, Ont. | glass pkg./dishware | Nov. 1989 | 600[23] |
| Domtar | Montreal, Que. | forest products/conglomerate (head office) | Nov. 1989 | 500 |
| Taurus Footwear | Montreal, Que. | footwear | Dec. 1989 | 150 |
| Taurus Footwear | Sherbrooke, Que. | footwear | Dec. 1989 | 80 |
| Weston | Longueuil, Que. | food processing | Nov. 1989 by Jan. 1991 | 180 |
| Canadian Wardair (PWA) | Toronto, Ont. | airline (head office) | Nov. 1989 | 600 |
| Industries Valcartier de Val Belair (SNC) | Valcartier, Que. | | Nov. 1989 by May 1990 | 100 |
| Alliance Canners | Scarborough, Ont. | beverage pkg. | Oct. 1989 by Feb. 1990 | 72 |
| Acco Canadian Co. (US) | Renfrew, Ont. | office products | Nov. 1989 by June 1990 | 90 |
| Saniland Forest Products | Sprague, Man. | forest products | Nov. 1989 | 60[24] |
| TNT Alltrans Express (Australia) | Various provinces | trucking | by Feb. 1990 | 1,000 |
| Faberge (Cheeseborough-Ponds UK) | Toronto, Ont. | cosmetics | Nov. 1989 | 150 |

23 Figure represents maximum number of jobs to be cut.   24 Figure includes 30 full-time and 30 contract jobs.

| Company/Ownership | Location(s) | Product(s) | Date | Job Loss |
|---|---|---|---|---|
| Westinghouse Canada | Renfrew, Ont. | power generating equipment | Dec. 1989 | 147 |
| Grafton Group | | apparel retailer | Dec. 1989 | n.a. |
| Emballages Paperboard Boxcraft | Montreal, Que. | paper products | Nov. 1989 | 100 |
| Montreal Standard (Thompson) | Montreal, Que. | printing | Nov. 1989 | 160 |
| Web Graphics | Winnipeg, Man. | printing | | 40 |
| Drill Systems Int. | Calgary, Alta. | oil & gas | Nov. 1989 | 12 |
| Weston Bakeries | Edmonton, Alta. | food processing | Nov. 1989 | 40[25] |
| General Electric (US) | Montreal, Que. | electrical products | Dec. 1989 by July 1990 | 200 |
| Ford Motor Company | Windsor, Ont. | auto (engine plant) | Dec. 1989 by Dec. 1990 | 900 |
| Gerber Canada (US) | Niagara Falls, Ont. | food processing (baby food) | Dec. 1989 | 150 |
| Indal Ltd. Technolite (PPG-US) | Mississauga, Ont. | glass | Dec. 1989 | 240 |
| Abitibi Price | Grandfalls, Nfld. | paper-newsprint | Dec. 1989 | 250 |
| PWA (Canadian Airlines) | Various provinces | airlines | Dec. 1989 by Spring 1990 | 800 |
| Motorola Canada (US) | Brampton, Ont. | electronics (circuit boards) | Dec. 1989 by Apr. 1990 | 186 |

[25] Figure includes 22 full-time and 18 part-time jobs.

| Company/Ownership | Location(s) | Product(s) | Date | Job Loss |
|---|---|---|---|---|
| GM (US) | St. Catharines, Ont. | auto (engines) | Dec. 1989 by Feb. 1990 | 400 |
| Budd Canada | Kitchener, Ont. | auto parts | by Nov. 1989 | 280 |
| St. Lawrence Starch Co. | Mississauga, Ont. | food processing | Dec. 1989 by Mar. 1991 | 230 |
| Lake Ontario Steel Co. | Whitby, Ont. | steel | Dec. 1989 | 184 |
| Rosita Shoe | Montreal, Que. | footwear | by Dec. 1989 | 300 |
| Tie Canada | Montreal, Que. | electronics products | Aug. 1989 | 75 |
| Square D | Edmundston, N.B. | electrical products | by Dec. 1989 | 156 |
| Courtalds | Cornwall, Ont. | plastics (cellophane) | Oct. 1989 | 250 |
| Kelsey-Hayes (Varity) | Windsor, Ont. | auto parts (wheels/ brakes) | Dec. 1989 | 379 |
| Cobi Foods Inc. (US) | Whitby, Ont. | food processing (vegetables) | Dec. 1989 | 250[26] |
| Schwitzers Canada (US) | Stratford, Ont. | construction equip. parts | by Feb. 1990 | 80 |
| SeaFair Enterprises | Wood Harbour, N.S. | fish processing | | 60[27] |
| Medway Fisheries | N.S. | fish processing | | 50[28] |
| National Sea Products | Canso, N.S. | fish processing | Dec. 1989 by Apr. 1990 | 625 |

[26] Figure includes 100 full-time and 150 seasonal jobs.     [27] Seasonal jobs.     [28] Seasonal jobs.

| Company/Ownership | Location(s) | Product(s) | Date | Job Loss |
|---|---|---|---|---|
| New Wave Fisheries Ltd. | Pte. de l'eglise, N.S. | fish processing | | 100 |
| Scotia Pride Seafoods Inc. | Saulnierville, N.S. | fish processing | | 20 |
| O.C. Marine Inc. | Short Beach, N.S. | fish processing | | 40 |
| Bon Portage Fisheries | Stag Harbour, N.S. | fish processing | | 20 |
| Lockeport Harbour Fisheries | Lockeport, N.S. | fish processing | | 40 |
| National Sea Products | St. John's, Nfld. | fish processing | Dec. 1989 by Apr. 1990 | 492 |
| National Sea Products | North Sydney, N.S. | fish processing | Dec. 1989 by Apr. 1990 | 345 |
| Ka-Mil Ltd. | Toronto, Ont. | clothing | Dec. 1989 | 25 |
| General Motors | Oshawa, Ont. | auto | Dec. 1989 by Jan. 1990 | 800 |
| General Motors | St. Therese, Que. | auto | Dec. 1989 by Mar. 1990 | 240 |
| Cargill Grain Co. | Port McNicholl, Ont. | grain handling | Dec. 1989 | 100 |
| Triman Industries | Morden, Man. | furniture | Nov. 1989 | 50 |
| Apple Canada Inc. (US) | | computers (sales staff) | Dec. 1989 | 60 |
| Canada Packers | Burlington, Ont. | meat processing | Sept. 1989 | 170 |
| F.W. Fearman | Burlington, Ont. | meat processing | Jan. 1990 | 47 |

| Company/Ownership | Location(s) | Product(s) | Date | Job Loss |
|---|---|---|---|---|
| Cer-Yass Rubber Inc. | Cornwall, Ont. | rubber products | Nov. 1989 | 40 |
| Colorization (Glenex Industries US) | Toronto, Ont. | motion picture film | Dec. 1989 | 140 |
| Biltmore Chesterfield | Montreal, Que. | furniture | Dec. 1989 | 150 |
| Black & Decker (US) | Trenton, Ont. | hardware — industrial locks | Jan. 1990 by June 1990 | 100 |
| Black & Decker (US) | Montreal, Que. | lawn & garden products | by Summer 1990 | 150 |
| Carter Automotive (US) | Bramalea, Ont. | auto parts | Feb. 1990 | 230 |
| Sunar-Hauserman (US) | Waterloo, Ont. | furniture | Feb. 1990 | 280 |
| Continental Canada (US) | Toronto and Etobicoke, Ont. | cans | Jan. 1990 | 480 |
| Alcan | Shawinigan, Que. | aluminum wire & cable | Jan. 1990 | 52 |
| Stone-Consolidated | Grandmere, Que. | boxboard | Jan. 1990 | 200 |
| Harding Carpets | Collingwood, Ont. | textiles (undyed spin yarns) | Jan. 1990 | 180 |
| Canadian Manoir Industries Ltd. (General Freezer Co.) | Woodbridge, Ont. | appliances, freezers | Jan. 1990 | 150 |
| CBC | Toronto, Ont.; Montreal, Que. | public broadcasting | Jan. 1990 | 500 |
| Rustshield Plating Ltd. | Windsor, Ont. | plastics (auto parts) | Jan. 1990 | 106 |

| Company/Ownership | Location(s) | Product(s) | Date | Job Loss |
|---|---|---|---|---|
| Direct Film | Various Quebec | film/camera retailing | Feb. 1990 | 800 |
| Queen Street Camera | Ontario | film/camera retailing | Dec. 1989 | 600 |
| Louverdrape of Canada | Mississauga, Ont. | window blinds | Feb. 1990 | 100 |
| Atlantique Video | Montreal, Que. | audio/video retail | Jan. 1990 | 100 |
| Singer Lighting Ltd. | Toronto, Ont. | lamps/tables furniture | Jan. 1990 | 40 |
| Preston Manufacturers | Cambridge, Ont. | toys | Jan. 1990 | 40 |
| Russell Morin Product Ltd. | Toronto, Ont. | clothing | Jan. 1990 | 20 |
| Playtex Apparel (US) | Renfrew, Ont. | clothing | Jan. 1990 by June 1990 | 160 |
| Woodward's | Vancouver, B.C. | retailer | Jan. 1990 | 623 |
| Basf | Cornwall, Ont. | industrial chemicals | Jan. 1990 by Apr. 1990 | 150 |
| Moose Jaw Packers | Moose Jaw, Sask. | meat processing (pork) | Feb. 1990 | 17 |
| Abitibi Price | Beaupry, Que. | forest products | Feb. 1990 | 20 |
| Canasphere Ltd. (Industries US) | Moose Jaw, Sask. | reflecting glass beads | Jan. 1990 | 5 |
| Canadian Steel Foundries | Montreal, Que. | steel foundries | Jan. 1990 by Apr. 1990 | 275 |
| Hume Publishing Co. Ltd. | Toronto, Ont. | publishing | Jan. 1990 by June 1990 | 44 |

| Company/Ownership | Location(s) | Product(s) | Date | Job Loss |
|---|---|---|---|---|
| Alcan Bldg. Products | Scarborough, Ont. | metal products | Feb. 1990 | 77 |
| Ventra Group (Reflex Div.) | Windsor, Ont. | auto parts | Feb. 1990 | 101 |
| Fletchers Fine Foods | Red Deer, Alta. | meat processing | Jan./Feb. 1990 | 275 |
| PPG Insulated Glass | Toronto, Ont. | auto parts | Jan. 1990 | 240 |
| IBL Industries | Burlington, Ont. | auto parts | Jan. 1990 by Mar. 1990 | 200 |
| Marimac Inc. | Cornwall, Ont. | textiles | Jan. 1990 by Mar. 1990 | 95 |
| Manutec Industries | Brampton, Ont. | auto parts | Jan. 1990 | 150 |
| Metro Richelieu | Various Quebec | food retailing | Jan. 1990 | 130 |
| Minerve Canada | Mirabel, Que. | charter airlines | Jan. 1990 | 120 |
| Canadian Pacific Forest Products | Gatineau, Que. | forest products, newsprint | Feb. 1990 by July 1990 | 100 |
| Falconbridge | Sudbury, Ont. | nickel mine | Feb. 1990 | 250 |
| J.E. Therrien | Abitibi, Que. | forest products | Mar. 1990 | 250 |
| Fundy Fresh Seafoods | Nova Scotia | fish processing | Jan. 1990 | 600 |
| StarKist | Bayside, N.B. | fish processing | Jan. 1990 | 100 |
| General Motors | Boisbriand, Que. | auto assembly | Mar. 1990 by July 1990 | 1,700 |

# SELECTED
# BIBLIOGRAPHY

**Books and Periodicals**

American Coalition For Trade Expansion With Canada. *Weekly Progress Report*, 17 June 1988.

American Gas Association. *Natural Gas Market Report,* Vol. 4, No. 24, January 1989.

Bocking, Richard. *Canada's Water: For Sale?* James Lewis & Samuel, 1972

Bottom Line Technologies Inc. *Advertising Package*, April 1989.

Brooks, Neil and McQuaig, Linda. "OK Michael Wilson Here's the Alternative." *This Magazine*, December 1989.

Business Council on National Issues. *Straight Talk on Free Trade*, November 1988.

Campagna, Paul. "Avro Arrow, An Aviation Chapter in Canadian History." *Engineering Dimensions*, September/October 1988.

"Canada Warms up to U.S. Business." *Fortune Magazine*, 4 March 1985.

Canadian Centre for Policy Alternatives. *Canada Under the Tory Government*, September 1988.

Canadian Council on Social Development. *Overview*, Vol. 6, No. 4, Summer 1989.

Canadian Environmental Law Association. *International Trade and the Environment*, October 1989.

*Canadian Labour Congress Trade Watch*, July/August 1989.

Canadian Union of Public Employees. *The Facts*, March/April 1987.

Canadian Union of Public Employees. *Project Ploughshares Monitor*, September 1989.

Cetron, Marvin, and Davies, Owen. *American Renaissance: Our Life at the Turn of the 21st Century.* New York: St. Martin's Press, 1989.

Clark, Mel, and Gamble, Don. *Canadian Water Exports and Free Trade.* Rawson Academy, Occasional Paper No. 2, December 1989.

Clarkson Gordon Woods Gordon. *Tomorrow's Customers*, 1989.

De la Fronter Norte, El Colegio. Survey in *Journal of Commerce*, 21 February 1989.

Diebel, Linda. "Free Trade: The Mexican Connection." *The Toronto Star*, 1 & 2 April 1989.

Dillon, John. *Report on Mexico and Free Trade.* Common Frontiers Project, 14 November 1989.

Fillmore, Nick. "The Big Oink." *This Magazine*, March/April 1989.

Foster, Cecil. "A Southern Threat." *Canadian Transportation Magazine*, January 1990.

GATT-FLY. "Maquiladoras and the Mulroney Trade Deal." *Pro-Canada Dossier*, 6 October 1989.

Gorrie, Peter. "The James Bay Project." *Canadian Geographic*, February/March 1990.

Gunton, Thomas. *Natural Resources and the Canada–U.S. Free Trade Agreement.* Canadian Centre for Policy Alternatives, October 1988.

Hall, Tony. "Warriors Forgotten on Remembrance Day." *The Globe and Mail*, 10 November 1989.

Hardin, Herschel. *The Privatization Putsch.* The Institute for Research on Public Policy, 1989.

Honderich, John. *The Arctic Imperative: Is Canada Losing the North?* Toronto: University of Toronto Press, 1987.

Hughes, Ann H. *World Trade Trends*, Vol. 2, No. 4, Summer 1988.

*Inside Guide: Corporate Strategy 1990*, Winter 1989.

Kneen, Brewster. *Trading Up: How Cargill, the World's Largest Grain Company is Changing Canadian Agriculture.* NC Press, 1990.

Langille David. "The BCNI and the Canadian State." *Studies in Political Economy*, Autumn 1987.

Lee, Steven. "Free Trade and the Arms Economy." *Canadian Institute for International Peace and Security*, 14 November 1988.

Litvak, A. Isaiah. "Free-Trade Strategies With Canada." *Journal of Business Strategy*, November/December 1988.

MacGregor, Roy. *Chief, The Fearless Vision of Billy Diamond.* Viking Penguin, 1989.

Marchak, Patricia. "Restructuring of the Forest Industry." *Forest Planning Canada*, Vol. 4:6, 1988.

McMahon, Kevin. Editorial in *The Toronto Star*, 23 May 1989.

McQuaig, Linda. *Behind Closed Doors.* Toronto: Penguin Books, 1988.

Milko, R. *Potential Ecological Effects of the Proposed GRAND Canal Diversion Project on Hudson and James Bays.* Library of Parliament, Arctic Vol. 36, December 1986.

Morton, Colleen. "Study for the Washington based National Planning Association." In *Subsidies Negotiations and the Policitics of Trade*, August 1989.

National Coalition Against the Misuse of Pesticides. *Information Brochure, Pesticide Safety: Myths and Facts*, 1990.

National Energy Board. *Export Impact Assessment: Illustrative Analysis*, 7 September 1989.

National Farmers Union. "Farmers on the Rack: Free Trade and the Farm Crisis." *The Pro-Canada Dossier*, No. 21, August 1989.

Newman, Peter C. "The Unknown Element." *Saturday Night*, January 1987.

Nikiforuk, Andrew, and Struzik, Ed. Editorial in *Report on Business*, November 1989.

One Voice. *News Bulletin, Seniors Press For Fairness in Budget*, 28 February 1980.

Orr. John L. "Letter to the Editor." In *Engineering Dimensions*, January/February 1989.

Orr, John L. *Job Creation in Canada, 1978-1985*. Study for The Council of Canadians, December 1987.

Parnas, David Lorge. "Free Trade: U.S. Department of Commerce Itemizes Canada's Loss of Sovereignty." *Kingston Whig Standard*, 26 August 1988.

Patented Medicine Prices Review Board. *First Annual Report*, 1989

Patrick, Lanie. "Global Economy, Global Communications: The Canada–U.S. Free Trade Agreement." In *Communication For and Against Democracy*. Edited by Mark Raboy and Peter Bruck. Montreal: Black Rose Books, 1989.

Postal Services Review Committee. *Report*, 1989.

Regehr, Ernie. *Arms Canada, the Deadly Business of Military Exports*. James Lorimer & Company, 1987.

*Report of the Defence Industrial Preparedness Task Force*, November 1987.

Ritchie, Laurell. "The Attack on UI." *This Magazine*, November 1989.

Saul, John Ralston. "The Secret Life of the Branch-Plant." *Report on Business*, January 1988.

Science Council of Canada. *Water 2020*, 1988.

"Selling Canada's Environment Short: The Environmental Case Against the Trade Deal." *Canadian Environmental Law Association*, Fall 1989.

Stothart, Paul. "How We Can Own Our Own Industry." *Policy Options*, July 1989.

Suthren, Victor. Introduction to *Canadian Military Anecdotes*. Don Mills: Oxford University Press, 1989.

Suzuki, David. Editorial in *The Toronto Star*, January 1990.

Tanner, James N., and Reinsch, Anthony E. *Canadian Crude Oil, Supply/Demand Balances*. Canadian Energy Research Institute, August 1989.

Tester, Frank James. *Green For Garbage: Free Trading the Canadian Environment*. Toronto: York University, 1988.

*The Brundtland Report of the World Commission on Environment and Development, Our Common Future*, 1987.

The Government of Canada. *Pro-Canada Dossier*. Special Edition, January 1990.

The Rawson Academy of Aquatic Science. *Water and the Canada–United States Free Trade Agreement, A Summary Assessment*, 29 July 1988.
Todd, Jack. "Why Canada is Losing Jobs to Mexico." *The Montreal Gazette*, 22 & 23 July 1989.
United Nations Centre on Transnational Corporations. *Environmental Aspects of the Activities of Transnational Corporations: A Survey*, 1985.
Uslander, Eric M. "Energy Policy and Free Trade in Canada." *Energy Policy*, August 1989.
Wood Gundy. *Monthly Indicators Bulletin*, April 1989.
Zarzeczny, Richard. Canadian Enerdata. Editorial in *The Financial Times*, 14 August 1989.

**Press releases, papers, briefs**

Agriculture Canada. *Pesticides Directorate.* Memorandum to Members of the Pesticides Technical Working Group, 6 December 1989.
*Amendments to NEB Act.* Subsections 119.3, 119.4 and 119.5.
American Coalition for Trade Expansion With Canada. *Statement of Purpose.*
*American Coalition for Trade Expansion With Canada. Press Release*, 4 October 1987.
*An Act to Implement the Free Trade Agreement Between Canada and the United States.* Article 142.
ANR Pipeline Company. *Submission to the NEB Review on Benefit Cost Analysis Methodology*, 25 January 1990.
Atlantic Regional Program Committee of the Canadian Council for International Cooperation. *Development in Maritime Canada & Newfoundland.*
BCNI. News Release: *Business Leaders Outline National Economic Priorities for 1987*, 21 January 1987.
BCNI. Statement of Purpose: *Economic Priorities and the National Agenda*, Ottawa, September 1986.
Beatty, Perrin. *Address to Canadian Export Association*, 5 October 1987.
Beatty, Perrin. Speech: "Building Canadian Capability: Defence Strategy for the 1990's", November 18, 1987 in *The Defence Industrial Base Review, Departmental Review*, Fall 1987.
Brymore Energy Ltd. *Submission to the NEB Hearing into Benefit Cost Analysis Methodology*, 25 January 1990.
Canadian Drug Manufacturers Association. *Analysis of the First Annual Report (1989) of the Patented Medicine Prices Review Board*, 4 December 1989.
Canadian Environmental Law Association. *Application to the National Energy Board Concerning the Matter of Applications to Export Natural Gas from the Mackenzie Delta*, November 1989.
Canadian Labour Congress. *Free Trade Briefing Document No. 1*, 16 April 1989.

Coop, Jack. *Free Trade and the Militarization of the Canadian Economy.* Submitted to the Annual Conference of Lawyers for Social Responsibility, 20 August 1988.

Council of Canadians. *Submission to the National Energy Board Concerning Exports of Natural Gas From the Mackenzie Delta,* April 1989.

Davidson, Roy. *Brief to Legislative Committee on Bill C-15, an Act Respecting Plant Breeders' Rights.* Bureau of Competition Policy, 21 September 1989.

Department of Fisheries and Oceans. *Memorandum to F.J. Fraser,* from *O.E. Langer,* 15 November 1989.

Devine, Grant. *Letter to Producers,* 8 November 1989.

Elliot, Ron. Statement of Purpose for GROW: *Sustainable Development in Jeopardy!*

Free Trade Operations Group, Office of the Minister for International Trade. *Memorandum to Progressive Conservative Members of Parliament and Senators,* 29 September 1988.

Freeman, Harry L. *Speech to the Brookings Institute,* Washington, 3 February 1987.

Friends of the Earth. *Demolishing the Fire Hall.* An Assessment of the Government's Environmental Record, 7 November 1988.

GATT-FLY. *News Conference Statement,* Halifax, 14 November 1988.

Harvey, Ross, New Democrat Energy Critic. *Speech Notes Delivered to the University of Calgary,* 10 March 1990.

Langille, Howard Peter. "Towards a Political Economy of Defence Regulations." Phd. thesis, University of Bradford, England, 1989.

Levitt, Arthur Jr. Press Release: *American Coalition For Trade Expansion With Canada.*

Lynk, Michael. "Trucking Deregulation — The Coming Strife in Industrial Relations." Paper delivered to the University of New Brunswick, 23 June 1987.

Manufacturers Association. *Letter to the U.S. Secretary of the Treasury,* 7 November 1988.

Morton, Colleen. *Subsidies Negotiations and the Politics of Trade.* Study for the Washington based National Planning Association, August 1989.

Newall, J. Edward. *Speech to an America's Society Conference,* 20 November 1986.

*Pro-Canada Dossier.* Special Edition, January 1990.

Pro-Canada Network. *A Position Statement on the Proposed Goods and Services Tax,* 23 October 1989.

Reisman, Simon. *Speech to the Ontario Economic Council,* April 1985.

Saskatchewan Energy and Mines. *Submission to the NEB Review on Benefit Cost Analysis Methodology,* 25 January 1990.

Standing Senate Committee on Foreign Affairs. *Report Monitoring the Implementation of the Canada–United States Free Trade Agreement*, March 1990.

Stanford, Jim. "Plugged in to the U.S.: The Shaky Case for Canadian Power Exports." Research paper for the Council of Canadians, July 1989.

Taylor, Allan R. *Remarks to the Americans Society.* Canada–U.S. Trade Conference, New York, 20 November 1986.

The Canadian Bankers' Association. *Letter to Michael Wilson*, 6 January 1980.

The Dené/Metis Negotiations Secretariat. *Presentation to the Alberta-Pacific Environment Impact Assessment Board*, 2 December 1989.

Trent, John, and Wilson, Bruce. *Submission to the Senate Committee on Energy and Natural Resources Concerning the Sale of Dome Petroleum*, 19 June 1987.

U.S. Free Trade Implementing Legislation. *Statement of Administrative Action*, 1988.

United Fishermen and Allied Workers Union, and the Prince Rupert Amalgamated Shoreworkers and Clerks Union. Brief: *The Case for Government Action to Protect and Develop the Fishing Industry*, June 1989.

United States International Trade Commission. *Fresh, Chilled or Frozen Pork From Canada.* Determination of the Commission in Investigation No. 701-TA-298 (Final) Under the Tariff Act of 1930, September 1989.

United Steelworkers of America. *Comments on Proposals for Accelerated Tariff Removal Under the Free Trade Agreement.* Submitted to Interdepartmental Committee on FTA Acceleration, Departments of External Affairs and Finance, 31 August 1989.

Veterans Against Nuclear War. Position Paper: *Towards a World Without War*, 1989.

# INDEX

Adams, Bruce, 177
Agriculture Canada, 35–37
Air Canada, 35, 41, 42
Alberta Government Telephones, 40
Alberta Medical Association, 154–55
Alberta Pacific Forest Industries, 154–55, 157
Alcan, 8, 53, 176, 177
Algoma Steel, 79
Allied-Signal, 10, 15
American Airlines, 42
American Coalition for Trade Expansion with Canada, 14, 18, 19, 22; corporate support, 103–4, 125, 126, 148
American Express, 14, 19, 20, 49–51
American Gas Association, 148
American Medical Association, 100
American Stock Exchange, 20
Amoco, 135, 148
Amtrak, 45–46
Andrew, Mary Adela, 107, 108–9
AT&T, 10, 15, 64, 125
Atlantic Canada Opportunities Agency, 88
Ault Foods, 95
Automotive Parts Manufacturers' Association, 53

Baker, James, 22
Bank of Canada, 75, 77–78
Barrett, Marlene, 93–94
Baucus, Max, 78
Bayer, 61
B.C. Council of Foresters, 155
B.C. Hydro, 146
Beatty, David, 58
Beatty, Perrin, 119

Bechtel, 10, 167
Bégin, Monique, 82
Beigic, Carl, 21
Bell, Dr. George, 123
Bell, Larry, 146
Bendix Safety Restraints Ltd., 69
Bentsen, Lloyd, 131
Bilt-Rite Upholstering, 57
Bio-Research, 73
Blenkarn, Don, 6, 33
Block, Walter, 175
Bocking, Richard, 169
Boeing Corp., 126
Bombardier, 45–46, 126
Bonine, John, 154
Borden Inc., 60, 61
Bottom Line Technologies Inc., 70–71
Bouchard, Benoit, 74
Bouchard, Lucien, 173, 175
Bourassa, Robert, 132, 162, 167, 168
BP Canada, 15, 138, 148
Braemore, 57
Brascan, 79
Bristol Aerospace, 126
British Gas, 73
Brooks, Neil, 187
Brouillard, Claude, 175
Burdick, Quentin, 169
Burney, Derek, 24, 174
Bush, George, 174
Business Council of B.C., 53, 70
Business Council on National Issues, 3, 4–11, 22, 31, 79, 80, 119; and defence production, 121–27; and energy policy, 148; and social programs, 6, 83, 85. See also Canadian Alliance for Trade and Job Opportunities

*Business Week*, 55–56
Butler, Bev, 90
Buzzelli, David, 80

C.D. Howe Institute, 5, 85
Caccia, Charles, 196
CAE Industries, 122, 125
Cameron, Duncan, 23
Campbell Soup, 16, 18, 59–60
Canada Council, 48
Canada Customs, 76, 98
Canada Packers, 59
Canada Post, 38–39
Canadian Airlines, 42
Canadian Alliance for Trade and
  Job Opportunities, 7–8, 9, 10–11,
  18, 19, 22, 83, 95; corporate
  support, 15, 65, 125–26, 148, 167,
  177, 182. *See also* Business
  Council on National Issues
Canadian Arsenals, 122, 125, 126
Canadian Association of University
  Teachers, 88
Canadian Auto Workers, 62
Canadian Bankers' Association,
  49–50
Canadian Centre for Arms Control
  and Disarmament, 197
Canadian Chamber of Commerce,
  7, 10, 85
Canadian Council of Furniture
  Manufacturers, 57
Canadian Council of Grocery
  Distributors, 76
Canadian Defence Preparedness
  Association, 124
Canadian Energy Research
  Institute, 137, 159
Canadian Environmental Law
  Association, 151–52, 160, 193
Canadian Forest Products, 175
Canadian Importers' Association,
  59
Canadian Institute of Strategic
  Studies, 124
Canadian Manufacturers'
  Association, 7, 83–84, 173

Canadian Marconi, 123, 126
Canadian Medical Association, 102
Canadian National, 44–45
Canadian Pacific, 44–45
Canadian Peace Alliance, 127
Canadian Petroleum Association,
  135, 175
Canadian Turkey Marketing Board,
  95
Canadian Wheat Board, 92, 97
Carey, Alex, 9
Cargill, Inc., 15, 36, 92–93, 97, 172
Carlucci, William, 65
Carney, Pat, 132
CBC, 34, 47–48
Chafee, John, 131
Cheney, Dick, 127
Ciba-Geigy, 36, 103
CIL, 61
Clark, David, 60
Clark, Joe, 25
Clarkson, Stephen, 185
CN Hotels, 35
CNCP Telecommunications, 35
Coates, Fred, 98
Cobi Foods, 60
Coca-Cola, 16
Commission on Future Health Care
  (Alberta), 101
Confectionery Manufacturers
  Association of Canada, 17
Conference Board of Canada, 80
Connaught Biosciences, 73
Consolidated-Bathurst, 72, 156
Consumers' Gas Co., 73
Control Data, 125
Coon-Come, Matthew, 163, 169
Coop, Jack, 120, 121
Corcoran, Terence, 70, 175
Cox, David, 113
Crestbrook, 154, 156
Crosbie, John, 31, 127–28
CRTC, 47–48
Cultural Survival Canada, 157
Culver, David, 123, 127
Cummings, Gordon, 89, 90

Cyanamid, 61

Daishowa Paper, 154, 157
d'Aquino, Thomas, 3, 7, 123, 175
Davidson, William, 106
Davis, Anthony, 190–91
de Chastelain, John, 122
Decima, 18, 23
Defence Industry Association of
   Canada, 127
de Grandpré, Jean, 53–54
de Havilland, 116, 126
Department of Energy (U.S.), 144
Department of National Defence
   (Canada), 109, 113, 124, 126
Desmarais, Paul, 11
Devine, Grant, 95, 96, 97
Diefenbaker, John, 113
Dingell, John, 49
Doddridge, John, 53
Domtar, 79
Dome Petroleum, 135
Dow Chemical, 15
Dow Corning, 61
Duloff, Art, 140
Du Pont Canada, 55, 61

Economic Council of Canada, 104
Edmonton Telephones, 40
Environment Canada, 176
Environmental Protection Agency,
   171
Epp, Jake, 141
Epps, Ken, 126–27
Esso, 138
Exxon, 148

Farm Credit Corporation, 94
Federal Pioneer, 73
Feldman, Elliot, 97
Financial Post, 31–32, 69–70
Finestone, Sheila, 47
Fitzgerald, Edmund, 66
Fleck Manufacturing, 69
Fletcher Challenge, 156, 158–59
Ford, 9
Foreign Investment Review
   Agency, 4, 72

Fraser Institute, 5, 175
Freeman, Harry, 14, 19, 23
Fulton, Jim, 111

Gablinger, Henry, 165
Gainers, 96
Gandhi, Prem, 58
Garrett, 125
GATT, 20, 22, 96, 99, 192–93, 194
General Electric, 15, 73, 74
General Foods, 15
General Motors, 15, 125
Gerber Baby Food, 16, 60
Getty, Don, 40, 155
Gillies, James, 21
Globe and Mail, 175
Goodyear Canada, 79
Government Research
   Corporation, 19
Grandy, Fred, 166
Gregg, Allan, 18, 23
Gregoire, Rose, 107
Grocery Products Manufacturers of
   Canada, 15–17, 60
GROW, 36
Gulf, 137, 138

Hall, Justice Emmett, 82, 100
Hall, Tony, 170
Hamel, Roger, 85
Harrington, John, 150
Hayes Dana, 53
HCR, 73
Heinz Canada, 52, 60
Hill & Knowlton, 23
Hockin, Tom, 50
Hodel, Donald, 149
Holmes, Mark, 22
Honeywell, 125
Hostess, 60
Hughes, Ann, 17–18, 131
Hydro-Québec, 145, 164, 173

IBM, 3, 15
Imperial Oil, 125, 148
Intair, 42
Interstate Natural Gas Association
   of America, 148

Investment Canada, 72
ITT, 3

J.B. Hunt, 44
Johnson, Daniel, 101
Johnson & Johnson, 103
Juneau, Pierre, 47

Kaufman, 57
Kellogg, 15
Kelly, William, 37
King, Brian, 73
Kluge, Dr. Eike, 102
Kneen, Brewster, 92, 93
Kodak, 61, 85
Korthals, Robert, 50
Kraft, 16, 60

Labatt's, 61
Lang, Stuart, 157
Langer, O.E., 176
Langille, David, 124
Laxer, Jim, 187
Le Hir, Richard, 173
Leigh Instruments, 73
Lewis, David, 4
Litton Industries, 121, 125
Litvak, Isaiah A., 71–72
Loewen, Bill, 186
Lougheed, Peter, 8, 65, 149
Lougheed Corp., 116
Louisiana-Pacific, 156
Lowney (Hershey), 17, 60
Lumonics, 73
Lynk, Michael, 43, 45

McCracken, Mike, 55
McDermid, John, 35
Macdonald, Donald, 8
McLean, Nancy, 18–19
McNaughton, David, 23
MacNeill, James, 161
McQuaig, Linda, 187
Magnus Aerospace, 121
Manson, Paul, 122
Maple Leaf, 59
Marchak, Patricia, 190
Mars, 17

Mathieson, Marion, 120
Mazankowski, Don, 98
Michael, Norma, 73
Mitel, 73
Mitsubishi, 154, 157
Mobil Oil, 148
Mulroney, Brian, 25, 27, 131, 132,
  166–67, 204
Murphy, Peter, 134

Nabisco Brands, 16, 74
National Council of Welfare, 86
National Energy Board, 47, 132–33,
  139, 190; hydroelectricity, 146–
  47, 163; oil and gas, 138, 141,
  142–22, 160, 169–70
National Energy Program, 4, 131–
  32
National Farmers' Union, 94
National Planning Association on
  Canada–U.S. Relations, 74
National Sea Products, 89–90
National Transportation Agency,
  44–45
NATO, 107, 110, 113, 197, 198
Nestlé, 16, 17
Neville, Bill, 50
New Democratic Party, 4
Newman, Peter, 58
Ney, Edward, 131
Nippon Telegraph and Telephone,
  64
Noranda, 8, 79, 157–58
Northern Telecom, 21, 62–64, 65–
  66
Nowlan, Pat, 44

One Voice, 86
Ontario Federation of Agriculture,
  94
Ontario Food Processors
  Association, 60
Ontario Trucking Association, 43
Orman, Rick, 134–35, 143
Orr, John, 116
Ostry, Sylvia, 194

Paradis, Pierre, 163

Patrick, Lanie, 22
Penashue, Greg, 109
Penn, Alan, 163
Pepsi, 16
Peters, Doug, 75
Petro-Canada, 35, 37–38
Petroleum Monitoring Agency, 136
Pfizer, 36, 104
Pharmaceutical Manufacturers
   Association of Canada, 102–3
Ply*Gem, 15
Polysar, 140
Power Corp., 11, 73, 79, 156
Powis, Alf, 10
Pratt, Buddy L., 61
Pratt & Whitney, 122
Priddle, Roland, 141
Prince Albert Pulp Company, 40
Prince Rupert Amalgamated
   Shoreworkers and Clerks Union,
   99
Pro-Canada Network, 80
Procter & Gamble, 16, 154
Progressive Conservative Party, 10,
   18; corporate support, 7, 15, 16,
   27, 125–26
Project Ploughshares, 126–27
Proulx, Jacques, 145
Public Affairs Communications
   Management, 18
Public Affairs International, 18, 19,
   23, 50
Public Affairs Resource Group, 18,
   19
Pyke, Brigid, 94

Ragab, Mageed, 77
Regehr, Ernie, 116, 196
Reisman, Simon, 31, 132, 165, 167
Rapap, 156
Rice, Lauretta, 91
Rill, James, 74–75
Ritchie, Mark, 93
Robinson, Barry, 99
Roche, Douglas, 114
Roman, Andrew, 41
Rowntree McIntosh, 17, 60

Royal Bank of Canada, 8
Royal Commission on Economic
   Union and Development
   Prospects for Canada
   (Macdonald Commission), 7, 8
Russell, Francis, 101
Russett, Edna, 93

St. Lawrence Starch, 60
Sandoz, 36
Sask. Power, 146
Sauvé, Maurice, 72
Schneider National, 44
Schultz, Kathy, 100
SCN Manufacturing, 125
Shell, 9, 15, 138, 148
Siddon, Tom, 177
Siemens, 73
Snelling, Richard, 166
Spar Aerospace, 126
Springer, William, 52
Spry, Graham, 34
Squibb, 103
Stern, Paul, 63, 65, 66
Stone, Roger, 72
Stone Container, 72, 156
Strangeland, Oscar, 72
Strauss, Bob, 14
Stubbert, Wesley, 88–89
Suthren, Victor, 117

Taylor, Allan, 20
Taylor, Gordon, 141
Tencer, Willy, 56
Texaco, 9, 148
Thibault, Laurent, 83–84
This Magazine, 9
Thompson, John, 37
3M, 15, 61
Thyssen, 121
Torrie, Ralph, 150
TransCanada PipeLines, 133, 140–
   41, 148
Transport 2000, 45
Triantis, Stephen, 86
Tricil, 173–74
Trudeau, Pierre, 4

Unisys Corp., 122
United Airlines, 42
United Fishermen and Allied
   Workers Union, 99
United Maple Products, 61
United Nations, 20–21, 151, 161,
   198
United Parcel Service, 44
United Steelworkers of America,
   61–62
Upjohn, 36
U.S.-Canada Business Studies, 23
U.S. International Trade
   Commission, 98
U.S. Manufacturers' Association,
   78
Utilicorp United, 146

Valenti, Jack, 48
Varity, 57
Veterans Against Nuclear Arms,
   120

VIA Rail, 44–45
Vice, David, 21, 64, 66
Vidal, Gore, 116

Wardair, 41
Watkins, Mel, 185
Webber, Neil, 149
Weinzweig, Daniel, 48
Wells, Clyde, 89
West Kootenay Power & Light, 146
Western Diversification Fund, 88
Westinghouse, 74
Weyerhaeuser, 15, 40
Wilson, Michael, 25, 30, 32, 55, 104
Wood Gundy, 53
Woodsworth, Jean, 86
Wright, James, 165

Xerox, 3

Yeutter, Clayton, 165

Zimmerman, Adam, 157–58